Women in the South African Parliament

Women in the South African Parliament

From Resistance to Governance

HANNAH EVELYN BRITTON

UNIVERSITY OF ILLINOIS PRESS

URBANA AND CHICAGO

Library of Congress Cataloging-in-Publication Data

Britton, Hannah Evelyn.
Women in the South African Parliament : from resistance to
governance / Hannah Evelyn Britton.
p. cm.
Includes bibliographical references and index.
ISBN 0-252-03013-3 (cloth : alk. paper)
1. Women in politics—South Africa. 2. Women legislators—South
Africa. 3. South Africa—Politics and government—1994– 4. South
Africa. Parliament (1994–) I. Title.
HQ1236.5.S6B75   2005
328.68'0082—dc22   2004030074

Portions of chapter 2 have previously appeared in "Coalition Building,
Election Rules, and Party Politics: South African Women's Path to Parliament," *Africa Today* 49, no. 4; used by permission.

Portions of chapter 4 have previously appeared in "Participate or
Withdraw? Women in South Africa," *International Politics* 38, no. 2
(June 2001); used by permission of Palgrave Macmillan.

Portions of chapter 5 have previously appeared in "Incomplete Revolution: South African Women's Struggle for Parliamentary Transformation," *International Feminist Journal of Politics* 4, no. 1 (2002); used by
permission of the journal (www.tandf.co.uk).

This work is dedicated to all the women of South Africa and most especially to the South African women in my life who have taught me lessons of grace, courage, and laughter.

Portia, Hermoine, Rose, Peggy, Nomzi, Karin, and Mergedis, I wish this work to be a tribute to your strength and your joy.

Contents

Preface

My relationship with South Africa began, oddly enough, in a high-school English class. The term *apartheid* was unknown to me until my senior year in the small, rural Appalachian town of Greeneville, Tennessee. As I sat on the kitchen counter at home one evening, reading a list of topics for our senior theses, my mother noticed one topic in particular: "Alan Paton's *Cry, the Beloved Country* as Political Propaganda." She said, "That is the best book I have ever read." Believing she had read every book ever written, I took this to be a strong recommendation.

Paton's narrative captured me instantly, and over the next several months I sought to learn all I could about apartheid, sanctions, and the international movement against South Africa's racist regime. Entering Wake Forest University in North Carolina the following fall, however, I faced culture shock. Wake Forest was an amazing place for cultivating the mind and pursuing a deep liberal-arts education, but I felt socially isolated by the privileged economic backgrounds of most students there. Fortunately, progressive organizations, such as Students Against Apartheid and a chapter of the National Association for the Advancement of Colored People, were emerging on campus at that time. I began participating in these new groups, and we worked hard that academic year to protest the university's investment policies. Activism filled all my time outside classes and part-time jobs. By my sophomore year we were building shanties and picketing the trustee meetings.

Collegiate antiapartheid activism led to my first two trips to South Africa: the first in 1990, on behalf of a student organization and the university's board of trustees to investigate divestment, and the second in 1992, as a research assistant for the director of women's studies at Wake Forest, Mary DeShazer.

Mary's book *A Poetics of Resistance: Women Writing in El Salvador, South Africa, and the United States* was a groundbreaking comparative analysis of resistance poetry. My work with Mary and her generous offer to allow me to observe her interviews with South African women poets and politicians helped me learn about the essential role women played in the struggle against apartheid, which was distinct from the role men played. These women were discussing a model of resistance politics that incorporated both the public and the private spheres; more broadly, they were redefining feminism and its relationship to the South African liberation struggle. By 1992 these activists were embarking on a new organization, the Women's National Coalition (WNC), that was to unite women from all political and ethnic backgrounds. The initial success of the WNC indicated that South African women were starting a new phase that could lead to the creation of a national women's movement. The context of women's politics in the transition to democracy was ripe for analysis.

Just as, according to Fonow and Cook (1991), feminist methodology is oriented toward action, my goals in researching women in South Africa cannot be separated from my history of antiapartheid activism. An activist by nature and a reluctant academician by necessity, I slowly began to recognize that my academic research could have a much wider impact on the struggles for national and women's liberation than my previously localized attempts to challenge corporate investment strategies could ever have achieved. Consequently, I began focusing my graduate work on gaining an understanding of women's roles in South Africa's transition to democracy, in the hopes of delineating and uncovering models and strategies that could be utilized in other African states. This book is an outgrowth of that process.

The major fieldwork for this project took place in 1996–97 and is supplemented by four other research trips: the previously mentioned two I made as an undergraduate, another in May 1998, and eleven weeks of fieldwork from May to July 2003. The Institute for Democracy in South Africa (IDASA) graciously hosted my research in 1996–97 and again in 2003. IDASA is one of the most prominent independent public-interest organizations in South Africa. It aims to promote a democratic and tolerant society, and its programs to foster sustainable development and democracy operate at the institutional, community, and individual levels. IDASA, which is politically nonaligned, has been a significant force in the eradication of apartheid and in the current transition to democracy. Its role in the nation's transition to democracy has been and will continue to be pivotal in securing a peaceful, legitimate, and equitable society.

In addition to working with parliamentarians in Cape Town, I carried out

month-long projects in each of the three major cities, Durban, Johannesburg, and Pretoria. These projects let me investigate additional spheres of
government, namely, the provincial and the local. My work tracked several
women's organizations in these areas. In 2003 my fieldwork research included six weeks in Cape Town interviewing women MPs and five weeks in
Pretoria and Johannesburg meeting with members of the government administration, the Office on the Status of Women, and the Commission on
Gender Equality.

I was partially connected to the women of South Africa in many ways. Specifically, we shared a gender identity, often a political orientation, and frequently class experiences. Despite these similarities, the differences between us
were much more apparent. I am a white American academician, whereas most
of these contacts were black African women with markedly different levels of
educational achievement. Mies's (1991) notion of "partial identification" cap-
tures my position in the research process: I could relate to the women in the
research project through shared roles and identities, but I remained cognizant
of the real differences and power imbalances that remained between us.

Race was of course a central fact of life in the apartheid era (as it still is in
modern South Africa), and it is a core concept in this book, but the boundaries as drawn there differ somewhat from those in the United States. The
apartheid government grouped people according to their racial backgrounds,
using classifications that included "white," "Indian/Asian," "Coloured," and
"Black." The "coloured" category comprised persons of mixed racial heritage
and was further divided into several subcategories. For example, persons were
categorized as "Cape Coloured" if they were coloured but spoke Afrikaans
as their first language, which was often the case for those in the Cape Town
area. Other such subcategories included "Cape Malay," "Other Asiatic," and
"Other Coloured." (Official discourse used *Coloured* to refer to the people
as a whole and *coloured* to indicate a property, as in "a coloured neighbor-
hood.")

My research was greatly affected by my living arrangements, which often
had racial ramifications. While I was in Cape Town, my host families lived
in Southfield, a community between areas that had been formally called
"coloured" and "white," and in Mitchells Plein, a deeply impoverished
coloured area. I took the "coloured trains" and was welcomed into Cape
Town's diverse and complex Muslim community as well as the coloured
community—as was often the case throughout South Africa, the coloured
and Asian areas there were close together and blended at the edges. Members of my host families were exceptionally well educated, informed, and active. In addition to offering their warmth and hospitality, they taught me

what life was like for socially active South Africans in marginalized communities. In Durban my host was a white activist professor who had a constant stream of youths from the violent Durban townships staying in his house, a living arrangement even more remarkable because his home was in a highly affluent white area. His dedication to the struggle at both an individual and an institutional level was remarkable.

While in Pretoria and Johannesburg I lived in the townships and frequently traveled to and stayed in rural areas and former homelands. My Sotho host family in Mamelodi, outside Pretoria, and my Zulu/Northern Sotho family in Soweto, outside Johannesburg, were a constant source of love, support, instruction, and encouragement. Despite the safety and security of their homes, the frequently harsh realities of their lives and those of their neighbors taught me that the work of Parliament is often far removed from families in the townships.

There is an intense debate within feminist epistemology and methodology concerning the level of intimacy and friendship developed between researcher and research participant, with some having claimed that such relationships may become more exploitative and manipulative than more distant research strategies are (Wolf 1996; Kirsch 1999; Reinharz 1992). However, the decision not to include my host families as direct research participants was more a personal decision than a professional one. Their lives and the lessons they continue to teach me have obviously provided a contextualizing framework for my research and created a deep understanding of the culture of South Africa. Nevertheless, these families welcomed me into their homes, not just offering me safety and shelter, but allowing me to develop deeply personal relationships that any objectification attendant to my research would have compromised.

As I became more attuned to myself as a researcher and to the locations occupied by researchers, I realized that most European and American scholars in South Africa were not living in black townships, coloured areas, or rural locations. Since my first encounters with South Africa came as an activist, it seemed incongruous to remain in all-white or predominately white areas or live exclusively with other Western researchers. Although this choice was a natural one given my prior relationships and political orientation, it did present extensive logistical challenges. For example, transportation to and from the cities was time-consuming, inconvenient, and on more than one occasion physically threatening. Similarly, I occasionally found myself meeting with high-ranking government officials in the executive branch on days when we had no electricity or water in the townships, which could make it difficult to present a professional appearance. Living with a family also brought the joys of being a part of that family, participating in both their social activities and their labors, which often occupied most of the time in the evenings. Finally, even the most versatile sleeper can find it difficult to get much sleep in a township setting. Depending on the township, traffic noise (Soweto and Gugulatu) or the sounds of livestock (Mamelodi) continue throughout the night. Winter evenings are filled with coal smoke; summer evenings, with mosquitoes. And because space is limited in the overcrowded townships, I occasionally shared a bed with another female family member.

Beyond providing a clear picture of the challenges of living in a township, this experience helped me understand the "doubling" that coexisting in two such vastly different worlds forces on black South African women in Parliament or the administration. Although these women's white colleagues had their own share of domestic duties and responsibilities, white members of Parliament often lived near their offices and employed domestic help; they most certainly had safe and physically pleasing places to rest their heads at night. Most black South African women in government had lived in conditions similar to mine night after night, yet they were expected to be in their offices rested, prepared, well fed, punctual, and polished. These women often commented that the marbled halls of Parliament or the administrative offices filled with high-level discussions and executive lunches were a jarring experience, especially after an evening of mealie-pap and tomato gravy. My temporary lifestyle was thus most similar to that of the women with whom I had the least in common, black women MPs, and their discoveries that I sometimes lived in townships affected our conversations significantly. Nevertheless, despite the insights my living conditions presented, these connections were momentary. As Wolf asserts, "the fieldworker has the ability and privilege to leave the field location once the research is over. Thus, immersion may be a useful strategy to attempt to view a culture from within, and it may position the researcher in a way that differs from a more distant participant-observer, but it does not basically alter the researcher's positionality" (1996, 10). And indeed, my experience in two worlds was temporary—theirs was most often permanent.

My host families became reference points and sounding boards for all the theories and ideas I gathered during interviews and participant-observations of women in Parliament. Women in Parliament had several assessments and perceptions of "life on the ground" for the average South African that could easily be checked against the realities of life in the townships. Living with families also provided me with a wealth of information regarding issues such as poverty, development, gender violence, and local party politics.

My research memos, interview transcripts, and fieldnotes trace a clear methodological path in the development of my codes and categories, the birth and revision of theories, and the formulation of conclusions, all of which are outlined in the appendix. Unlike many quantitative studies within political science, however, my research is not replicable in the traditional sense. My color, gender, socioeconomic background, nationality, age, and political orientation are all factors that affected how research questions were received and how they were answered. While there was no way to control for these factors, it is important that I mark how they influenced the work and research. My research findings would have been dramatically different had I been black, male, or older. My experiences and beliefs as a former anti-apartheid activist and as a temporary member of townships certainly helped shape the questions, theories, and focus of this research. Finally, the gendered nature of the project affected the work and the ways others viewed it.

First, my age and gender were invaluable in establishing rapport and building trust. When I met MPs or delegates face to face and not over the phone, they often viewed me as a young, eager student rather than as a doctoral candidate. My level of education became much less intimidating to many women when they saw me as a younger person with less life experience. Because of my gender, these women shared their stories of rape, abuse in their homes, sexual harassment in the workplace, and discrimination in their parties. Moreover, they often asked questions about violence against women or sexual harassment in my own life specifically or in the United States generally.

Second, the tone of the interviews shifted sharply when we discussed my living arrangements, political background, or language ability. (While the interviews were conducted in English, my language training often became evident in conversation.) Gender and age go only so far to break through the racial barriers of the ethnically polarized postapartheid South Africa. My race, undoubtedly and understandably, inhibited some women's full disclosures during the interviews. My living arrangements and language training, however, did help to break through some areas of tensions. Thus, when women discovered that I lived in black townships in Gauteng and in the formerly coloured areas of the Cape Flats and Mitchells Plein, their attitudes and comfort levels improved significantly. Often there was an immediate and noticeable change in the tone of our conversations as the discussion became more open. For women especially in the African National Congress (ANC) and Pan Africanist Congress but also (refreshingly) in the Democratic Party, my firsthand knowledge of the lives of people in townships and homelands made me more of an ally and a trustworthy interviewer. (The opposite was true, however, for a few women in conservative parties who told me my living arrangements were unsuitable and unsafe.) In addition, my knowledge of IsiXhosa was meaningful to ANC and Inkatha Freedom Party members, for they feel the majority of white South Africans are unable and unwilling to learn even the basic greetings of an indigenous language. Other women mentioned language within the context of their work in Parliament or in terms of race relations.

As my project's activist origins suggest, I intend this work to have implications for women's movements globally but especially for the women in South Africa. In it, I chronicle the continued challenges facing women in the movement as they struggle, often successfully, for empowerment, equality, and basic needs. No one else has focused on the stories of the women in this nation's first democratically elected parliament. Moreover, as became clear during interviews, these women rarely had the occasion to reflect individually or collectively about their progress and their strategies. I hope this text will provide both a record of what has already happened and insights into what is yet to come.

Acknowledgments

This project has been anything but a solitary endeavor. First of all, IDASA staff members in Cape Town, Pretoria, and Durban have been essential to my work logistically and intellectually. Indeed, my work would have been impossible without the support and interest of IDASA's Executive Staff, especially Ivor Jenkins in Pretoria, Paul Graham in Pretoria, and Vincent Williams in Cape Town. The members of IDASA, under the dedicated and ethical leadership of Executive Director Paul Graham, have numbered among the most committed and effective leaders in helping all levels of civil society and government move from authoritarian rule to a government based on accountability, transparency, and participation. I am also personally grateful to Ivor Jenkins and his family, who have been the touchstones for each of my trips and facilitated contact with my host families as well as with several organizations and officials. Ivor's warmth and commitment to building a new South Africa and to promoting reconciliation are a testament to the people of his nation.

Some of my most beneficial contacts in Cape Town included members of the parliamentary staff, political parties, women's groups, and labor unions. This broad spectrum of highly engaged and insightful women and men was central to my understanding of parliamentary life, party politics, and gender issues in South Africa. The women especially offered vital support, both personal and professional, providing important criticism of my research and theories as the work progressed. In particular, I am indebted to Philemon Mahlangu of the Public Relations Unit of the Parliament of South Africa, who was invaluable in arranging interviews during 2003. In addition, I wish to give special thanks to Joe Crawford, Rebecca Holmes, Vivieen Smith, and Patricia Van Stavel of the staff of Parliament; Debbie Budlender of the Women's

Budget; Colleen Lowe Morna and Ayanda Bekwa of Gender Links; Janine Hicks of the Center for Public Participation; Penny Parenzee, Christina Nomdo, Samantha Fleming, Judith February, and Nomzi Ndyamara of IDASA Cape Town; and Bertie van Eck of the parliamentary library.

To the countless South Africans who opened their homes and lives to me during my many trips: I want to thank you for your generosity. Your kindness provided me a place of learning, support, community, and family. I wish especially to thank my hosts in Cape Town, Abu and Hermione Solomons and their family and friends, and all those elsewhere: Mergedis Nathan and her warm and generous parents (Mitchells Plein); Nomzi Ndyamara and her children (Gugulatu); Ivor and Karin Jenkins and their family, as well as Michele Ruiters, Reinette Erkan, and Paul Graham (Pretoria); Crispin Hemson and his family, as well as Nise Mahlangu (Durban); Peggy and Mike Twala and their children, as well as their loving friends Sheila and John (Soweto); and the Manasoe and Kekana families, who welcomed me into their homes more times than I can imagine (Mamelodi). Finally, the family and friends of Rose, Isaac, Portia, Holly, Robert, Kgothatso, Mpho, Nkosi, and our dear Tshepo have been invaluable in shaping who I am today.

Three institutions supported my research either financially or professionally: Syracuse University; Winthrop University; and my current institution, Mississippi State University. The 1996–97 fieldwork portion of this study was generously funded by the U.S. Department of Education through a Fulbright-Hays Doctoral Dissertation Research Abroad Fellowship. Time and resources to complete this project were made available by Mississippi State University in the form of a summer research grant. I am indebted to the dean of the College of Arts and Sciences, the vice president for research, and the Department of Political Science and Public Administration for their support of my 2003 fieldwork.

I am deeply indebted to my dissertation committee at Syracuse University—Mark Rupert, Marie Provine, Peg Hermann, and most especially Deborah Pellow and Patricia Ingraham—for their constant support and careful reading of my work. I am also deeply grateful for early mentors of this project, such as Mary DeShazer, Alton Pollard, Katy Harriger, and Ed Wilson of Wake Forest University. The project's success has further depended on the resources and professional support of several other faculty members at Syracuse, including Jeff Stonecash, Kristi Anderson, Sue Wadley, Bob McClure, and Stu Thorson.

The book's strengths are due in great measure to careful reviews by Anne Sisson Runyan, Aili Mari Tripp, and Sylvia Bashevkin, who read portions of the manuscript, and Kathleen Staudt, Karen Beckwith, and two anonymous readers, who read it in its entirety. I wish to thank especially my editor at University of Illinois Press, Kerry P. Callahan, for her thoughtful reading of this work, her enthusiasm for this project, and her professionalism at every stage of the review process. I owe special thanks to Bruce Bethell of the UI Press for his meticulous, generous, and comprehensive copy editing of the final manuscript. His professionalism and thoughtful suggestions led to a clear improvement of this book as a whole. Additionally, Volker Franke, Jessica Kulynych, Lynn Hemple, Sorayya Khan, Naeem Inayatullah, and Dottie Moore have all been reliable sounding boards during the various stages of my proposal and my writing. Three graduate students at Mississippi State University, Mandy Mitchell, Hilary Brannan Gresham, and Barbara Patrick, provided valuable assistance during my revisions. I am also especially grateful to the library staff at MSU, particularly Ida Cunetto and Summer Mord, for their assistance in finding obscure titles and articles.

The most valuable contributions to the overall success of this project come from my parents, Sandra and Gordon Britton, who are the inspiration for my life's work and my untiring advocates. I owe a special debt to my chosen family, especially Robin Riley, my sister-friend who has spent countless hours on the phone and on e-mail working through the most critical aspects of this project as well as discussing our teaching, politics, and careers. And most important, I owe the ultimate completion of this book to Bob Tryanski, my husband and partner, who graciously relocates his professional and personal life based on the vagabond nature of my academic career and who remains my most constant source of support, courage, and strength.

Abbreviations

AEB	Afrikaner EenheidsBeweging (Afrikaner Unity Movement)
ACDP	African Christian Democratic Party
ANC	African National Congress
ANCWL	African National Congress Women's League
APO	African People's [formerly "Political"] Organization
AZAPO	Azanian People's Organization
BWF	Black Women's Federation
CEDAW	Convention on the Elimination of All Forms of Discrimination against Women
Codesa	Convention for a Democratic South Africa
COSATU	Congress of South African Trade Unions
CP	Conservative Party
CGE	Commission on Gender Equality
DA	Democratic Alliance
DP	Democratic Party
FEDSAW	Federation of South African Women
FF	Freedom Front
GAC	Gender Advisory Committee
IDASA	Institute for Democracy [formerly "a Democratic Alternative"] in South Africa
IFP	Inkatha Freedom Party
JMC	Joint Monitoring Committee on the Improvement of the Quality of Life and Status of Women
MF	Minority Front
MMD	Multimember District
MP	Member of Parliament
MPNP	Multiparty Negotiating Process

NA	National Assembly
NCOP	National Council of Provinces
NGM	National Gender Machinery
NGO	Nongovernmental organization
NOW	Natal Organization of Women
NP	National Party
NNP	New National Party
OSW	Office on the Status of Women
PAC	Pan Africanist Congress
PFP	Progressive Federal Party
PWG	Parliamentary Women's Group
SACP	South African Communist Party
SADF	South African Defense Force
SAP	South African Police
UCDP	United Christian Democratic Party
UDF	United Democratic Front
UDM	United Democratic Movement
WBI	Women's Budget Initiative
WNC	Women's National Coalition

Women in the South African Parliament

1.   Women and the Struggle for Liberation

Through its history of identity politics, the legacy of apartheid, and the methods of its liberation struggle, South Africa demonstrates how processes of liberalization, negotiation, and consolidation can be manifested within a potentially explosive atmosphere. The 1994 elections saw South Africa make dramatic progress in terms of the percentage of women in national office, moving from 2.4 percent before the elections to over 26 percent. This impressive gain was further enhanced with the 1999 elections, bringing the percentage of women in office to 29.8 (Ballington 2002, 76). The South African case suggests that in societies moving to newly democratic governments, pretransition mobilization by women fosters their posttransition success in influencing constitutional mandates, playing roles in party politics, and winning office. In winning political office South African women followed a path of several stages: multiparty coalition building, revising the electoral system to facilitate the election of women candidates, and pressuring the leadership of political parties to advance the status of women through the use of affirmative-action measures and gender quotas.

This case, resting firmly in a postcolonial African context, demonstrates that the power and influence women developed during a liberation struggle may be used to transcend some but not all of the public/private political distinctions within the new regime. Although the South African parliament has shifted to reflect some of the needs of women, the requirements necessary to be an MP or delegate remain fundamentally unchanged. Some women have adapted well to the institution, but they are not representative socioeconomically, educationally, or ethnically. Despite the obstacles, women have created internationally emulated governmental institutions and implemented far-reaching pieces of legislation intended to promote gender equity.

The South African case is an important addition to the field of women and democratization. Currently, studies concerning the impact of women's movements and women's activism on government have produced contradictory findings. Early research on women's roles in democratization focused on women's gaining office and on women in the transition to, not the consolidation of, democracy. Even as late as the early 1990s, the dominant narrative in the study of gender and comparative development was that women were left out of the consolidation phase. Waylen (1994), for example, compares democratization movements in Latin America and Eastern Europe and finds that women's participation in liberation and reform movements did not ensure their place in conventional political roles after the transition. In their global case studies Nelson and Chowdhury (1994) similarly found that women's activism typically falters in the democratic consolidation phase and that women's political power is not translated into office holding or institutional representation.

New research on more recent democratic transitions is challenging these previously held beliefs. Increasingly, women's movements are significantly influencing the creation of democracy and, more important, its subsequent consolidation. This new success is fueled in part by a global women's movement for representation (Brown et al. 2002, 72). Women worldwide are seeking a sustained voice in formal politics, and the movement continues to analyze and reproduce models of women's activism internationally. For the first time, women across the globe are talking to one another and learning from one another's successes and failures through improved communications technologies, at international conferences, and by direct activist networking. Their new goal is to use state institutions to secure lasting change during the consolidation phases of transitions (Byanyima 1994; Beckwith 2000; Tamale 1999; Tripp 2000b; Baldez 2001). Despite the enormous pressure in postwar contexts for the "re-creation of patriarchal domination in new forms," women are working with the "seeds of transformation" and the "role of solidarity with women" in creating new democratic institutions and practices (Meintjes, Pillay, and Turshen 2001, 18).

The South African model extends this new pattern in the gender and democratization literature; specifically, women in South Africa have been singularly focused on securing a sustained voice in elected office and in the legislative and policy implementation process. In fact, I will show that women were focused on ensuring their political presence long after democratization had moved into the consolidation phase. And this posttransition focus on state feminism was informed by sister struggles throughout Africa. Women in South Africa specifically and intentionally acknowledge their awareness of failed women's movements and unrewarded efforts by African women's groups elsewhere on the continent. As Lindiwe Zulu, an MP from the ANC, asserts: "When the negotiations process led by the ANC started in 1994, women were not involved—not because of unwillingness on their part but because the negotiators had not thought it necessary to involve women. This was nothing new for women, because we had seen the same process in Zimbabwe, Angola, and Mozambique" (1998, 148). The women I interviewed in South Africa had watched similar liberation movements and learned several key lessons about tactics to avoid during the transition. Women there are deeply aware of the problems that can arise when Western studies of gender and democratization are applied to the African context.

This book examines women's roles in democratization, reflectively analyzing the significant accomplishments of women in South Africa and the remaining challenges still facing them. Through interviews, participant observation, and archival research, I analyze the experiences of South African women who were part of the destruction of apartheid, the formulation of the first two democratic parliaments, and the growing consolidation of the democracy.[1] Specifically, I delineate how women secured national office, changed both the processes and outcomes of Parliament, and have been affected individually and as a group by the transition to institutionalized politics. This project is rooted in South African women's stories of how they achieved electoral success, learned to work with lifelong enemies, and began to transform Parliament to create more space for women's voices.

The following pages reveal that, despite the numerical increase in representation, women in the South African parliament continue to face substantial challenges that may hinder their full participation in the nation's political life. Because of these challenges, over one-half the women I interviewed did not return to Parliament, for their skills as grassroots activists did not match the professional skills Parliament demanded. This pattern of attrition emerged even within the ANC, which is widely recognized to be the political party most committed to gender equality. The attrition rate within the ANC was quite high, with over one-third of its female representatives leaving Parliament during the 1999 election (Ballington 2002); several other women MPs had left before then. My research also indicates that the most demographically representative women are choosing to leave office. In fact, the "second-generation" women MPs who entered Parliament following the 1999 elections are markedly distinct from the 1994 cohort in terms of occupational and educational backgrounds. Those in the 1999 cohort are increasingly "professionalized" and prepared to work within the existing parliamentary culture.

Given the long history of the study of democratization and the more recent introduction of an analysis of gender in such transitions, the South African story provides researchers, activists, and legislators with multiple new lessons for the transition to democracy and its eventual consolidation. Although the story of South African women is far from complete, I provide a step-by-step analysis of how they gained office and functioned within it and what challenges they still face. The preponderance of literature in this field has come from Latin America or Central Europe, but cases from Africa are increasingly numerous (Tripp 2000b; Tamale 1999). The South African case provides researchers and practitioners a window into these debates within the African continent.

South Africa's transition occurred at the ideal time to implement the newer models of success and to draw on a collective international history of women's roles in democratization. There are particular moments that enhance women's opportunities for success in gaining office, such as regime changes, political realignments, periods of decrease in political repression, and periods during and after revolutions (Bop 2001; Beckwith 2000; Basu 1995). The South African regime change was aligned with democratization; thus, the women's movement had a chance to secure key elements of state power. Because of the history of apartheid, South African women were in a unique position to utilize their dramatic history of identity politics, their political training during the liberation struggle, their educational exile backgrounds, and their multiracial coalition-building experiences. They were able to use these different sources of political learning to pressure the state for symbolic and substantive representation. The remainder of this chapter will outline the major trends within women's political participation before and during the antiapartheid struggle, especially within social movements and coalition building.

Paradoxes of South African Women's Political Participation

Each stage of the history of women in South Africa is replete with highly contested visions of how and why women participate in the political sphere. Historians, anthropologists, and gender activists are locked in a deeply politicized debate concerning the power, agency, and identity of women from precolonial times through the end of apartheid. Central to this debate, especially with respect to the precolonial period, is the lack of historical records and verifiable research. Because the first written records began with the arrival of European explorers, much of this research involves the interpretation of oral histories, and much of the colonial documentation is suspect for its potential Western bias. Even contemporary and purportedly progressive African studies researchers are, as Oyewumi argues, still trapped within their ethnocentric biases: "Whether the discussion focuses on history or historylessness . . . , it is clear that the West is the norm against which Africans continue to be measured by others and often themselves" (1997, 17–18).

Despite these gaps in material, there is a solid consensus that women's status and power were permanently altered by the imposition of colonial and religious hierarchies of gender. Precapitalist societies are often organized around the accumulation not of material wealth but of productive potential—that is, the potential labor a household has at its disposal. Women are the pivotal organizing factor of such societies because of the potential productive labor they offer and the powerful reproductive potential they provide (Guy 1990; Parpart and Staudt 1989; Amadiume 1997).[2]

The colonial powers' introduction of Christianity and capitalism to Africa affected women's status and power enormously. Colonialism brought with it a particular version of Christianity that worked to marginalize women's roles within both the public and the private spheres, much as the spread of Islam had done earlier in African history. As Deborah Gaitskell (1990) argues, however, colonial Christianity also lessened women's status and power through missionary organizations established to ensure Victorian female virtues and social roles, especially the centrality of marriage for women's identity. Capitalism further reified the notion of women as secondary members of the household economy, a sexual division that allowed men to operate freely in the economy while severely restricting women's access to it. Although a sexual division of labor may have existed before colonialism and capitalism, it was only with their introduction that the division became a power imbalance and led to the domination of women (Geisler 1995; Gordon 1996). Because such patriarchal gender systems were already in place, capitalism served to strip women of the main sources of power they had before colonialism.

Beyond wrestling with these gaps in the historical material, researchers, political scientists, and historians also struggle to define power and status. Questions persist concerning how much power women held, how much they were allowed to have, and how much they tried to achieve. Power is culturally defined, and African women maintain that early Western researchers underestimated the power African women derived from their domestic roles because such strength was designated by the patriarchy.

This complex vision of women in South African history embraces two central themes: the definition of women's leadership and the construction of women's identity and activism. First, researchers and activists debate women's leadership roles during the antiapartheid movement. They see women during the antiapartheid struggle either as leaders of the movement or as its backbone and "silent strength." In many ways, both interpretations are correct. Women did push the antiapartheid struggle into a phase of mass action and national mobilization long before their male counterparts were prepared to do so. At the same time, official leadership positions within all political parties were overwhelming and almost exclusively filled by men.

Women's identity has also been contested, in that some researchers argue that women activists maintained and perpetuated their identities as mothers and wives instead of challenging those scripted positions (see, e.g., Walker 1982). Women in the resistance often did unite in attempts to save the country for their children or worked alongside their husbands, who were at the front of the struggle. Women's organizations consciously and voluntarily subordinated their quest for gender equality to the quest for racial equality. Even as they accepted these traditional and conservative gender identities, however, women were simultaneously working to change their parties' gender policies. Several women acquired significant leadership positions after their husbands were imprisoned. Women in exile achieved top positions in their parties and received extensive educational and political experience. Women never fully abandoned their struggle against patriarchy. They continually fought to win the support of male leadership and to gain party commitments for gender equality. These contested visions in many ways are a precursor to the reality of women's lives during the current transition to democracy.

Apartheid's Extension of Ethnic and Racial Hierarchies

Apartheid was founded on over one hundred years of colonial domination and racial exclusion. Starting in the late fifteenth century, European traders and explorers sailed around the coast of southern Africa on the way to Asia. The area soon became a victualing and refreshment station for these explorers, and in 1652 its Dutch settlers established livestock farms and gardens to replenish fresh fruit, vegetables, and meat supplies for the long journey between Asia and Europe. Trade relations with the Khoikhoi people were relatively stable,[3] because they were the settlers' main source of iron, copper, and livestock (Saunders 1994, 11–62). The Dutch, however, never recognized the Khoikhoi's ownership of the land.

The fertile land and the mild climate soon attracted numerous Dutch, German, and French settlers to the region. These settlers eventually created their own unique culture and distinctive language, Afrikaans, which developed from the European languages, chiefly Dutch. Rapidly losing connections to their European past, the Afrikaners considered themselves to be more African than European (Mallaby 1993, 71–73). The "trek Boers," or wandering farmers, pushed farther north and east to acquire more land, eventually destroying the Khoikhoi population through conquest. Slaves were brought to the area from West Africa and from Asian countries including Malaysia, Burma, and Timor. Children of white settler men and indigenous black women were the next group to be enslaved. This Afrikaans-speaking mixed-race group was later to be known as the Cape Coloured (Saunders 1992, 48–51).

British explorers occupied the western cape in 1795. Unlike their Afrikaner counterparts, the British claimed the land for their country and worked to establish colonial control over southern Africa. The colonists brought with them the ideas and practices of a modernizing Europe. They established industry and advanced farming techniques, and they also abolished slavery in 1834, because slavery impeded the implementation of capitalism.[4] These practices immediately led to conflict with the Afrikaner people, who had modestly prospered during their hundred years of self-governance and freedom from governmental or colonial control.

Although they outlawed slavery, the British believed they should remain separate from, and in control of, the African people. When the British encountered the Xhosa people, the African people living closest to the cape, they worked to bring them into their colonial workforce and under their rule. The Xhosa nation fought first against enslavement by the Afrikaners and second against colonial domination by the British. The British eventually divided the Xhosa nation in 1853 after the Eight Frontiers War (Peires 1991, 30), and following the Nongqawuse Catastrophe, they ultimately conquered the independent half of the Xhosa nation.[5] This pattern, in which the British and Afrikaners fought with and then conquered these eight African nations, occurred throughout the colonial period.

Goldblatt and Meintjes argue that colonialism and later apartheid relied on both racial and gender hierarchies: "Patriarchy was embedded within the social fabric of apartheid in particular ways and meant that women and men from different racial, class and cultural backgrounds experienced life very differently" (1998, 29–30). Although elements of patriarchal rule or male domination were certainly evident before colonial times, these patterns were heightened, deepened, and ingrained to ensure white male power, especially within the South African context.

Violence, too, lay at the heart of the colonial attempt to control African nations, and women experienced an additional, sexual layer of exploitation at the hands of colonial authorities. Conquest of land went hand in hand with the violation of women in Africa, and this strategy continues today in the ethnically based rape found in Rwanda, the Sudan, Bosnia, and Serbia.[6]

At the very least, it is now evident that colonial conquest, authority, and governance constituted "both a violent and [a] gendered process, which exploited preexisting social divisions within African culture . . . [and led to] an increased vulnerability of African women" (Mama 1996, 48). Many patriarchal conditions undoubtedly existed before colonization, but these patterns were exacerbated by externally imposed institutions within politics, economics, education, and religion.

Battles for Control: The Great Trek and Anglo-Boer War

From 1835 to 1837 the majority of the Afrikaner population migrated away from the cape—and British influence—in what is known as the Great Trek.[7] Riding armed ox-drawn wagons through harsh conditions, the Afrikaners pushed through one thousand miles to establish independent republics in the interior of South Africa (Mallaby 1993, 73).[8] The Great Trek has become a cornerstone of Afrikaner identity. Throughout the trek, Afrikaners battled with indigenous populations,[9] seizing their land to form the new Afrikaner state. Saunders asserts that the "Great Trek was a landmark in an era of expansionism and bloodshed, of land seizure and labour coercion" (1992, 114). One of the most savage battles took place between the Afrikaners and the Zulu at the Battle of Blood River. Although previous conflicts had left them with depleted resources and diminished health, the Afrikaners vowed to defeat the Zulu nation. Led by Andries Pretorious, the Afrikaners prayed and vowed that, if they won, they "would note the date of the victory . . . to make it known even to [their] latest posterity in order that it might be celebrated to the honour of God" (qtd. in Saunders 1992, 119). On December 16, 1838, the Afrikaners fought the Zulu and their spears with cannon, rifles, and pistols. At the end of the battle three Afrikaners had been injured; over 3,000 Zulus had been killed, their blood turning the river red. This battle established the second cornerstone of Afrikaner identity, for they saw their victory as a sign from God that they were a chosen people.[10]

The Great Trek did not end the conflict between the British and the Afrikaners. With the discoveries of diamonds in 1867 and gold in 1886, settlers and fortune seekers flocked from Europe. These valuable natural resources made South Africa more important than the other African colonies, and British dominance of the nation became a priority. The Afrikaners resisted the British in the Anglo-Boer War,[11] even though they were outnumbered and had inferior military training and weapons. In pursuing victory the British invented the first concentration camps, imprisoning 136,000 Afrikaner women and children and 115,000 Africans who had been laborers for the whites.[12] Although not designed as genocidal execution centers, the prison camps had unsanitary and inhumane conditions that led to the deaths of over 28,000 whites and 14,000 blacks (Mallaby 1993, 72; Saunders 1994, 256). This resistance to the British became the third cornerstone of the Afrikaner identity: Africans fighting against colonial domination (Mallaby 1993, 73–74).

The Birth of Apartheid

Great Britain granted the colony self-rule as the Union of South Africa in 1910. Although the British worked to end slavery in the cape upon their arrival, the colonists never intended to give the indigenous African nations equal protection under British law, nor did they intend to mix freely with the African population in any social, religious, educational, or political sphere. The inspiration for apartheid came from the British, not the Afrikaners, in Natal in 1845. Theophilus Shepstone created ten locations to house the African population away from the white city. Shepstone envisioned a primitive form of self-governance in these locations, "the recognition of hereditary chiefs and the perpetuation of, on his own terms, a modified form of clan existence" (Saunders 1992, 156).

The Afrikaners gained control of the South African parliament in the 1940s with "a promise to preserve white power in general—and Afrikaner power in particular" (Saunders 1992, 367). The Afrikaner-controlled government quickly extended the policy of apartheid ("separation") nationwide and created separate spheres of development for each race.[13] During the apartheid era the Population Registration Act categorized all South Africans by race.[14] All decisions about education, housing, and employment were determined by that categorization. The broadest categories included white, colored (of mixed ancestry), and African. Assigned at birth, a child's status was "determined by criteria such as descent, appearance (hair, lips, nails, etc.), social acceptance, habits, speech and education" (McLachlan 1987, 76). The apartheid regime afforded the most privilege to the white minority, with decreasing degrees of opportunity given to Indian, coloured, and African populations in that order. Cock asserts apartheid did more than separate the races; it served to "maintain Blacks in a subordinate position . . . [in] five critical areas: political rights, property and residence rights, employment, education, and income" (1980, 232).

The Group Areas Act divided the nation into separate living areas based on race. Whites lived near urban centers, while blacks were forced to the outskirts of town (McLachlan 1987, 76–77). Apartheid legislated separation throughout the nation, assigning each race its own separate hospitals, buses and trains, housing areas, schools, and recreational facilities. Black South Africans were not allowed to own land, and they were relocated to "homelands," or land reserves, unless they secured labor documents to work in the white areas. The apartheid government and its officials deemed these homelands to be the "reincarnations of ancient tribal kingdoms that Blacks yearned to revive" (Mallaby 1993, 76). These small underdeveloped reservations constituted only 13 percent of the land of South Africa, yet they were intended to hold and sustain over 70 percent of the population (McLachlan 1987, 77). As I will show, the Group Areas Act exacerbated the impact of the migratory labor system and within it the foundation for resistance among black South African women.

The Migrant Labor System

The migrant labor system permanently altered women's status and power as well as familial structures and systems throughout the region (Bozzoli 1991; Murray 1981). This system, which started with colonialism and accelerated during apartheid, extracted young, productive males from the rural society, leaving disproportionately large numbers of women and children in rural areas (Guy 1990, 28). These rural areas, also known as Bantustans or homelands, were severely underdeveloped and lacked the basic infrastructure found elsewhere throughout the nation: "Whole communities were uprooted from their land and were dumped in inhospitable environments—ironically labeled 'homelands.' . . . Women found themselves in a less secure position than men," most specifically in the control of or access to economic opportunities, jobs, and land (Goldblatt and Meintjes 1998, 30). In fact, this physical isolation has had broad and longlasting effects on black South African women, affecting not only their family systems and employment opportunities but also their access to basic educational and health resources (Kemp et al. 1995; Sibisi 1977). This legacy has had dramatic implications for the physical lives of most black South African women. The apartheid state forced the black population into areas lacking proper health facilities, imposed unsafe forms of birth control specifically on the black population, limited women's control over their reproductive lives, and used physical violence and rape to intimidate and silence women's protests (Kemp et al. 1995, 135–36). Black women were forced to take on all the roles that they had traditionally shared with men, including management of the household, production of all food and necessities, and negotiations with local governments and communities. They had to face "a gradual and significant deterioration of rural family welfare. Indeed, the extremely impoverished female headed households of [southern Africa] are the contemporary result of more than a century of South African capitalist 'growth' based on migrant labor" (Henn 1984, 15).

Soon industrialization and capitalist progress created a demand for labor that exceeded the capacity of the African male population, so black women were brought into the industrial and domestic labor force. This "industrialization, urbanization, the restructuring of rural social relations, and a fresh intervention by the state into the lives of African women all helped to create a vast new political constituency . . . [and] the base for one of the most militant and disciplined political movements of the decade" (Lodge 1983, 150). Although black South African women would undoubtedly have become active in politics eventually, colonization and industrialization propelled them to action much sooner than white women or even black men began to mobilize. This increasing responsibility was a source of class consciousness that later became the foundation for women's participation in labor movements (Berger 1983). According to Winnie Mandela, this is the central reason black women became politically active long before white women did: "When they removed our husbands and our fathers from the rural areas to work in the mines . . . , the Black woman found herself acting as head of her family. As well as raising her family, she had to look after the cattle and till the land. So it has not required any special transformation for women in the urban areas to be in the forefront of the struggle" (qtd. in Russell 1989, 341). As Mandela states, the increase in women's responsibilities and repression led to an increase in women's activism and resistance. Black South African women worked, protested, and fought for racial equality despite violent state oppression and weighty domestic obligations. Indeed, according to Hilda Bernstein, a South African activist and the founder of the Federation of South African Women, they "emerged as primary catalysts for protest and challengers of the apartheid regime" (1985, 81). I again heard this sentiment about black women's strength in my interview with Mandisa,[15] one of the ANC women who had long been active in the struggle and was able to give a historical perspective on women's resistance:

> At the beginning of things, man lost their land because the state took the lands, took their cows. . . . So, that made most men leave the countryside and come into the towns and look for jobs . . . [at] places called locations, where blacks were kept, the now townships. They got lost in the locations and met other women and stayed with them. But at the home base, the women would carry on with her chores, and the men would send money from where he was working. And she looked after everything. . . . And they developed to be very strong women. And when the men didn't come back, they said, "I have a family to care for, and I can't worry about somebody who is being irresponsible." . . . They were determined that their own children were not going to be like them. They were going to have an education. So they worked for missions, and they sent their kids to missionary schools. They plowed the fields. They sold the cattle,

chickens, sheep, and all that. And that is how President Mandela is president today. That is how my husband became a doctor, and others became lawyers, and all that—because of the women.

What is most striking about this narrative—one central to the women's movement—is the connection Mandisa draws between women's power and women's roles as mothers and leaders of the household. Women were able to use this connection between household power and political strength to confront the apartheid regime. Nor has this pattern been limited to South Africa. Across the continent forces such as capitalism, urbanization, and industrialization have long pushed men into urban centers before women or entire families moved there (Gordon 1996, 47–48; Berger 1983). These forces regularly present women with increasing responsibilities and leadership roles within the household and rural power hierarchies. Similar patterns emerge during war, which draws away men and leaves women, whether in industrialized or preindustrialized settings, in charge of both the public and the private spheres. These gaps in patriarchal power allow women to develop the female consciousness described by Kaplan (1982).

Nonetheless, South Africa's version of this pattern is unusual, if not unique, in the lengths to which the apartheid government went in attempting to keep women in the Bantustans and restricting their movement through so-called pass laws governing travel across racially defined borders. Because such migration was not strictly prohibited to them, large numbers of black women elsewhere in Africa often migrated to the cities to find employment, leave abusive relationships, or escape the harsh realities of rural life (Mama 1996, 51). Their presence in the towns was often seen as a threat to the colonial systems, however, because women could distract men from their jobs. Consequently, colonial powers would engage in forced removals. Additionally, as Gay Seidman argues, the migrant labor system and its destruction of the indigenous subsistence lifestyle propelled women into the paid labor force after the 1970s, giving them some level of economic self-sufficiency for the first time. The migrant labor system thus led to increased political and economic participation for women, which provided a foundation from which they could demand a greater role in postapartheid South Africa (G. Seidman, 1993, 292–93).

White Nationalism and Gender Hierarchies

Within the colonization period leading to the apartheid era of the 1950s, gender expressions within both white and black groups romanticized and reinforced the notion of women as mothers and wives. Women were often relegated to the domestic sphere and discouraged from engaging in public life. As Mangaliso asserts, although white and black women had similarities "based on in-group hierarchical gender arrangements," each group's gender experiences differed from the other's (1997, 131). White and black South Africa each had its own social and political history, its own national and ethnic identity, and its own gender hierarchies.

Although many white women have become leaders in the struggle for racial and gender equality, as a group their involvement has been limited. Except for a few individual leaders and a few women's organizations that were originally mainstream and nonconfrontational,[16] white women usually stood apart not only from activity against the apartheid state but also from women's movements and gender activism (Bernstein 1985). White women may have been an oppressed class within South African patriarchy, but apartheid gave them a level of privilege and comfort that inhibited their widespread involvement in the resistance movement. Of course, their comfort and relief from domestic labor were provided by an endless supply of exploited black domestic labor. This arrangement increased the economic potential of many white women, who were thus free to pursue employment in the waged economy, and consequently decreased their resistance to their subordination to white men. As Cock asserts, "while both Black and white women are subject to discrimination on the basis of sex, the system of racial domination provides white women with mechanisms of escape from this structure of constraints" (240–41). Still, although whites did not typically participate in the liberation, white women were consistently more active in it than white men were (Cock 1991, 150).

Afrikaner women were excluded from both formal wage employment (Marks and Trapido 1987) and the institutional stronghold of Afrikaner power and advancement called the Broederbond. The Broederbond, otherwise known as the Afrikaner Brotherhood, was a secret male society focused on preserving the Afrikaners' culture and heritage and promoting their economic and political strength following decades of British domination. Instead of being a part of the brotherhood, women had the complementary and equally significant role of preserving Afrikaner language and culture and therein a particular version of Afrikaner nationalism. Rather than focus on the public, political, and economic spheres of life, Afrikaner women were supposed to promote, preserve, and uplift Afrikaner culture by raising children and making a home for their families. This feminine role is most clearly mythologized in the stories of women in the Great Trek, who are portrayed as strong pioneer women supporting their husbands' push through the wilderness,[17] and of women in the Anglo-Boer War, who appear as inspirations for their soldier-husbands and as victims interned in British concentration camps.

Afrikaner women were not permanently trapped within a traditional domestic role, however. In the poverty following the Anglo-Boer War, many Afrikaner women were forced to pursue waged employment, often in factories with extremely poor working conditions. These conditions created a level of class consciousness that propelled Afrikaner women to take action and participate in the union movement, although often in ways designed to preserve their Afrikaner identity through language, custom, and dress (Marks and Trapido 1987). Afrikaner women militantly agitated for better working conditions while working to preserve their traditional identity. This militant preservation of traditional identity becomes a trend throughout women's history in South Africa, a development I discuss later in greater detail.

More recently Afrikaner women have created organizations to support the notion of Afrikaner nationalism and even the extreme right-wing desires for a separate Afrikaner homeland, or *volkstaat*. These activities, most prevalent during the 1980s and early 1990s, are rooted in the Afrikaners' devotion to Calvinism and their acceptance of men as "the head of the household and the movement" (Klugman 1994, 654). Afrikaner women remain largely confined within these roles: "Even though Afrikaner women had supported Afrikaner men during the war, as the men ascended to power, the women were assigned to motherhood, self-sacrifice, and stoicism" (Mangaliso 1997, 132).

Despite their second-class position in Afrikaner society, these women were significantly privileged because of their race, especially as the Afrikaner population began to excel in business, agriculture, and civil service from the 1950s through the 1990s. Although consistently second to their husbands in terms of political and economic power, they occupied positions of considerable power, privilege, and influence simply as white South Africans.

English-speaking white women have historically enjoyed considerably more freedom and choices than the women of the "Afrikaner nation" have.[18] Certainly English-speaking South Africans maintained distinct gender roles, but English-speaking women have made more advances in their political parties and professions than have Afrikaner women of the same period. Moreover, it was English-speaking women who pushed for women's suffrage for nearly three decades until it was won in 1930, and they succeeded in electing the first woman to Parliament in 1933 (Ballington 2002). Within national parliamentary politics the English-speaking population has been more often linked to the opposition to apartheid in the 1970s and 1980s, as embodied in the work of the Progressive Party. This precursor to today's Democratic Alliance had a woman as its single representative: Helen Suzman, whose persistent opposition to apartheid became a rallying point for the resistance. Despite these apparent nods toward progressive politics, however, both the English- and the Afrikaans-speaking populations perpetuated apartheid politics and the conservative, traditional ideologies that "ensured that women were principally relegated to the private sphere" (Ballington 2002, 81).

Conservative Militancy of Women's Resistance to Apartheid

Although black and coloured South African women did not directly counter the gender hierarchies that relegated them to the domestic sphere, they began to challenge the apartheid state's control over their lives. These challenges took the form of mass-based protests, such as consumer boycotts and protests against the pass laws. Women began to occupy several areas of political activism, including labor unions, women's organizations, and political parties. Rather than eschew their traditional roles, women often preserved and drew strength from their domestic lives and maternal identities. They did this, however, using highly militant, aggressive, and nontraditional methods—what one might call "conservative militancy," which was to guide the activism of South African women throughout the apartheid era. Julia Wells was the first to observe this pattern in South African women's resistance to apartheid during their protests of the pass laws, discussed in a later section. This pattern is remarkably similar to those found in other instances of women's mass mobilizations within highly patriarchal societies.[19] Cock (1991, 182) has found that "'motherhood' was a mobilizing role. It seems to have led to support for radical political change and sometimes to support for revolutionary violence" in South Africa.

Within the antiapartheid struggle maternal identity has repeatedly been used to legitimize radical action. Goldblatt and Meintjes concur, asserting that the focus on South African women's maternal functions has been revolutionary, not limiting: "Women have used this as a means . . . of entering the public arena. This has had the effect of politicizing private issues and placing women's pain at the loss, abduction, and attack on themselves and their families on the oppositional agenda" (1998, 31). This pattern of a revolutionary female consciousness[20] and conservative militancy has recurred throughout Africa and elsewhere. Women have been pivotal actors in wars of liberation because of their maternal identity and responsibilities. From Mozambique to Zimbabwe, from Kenya to Nicaragua, women become combatants because they are caretakers.

The Pass Laws Protests

Nowhere is the notion of conservative militancy more evident than in Wells's (1993) analysis of the protests against South Africa's pass laws. The pass laws were used to regulate the movement of black South Africans between and within the color zones designated by the Group Areas Act. Black men had to carry passes demonstrating they had contracts to work in a particular area or industry. Women were not subject to the passes until the 1890s, and they successfully protested for exemption to them in 1913. Women maintained a strong and unified resistance to the passes until the late 1950s, when the government decided again to enforce the laws for women and used tactics too violent for the women to oppose.

Wells asserts that the women's efforts to repeal the pass laws charted a paradoxical path between the potent and explosive militancy of their protest methods, which "far exceeded the actions of their male counterparts," and the conservative and traditional impetus for the protests, which defended "the primacy of their roles as mothers and homemakers" (1993, 1). In Wells's estimation this pattern continued throughout the subsequent antiapartheid struggle as women separated their racial oppression from their gender oppression: "Racial oppression was tackled while traditional gender-defined roles were reinforced" (1).

Unlike Walker (1982), Wells does not see this conservative militancy as a failure to resist patriarchal oppression. Rather, this duality emerges from the complex history of women's lives under colonialism and apartheid. In many ways "early twentieth-century Black women were neither sophisticated politicians nor stumbling feminists" (Wells 1993, 1). Throughout their history black South African women stridently maintained their domestic roles; they resisted the pass laws, however, because these laws affected the private sphere, which was their primary and often only source of power and identity. Within the household and the informal economy, African women were in control of their economic, political, and social activities. Here they were in charge of managing household labor, generating income, and maintaining the family. Wells asserts that the women's resistance, which reinforced their domestic power and not their public power, was in fact an attempt to maintain women's freedom (9). Having witnessed wage labor significantly disadvantaging their male counterparts both economically and psychologically, women recognized the power and mobility they had within the informal sector of the second economy. South African women maintained their domestic roles to preserve power and control over their economic and, subsequently, their political and social lives. This defense of traditional economic and domestic roles continued to be marked by militant and nontraditional methods, which became the pattern for women's involvement in all their antiapartheid activities.

Consumer Boycotts and Labor Unions

This pattern of conservative militancy is also apparent in other mass-based actions opposing apartheid. Apartheid's discriminatory labor practices, wages, and product pricing affected black South African women directly, because they managed household finances. South African women have been involved in labor-movement struggles from as early as the 1920s, in their work with the Industrial and Commercial Workers' Union and the Women's Workers' General. Beginning in the 1930s regional and national unionization campaigns and work with the Communist Party imparted tremendous momentum to union mobilization (Berger 1983, 1987). In addition to furthering such mobilization efforts, especially within the textile and garment industries, women in the labor struggle introduced mass action, including strikes, boycotts, marches, and rallies, which set the tone for the movement as a whole. Leadership in union activities brought national prominence to several key women, such as Ray Alexander, Mary Mafeking, Emma Mashinini, Lydia Kompe, Liz Abrahams, and Florence de Villiers.

Black South African women began widespread national consumer boycotts and labor protests in the 1950s.[21] After a time of intense repression by the apartheid government in the 1960s (Berger 1983), women's involvement in trade unions soared in 1970–90. The Congress of South African Trade Unions (COSATU) was at the forefront of protests against unfair labor practices. Mangaliso states that COSATU also addressed "issues affecting [women] as women, such as night shifts, maternity leave and the implications of such leave, and sexual harassment in the workplace" (1997, 135).[22] The African National Congress Women's League (ANCWL) had numerous consumer boycotts nationwide. For example, in 1957 it organized a boycott against a penny rate increase for busfare in three townships. Ultimately the protest involved over 45,000 individuals, and some women walked almost ten hours to reach their places of employment in the cities and return home. The protesters regularly encountered swift and violent police repression, yet the boycott's economic pressure forced the government to rescind the rate increase in less than six months (Terborg-Penn 1990).

The women I interviewed discussed several consumer boycotts in which they had participated. For example, Abongile told me about "Operation Lollipop" to support workers in the meat industry, who experienced poor working conditions and received exceptionally low wages. She stated: "We went into the supermarkets. Because of our involvement [in party structures], we weren't supposed to be in the front lines, but [we] did [participate in Operation Lollipop]. We went to the Grand Bazaar. [Women] would fill their trolleys with red meat and go to the tills and only pay for a lollipop." Such creative and costly protests were effective and media friendly. They also utilized women's roles as food consumers and producers to highlight how unfair labor practices and product pricing affected women. The police often arrested and jailed participants in the protest.

In another protest, the potato boycotts, women fought against the exceedingly harsh treatment of political prisoners in labor camps. Nobanzi told me the reasons behind the boycott and explained the impact of protest on her maternal responsibilities:

> I had my first boy in '58. Terrible time when we were boycotting potatoes. Terrible thing, because when you are weaning a child, the first thing you give him is mashed potatoes and so forth. No mashed potatoes to give them. Boycotting potatoes because people being arrested for passes and taken to these notorious farms to work there. And many people were killed there, and nobody took up the problem. They would be killed there. And when they were killed there, they would be dug into the fields to manure those fields—which brought up very, very good potatoes. *Big* potatoes. But then our organization decided that, *no,* we should not eat potatoes anymore because it is the blood of our relatives, of our people.[23]

Nobanzi's narrative shows how apartheid disrupted even the most intimate and natural processes of life for a mother and child.[24] Women used their buying power to protest the horrific acts of the apartheid government and to honor the deaths of their relatives and fellow activists. The potato boycotts show how the overlapping identities of mother, household consumer, and activist can come together to oppose the regime.

Throughout this period women were often referred to as the "backbone" of the antiapartheid struggle or the "silent strength" of the resistance. One former ANC activist in Parliament recounted how women supported the movement:

> When the struggle intensified, the women played a part at conferences. They raised funds for the organization. They received guests. We had no hotels.[25] They catered for them, washed for them, ironed for them. They became the backbone of the political movement. We said in our freedom charter that when we were tabulating our human rights, that we were going to fight for these rights. We fight for side by side with our men until freedom is won.

The backbone metaphor is in many ways complimentary and respectful of women's work. A human body would be incapable of functioning, standing, or moving forward without a backbone. The trope is also disabling, however, for women provided voices, hands, eyes, legs, and brains, too.

Indeed, this designation of women as the silent strength or the backbone of the movement is only one interpretation of their activism. Women were also seen as pivotal antiapartheid leaders. Women were far from the silent or passive background. More than just the backbone of the struggle, they *were* the struggle. They kept the movement progressing, and they supported one another and kept one another's children alive.[26] Lilian Ngoyi, Helen Joseph, Ruth First, Emma Mashinini, and Ellen Kuzwayo were all visible leaders in the struggle.[27] Other, lesser-known women, too, were implicated, arrested, and convicted for their roles in protests. The women I interviewed related story after story of state harassment and threats, of exile and imprisonment. One woman told me how her house was destroyed by a policeman's fire-bomb. Many lost family members in violence with the police or rival parties. Others discussed suspicious "accidental deaths" at the hands of the police or in unexplained car accidents. Women told me how they were subject to discrimination and excluded from employment or housing opportunities.

Beyond the threats to their lives by the police or rival parties, women faced opposition from their own husbands. Siboniso recalled that her involvement in resistance politics began after she experienced violent police intimidation, but her involvement then resulted in violence from her husband:

> [The Monday after the Soweto Uprising], when I was cleaning my stoop, which faced the [police] station, I just heard something on the wall, and I looked and it was a bullet. The police were firing at me from the station. That is where I took it from. I said to my husband, "I want to join this organization." And he said, "Oh! Over my dead body! I want no organization. I want no woman. I want no friend. You are just my wife." Just such a rude man. I lived under those circumstances for years. Hitting me and chasing me away from the children. And he was a nondrinker.

When I asked how she joined the organization, she replied: "Out of my powers. I was not that active, because I was under strict observation. The minute I get a child, I was involved in women. I was very good at helping people even though I was very poor." Despite severe oppression and control by her husband, Siboniso found a way to be involved. She was able to use her identity as a mother to network with other women and to hide her political activities from her husband. In our interview she often linked her work in resistance politics to community development and social welfare work. As with many women involved at the grassroots level, she understood the struggle to be against apartheid, poverty, sexism, and gender violence all at the same time. The point was to improve life for her children, for herself, and for the nation. The intersections of race, class, and gender simultaneously inhibited women's participation in South African society yet also propelled their engagement with the resistance.[28] Here we again see how women were able to use gender systems to challenge South Africa's multiple patriarchies.

Two Visions of African Women's Activism

Like many of the women I interviewed, Wells believes that the history of South African women's political participation is captured within two narratives, two incomplete interpretations, two myths that eclipse a clear picture of their actions. The first of these incomplete interpretations asserts that women were crucial political agents who were fully actualized in their public roles and aware of their power. This interpretation, which was repeated to me by many of the women I interviewed, is substantially true in several respects. Women were a powerful force; women were a primary agent of resistance. As Wells and others have been quick to note, however, women remained in the background, and male leadership was the norm. Women also never directly challenged the sexual division of labor; rather, they often reinforced this gender system. As Moodley asserts, "When I look back, I think the concept of gender was always on the periphery of one's consciousness— inchoate and ephemeral. To put it bluntly, no one was making any audible noises around gender issues—if they were, they must have been whispering" (Kemp et al. 1995, 138).

The second myth, or incomplete interpretation of women's collective action in South Africa, has most often come from a feminist lens and asserts that women were either unwilling or unable to attack the layers of patriarchy. Wells (1993) is critical, for example, of Cherryl Walker, a South African feminist sociologist whose pivotal work Wells takes as a primary example of this misinterpretation. Although not disagreeing with Walker's extensive and groundbreaking research, Wells questions her ultimate analysis: "While she recognized the conservative aspects of these movements, she could not reconcile them with the otherwise militant actions. This struck her as contradictory and led to her ultimate judgment of the women as having failed" (1993, 1).

The critiques launched against feminism, especially those by black South African women, seem particularly important and are extensively documented elsewhere (Steyn 1998; Ginwala 1991; Hendricks and Lewis 1994). Steyn argues that most South African women's refusal to accept the label *feminism* comes from legitimate complaints of ethnocentrism: "Feminism has often been viewed as intellectual imperialism, divisive of the struggle, and an assault on non-Western cultures. . . . Those women who have called themselves feminist have been, for the most part, white middle-class, left-wing intellectuals . . . , and their tendency to speak on behalf of Black women has been resented" (1998, 43). The phenomenon of women actively working for women's rights and liberation but rejecting the label *feminism* is global in scale, although the reasons differ considerably from place to place (Basu 1995). Feminism is often associated with Western ideology—in South Africa, then, with the apartheid state and the domination of the African people. Although important steps have been taken to articulate an "African feminism" (Mikell 1997; Mbire-Barungi 1999; Tripp 2000a), resistance to an undifferentiated feminism is widespread.

Clearly South African women's participation in the antiapartheid movement was not fully revolutionary in its goals, yet neither did these women fail to challenge the state, patriarchal power, or prescribed notions of feminine behavior. After all, the underlying propositions are not mutually exclusive. As Kaplan (1982) and Wells (1993) claim, the layers of women's consciousness and the revolutionary methods of their resistance defy such simplistic accounts. Women neither completely failed nor fully triumphed. Their propagation and defense of the gender system served to undermine, but not destroy, the authority of the state and the patriarchies of power.

South African women themselves are struggling with these competing identities. Grace, a white, English-speaking former antiapartheid activist and current ANC MP, urged me not to be blinded by the first myth:

> You should not get caught up in the myth that women were in the forefront. This is the myth we perpetuated abroad, and it won us a lot of solidarity and a lot of financial support. But do not decry it either, because it has won women positions in Parliament. . . . Women came [in from the homelands] and occupied territory and were deported and redeposited back to the Transkei. And, in that sense, women were in the forefront. They were the soldiers on the ground, but the generals remained men.

Grace explained that this myth started with women in exile who were greatly influenced by the international women's movement and the United Nations' "Decade for Women," 1975–85. The "woman question" began to filter through the organization, and women started to ask uncomfortable questions about tokenism and rapes in the exile camps. Eventually the ANC leadership, under Thabo Mbeki, adopted a progressive gender platform and agenda. Still, Grace insisted that the myth was necessary and partially true and must be not only critiqued but also upheld.

My own work shows that this account continues to both help and harm the women's movement and the struggle for national liberation. Women were leaders in the struggle, but they were excluded from the leadership.

Women have been able to make significant electoral gains, but they have been unable to fulfill promises of widespread social empowerment and gender equality since the fall of apartheid. If women are to move forward in the new South Africa, they must come to terms with their history of conservative militancy. They were progressive, aggressive, and influential yet restricted by patriarchies in their homes, their political parties, and the state.

Women's Organizations and Evolving Collective Identities

The same conservative militant identity shaped the composition and structure of women's organizations during the apartheid era. There were two notably distinct generations of women's organizations in this period. As previously discussed, South African women experienced varied levels of societal oppression, depending on their racial backgrounds (Henn 1984; Gaitskell 1990; Guy 1990). Women of different races mobilized at different times and in different ways. These differences created two generations of women's organizations that were distinguishable not only by race and time but also by the extremism of their agendas and methods (Sideris 2001; Lodge 1983; Bernstein 1985).

Women as Mothers: First-Generation Women's Organizations

Women of all races that espoused traditional domestic roles and attitudes formed the first generation of women's organizations, which appeared between 1940 and 1970. Initially these groups focused on women's needs and demands, but they were willing to sublimate their agendas to those of the male-dominated antiapartheid movement. These women militantly fought to reinforce their traditional roles and position in the domestic sphere, from which their power and influence grew, thereby embodying the pattern of conservative militancy. Above all, they sought to create a "special position for 'mothers of the nation,'" an "'iconography of women'" that could offer them a meaningful role within traditionally circumscribed identities (Marks and Trapido 1987, 23). Yet women from all races were sometimes able to use their "traditional" roles to assert their rights and demand protection.

One of the first organizations from this period was the Federation of South African Women (FEDSAW), formed in 1954, which focused on protesting the pass laws. Although the organization comprised women from numerous ethnic groups and political backgrounds, its members managed to find a common unifying maternal identity: "There were no differences between us as

mothers. . . . We all wanted to bring up our children to be happy and to protect them from the brutalities of life" (Mompati 1991, 114). They thus emphasized their roles as mothers, characterizing their activities as efforts to free
the nation for their children. Debbie Budlender, a South African activist and
social scientist, told me that she believes this stress on motherhood to have
been as much a tactic of the leadership as anything else. Budlender's assertions are supported by Steyn, who finds that the FEDSAW founder and current ANC MP Albertina Sisulu, who was "often regarded as having a feminist
agenda, actually saw the purpose of the Federation as guarding against in-
justices aimed at traditional homes and families" (1998, 43). FEDSAW protests
against the pass laws took on a level of engagement not anticipated by the
male antiapartheid leadership: "Despite the discouragement of male comrades, the ANCWL and the Federation of South African Women (FEDSAW)
led this campaign, utilizing mass action techniques, including the historic
march of twenty thousand women on the Union Building in Pretoria to present their demands. This is an extraordinary number considering the lack of
transportation infrastructure, the repression of the state, and the resistance
women faced at home" (Kemp et al. 1995, 136–37).

Over the years FEDSAW's agenda expanded to attack other apartheid laws,
including the Group Areas Act and the Population Registration Act (Joseph
1991, 206). It fought a pivotal battle against Bantu Education, the educational
system that trained black South Africans to perform only the tasks required
to support white South African industry and lifestyles. The oppressive system "was instituted to make it very clear that Black children had to be educated to know their place in South Africa" (Mompati 1991, 115). But FEDSAW
faced destabilizing government repression of its leadership and activities. As
a result, the organization often had to work underground in the 1960s and
1970s. In the early 1990s FEDSAW worked to challenge violence against
women, and it has been credited with bringing women together across ethnic lines to fight for equality (Klugman 1994, 649–50).

The Black Sash, another first-generation women's organization, was formed
in 1955. Six white South African women who were outraged by a government
bill excluding the coloured population from voting started the Black Sash, which
has become one of the most progressive legal assistance groups for black South
Africans. Their primary concern was that the Afrikaner-controlled government
would eventually exclude the English-speaking population from voting rights
through similar legislation (Duncan 1991). Initially focusing on human rights
and voting rights, the organization has since addressed the pass laws, forced
resettlement, legal assistance, and bail funds for political prisoners (Michelman
1975). Although the organization was originally a white organization, its mem-

bers "have engaged racial politics by using their whiteness where it is most powerful—in challenging the white minority government by showing that not all whites support[ed] apartheid and by standing between African communities and members of the South African Defense Force or its puppet vigilantes" (Klugman 1994, 643). The Black Sash radicalized its activities during the 1980s and 1990s and is now primarily staffed by black and coloured South Africans. From the late 1980s through today, the Black Sash has maintained nationwide legal-advice offices for those South Africans whose lives have been destroyed by, for example, forced resettlement or imprisonment.[29]

Expanding Identities: Second-Generation Women's Organizations

Second-generation women's organizations, formed between 1970 and 1990, were primarily founded by black South African women who "saw renewed attempts to establish women's organizations that would resist the state at the grassroots level by addressing local concerns and engaging in local struggles" (Kemp et al. 1995, 139). These groups place meeting the material and political needs of black, coloured, and Indian women at the forefront of their activities, and this generation's conception of woman's identity extends beyond the traditional domestic and maternal notions. Women are seen as activists, poets, industrial workers, trade unionists, spokespeople, soldiers, and political prisoners. Instead of moving away from conservative militancy, this stage broadened that model and extended women's dedications to both their maternal roles and their militancy. The ANC member and trained guerrilla Thandi Modise stated, "I'm a guerrilla because I'm a mother" (qtd. in Cock 1991, 153).

The tenure and direction of the antiapartheid movement as a whole had shifted during the 1980s, especially because of international pressure against the state. Opposition groups inside the country began full-force mass-action movements against the state. Although most of these actions remained nonviolent, the level of state repression continued to increase. The conflict never reached the status of civil war, but resistance organizations increased their attacks on state targets, and the state increased its violent repression and supported forces of instability within the black areas. Goldblatt and Meintjes found that during this period, "militarized constructions of masculinity and femininity became more pronounced. . . . it was well known that women were soldiers and commanders. Women increasingly became drawn into the violence that grew throughout South Africa, as activists themselves, or as indirect victims" (1998, 31). Nevertheless, the numbers of women participating in armed struggle remained relatively small,[30] in both the white government's South African Defense Force (SADF) and the ANC's guerrilla army,

Umkhonto we Sizwe (known as "MK"). At the height of their military operations in 1989, the SADF had only 14 percent women and the MK had only 20 percent, and neither placed more than a handful of women in leadership roles (Cock 1991, 162).

This newer generation of women's groups increasingly presented the links between their quest for racial justice and gender equality. In Temma Kaplan's estimation, this group of women activists moved beyond her notion of "female consciousness" toward a larger struggle for "social citizenship" that women define as "economic and social rights conceived as human rights" (1996, 159).

The Black Women's Federation (BWF), formed in 1975 and banned in 1977, directly focused on the needs of black women and was linked to the black consciousness movement. As the political activist Shahieda Issel stated in her assessment of the BWF, "most men still think that women should play a subordinate role. . . . I'm not going to stand down because I'm female. . . . it really helped me to be in the Black Women's Federation. . . . women need to get the confidence to speak up" (1991, 68). The BWF was tied directly to the liberation movement. As the former BWF member Asha Moodley remembers, those seeking to further black consciousness and black women's empowerment needed to work together but also to recognize the movements' internal tensions (Kemp et al. 1995, 138–39). These new, more fervent groups continued to fight for racial equality but added the goal of gender equality. Women recognized the need to address the violence and dominance of the white regime before all else, yet they now planned to demand recognition in the future.

The Natal Organization of Women (NOW) formed in 1983 "to remind people that [women's] struggle [for gender equality] is very much part of the rest of the struggle" (Ramgobin 1991, 140). A former member of NOW, Nozizwe Madlala, states that the organization foregrounded the material and strategic needs of black South African women and extended the notion that women's rights are human rights:

> As the level of political awareness grew, we began to demand that issues of the specific oppression of women be integrated into the national agenda. As we did so, however, we were conscious of the specific context in which women experienced oppression in South Africa, where gender, race, and class are intertwined. It was this specific context which influenced our decision to adopt an approach that sought to integrate gender issues into those of national oppression and class exploitation. (In Kemp et al. 1995, 139)

This pattern of linking gender rights to human rights is seen throughout Africa, although methods of actualizing such rights remain elusive in most contexts because the abuses often occur within families and cultures (Fox and Hasci 1999). In South Africa two other organizations formed in protest to violence against women: Women Against Repression, formed in 1986 by five black women, and Rape Crisis, formed in 1976. Rape Crisis has been particularly successful in helping women of all races to obtain medical treatment, abortions, and counseling (Mayne 1991, 230–32). Also exemplary of the philosophy and agenda of the second generation was the United Women's Organization, formed in 1979, which helped women meet their basic needs. For example, the organization helped to get more communal water taps in the squatter communities and developed child-care facilities. Their meetings include numerous translators so that they may reach all women of all ethnic groups. They recognize that "this is part of being in a women's movement. It [is] a political training ground for women. It has to be slower if you want to bring all your members with you" (Fester 1991, 249–51).

Gender and the Transition to Democracy

This emphasis on a broad conceptualization of women's rights as human rights and the lessons drawn from "female consciousness" and women's plans for "social citizenship" created the groundwork for the role of women in South Africa's transition to democracy. Drawing on their history of conservative yet militant activities, South African women had both the identities and the methodologies necessary to make critical political claims on the constitutional negotiations and the new government. Throughout history South African women have tenaciously defended their power and influence in the domestic sphere and their private lives. Some researchers have dismissed such actions by arguing that women did not directly challenge the patriarchy. Other researchers have exalted these actions as progressive, militant, and transformative. Clearly both interpretations have elements of truth.

Colonialism, capitalism, religion, apartheid, and war led women to new forms of political action and resistance. As the migratory labor system dumped leadership responsibilities in the laps of women in the Bantustans, so too did military service. Civil war and revolution often increase "women's household burdens . . . and transform the traditional division of labor between men and women, with women assuming male roles" in the home, in politics, and in the economy (Kumar 2001, 13). As Cock asserts, "wars alter social maps" (1991, 183). These new social maps provide opportunities for women to renegotiate their societies' gender systems, as seen in contexts as diverse as Eritrea (Hale 2001; Meintjes 2001), Central America (Luciak 2001), Israel-Palestine, and Northern Ireland (Sharoni 2001). A similar case can be made for South Africa, although the long-term implications of this activity are still uncertain. The SADF provided Afrikaner women social mobility un-known outside marriage; participation in MK provided black women op-portunities to break through gender stereotypes and demonstrate women's parity with men in combat training (Cock 1991).[31] Despite the totalitarian nature of apartheid South Africa, women regularly utilized these various rifts within the gender system. They were able to exploit such gaps to make claims for their own rights or the rights of their people. State repression intended to control and suppress all South Africans. State violence and patriarchal violence are supposed to keep people and women suppressed, yet the op-posite occurred. Women were able to turn the state's conservative preser-vation of the status quo to make new demands and assert their rights.

These competing visions, while clearly global in scale, establish a pattern that continues throughout women's participation in the transition to de-mocracy in South Africa. Nevertheless, although Steyn argues that "a femi-nist agenda is being created that is authentically South African" (1998, 43), women there must come to terms with their pattern of female consciousness and conservative militancy. Since most African nations have thanked women for their participation in liberation and promptly sent them back to the kitchen, South African women have had to work hard to actualize the prom-ises made by the male leaders of the democracy movement. Indeed, they have continued to redefine leadership, feminism, and power on their own terms and in their own cultural contexts. Unfortunately, for every significant gain women have made in the national political arena, their male colleagues have posed a parallel challenge or obstacle to their advancement. If they are able to achieve all that has been promised, they will differ from their sisters in most other postliberation struggles in Africa.

Whereas much of the early work in transitionology was filled with cau-tionary tales of the assimilation and co-optation of women's activism, newer research is challenging this notion with recent evidence that women play piv-otal roles in the creation and the consolidation of democracy. The South Af-rican experience provides an important new position within this debate. Al-though the gender revolution is not yet complete and many obstacles still remain, South African women have succeeded in using electoral politics to sig-nificantly and enduringly improve the lives of women. This case provides the field with a new source of models for women's activism, new modes of women's political participation in office, and new methods for future libera-tion struggles.

* * *

The following chapters examine women's roles in the South African parlia-ment, from the transition to democracy to the more recent progress toward democratic consolidation. Chapter 2 continues the historical analysis of women's roles in the antiapartheid struggle, but it focuses specifically on the transition period, the late 1980s and early 1990s. Infused with narratives obtained during the fieldwork, this chapter relates the mobilization strategies and pressure tactics women used to influence their parties' male leadership to include women's voices in the transition and in the future government. The chapter details how women gained a voice in the constitutional negotiations and secured over 26 percent of the seats in the national parliament. It also explores how the increased participation of women affected political parties' gender compositions and attitudes. Most important, this chapter examines how women's movements in Africa and elsewhere in the developing world are beginning to establish an international network to share their accomplishments and failures. Without this dialogue with their African sisters, the women of South Africa could have missed a unique opportunity to press for national political change.

Chapter 3 discusses the integration of women into parliamentary life and culture. Again, using the voices of the women, the chapter begins with a collection of "first-day" stories in which women relate the culture shock and identity crises they experienced when they entered the chambers of Parliament. The chapter maps this process of political learning, as women moved from this initial confusion into their new roles as policy makers and national politicians. Finally, it summarizes both the obstacles women faced as a group during their integration process and those they continue to experience as legislators. This chapter raises significant challenges to the "critical-mass" theory predominant in the field of women and comparative politics.

Chapter 4 examines how women operate as political actors in their parliamentary lives. South African women have developed numerous ways to participate in the political life of their nation, and they have a wide range of responses to women's issues and gender politics. This chapter maps the continuum of women's participation strategies and gender attitudes. It relates this range of roles and attitudes to the lives and experiences of women before they entered Parliament and before the transition to democracy. It furthermore explains which types of women are leaving the institution and predicts how this exodus will affect Parliament, the parties, and gender politics. These issues are particularly relevant for comparativists studying women's recruitment, integration, and retention in legislatures worldwide, and this chapter concludes with a discussion of these trends.

Chapters 5 and 6 consider the accomplishments that women as a group have made during their first tenure as parliamentarians. Chapter 5 begins with changes in parliamentary culture that were intended to make the institution more "woman friendly." It then analyzes how women are incorporating gender issues into legislative debates and policy creation. Chapter 6 examines women's attempts to mainstream gender within state institutions, Parliament, and civil society.

Chapter 7 details the emerging trend of "professionalization" within the South Africa parliament. Based on fieldwork conducted in May–July 2003, this chapter examines the noticeable differences between women in the first democratic parliament and those in the second. Women with advanced educational degrees, professional occupational backgrounds, and higher socioeconomic statuses are rapidly altering the vast class diversity represented in the 1994 cohort. Although this trend shows up in legislatures internationally, it is remarkable that this transition seems to happening so rapidly within the South African case. The chapter concludes with an overview of the major successes and continued challenges facing women in the South Africa parliament and raises key theories and themes that are widely applicable to international case studies of women in the politics of social movements, democratization, and parliamentary life.

2. Party Politics in the Transition to Democracy

Nobanzi, a former activist and current MP, spoke with me about her first time inside the walls of Parliament, which she initially entered as an antiapartheid activist two years before the 1994 elections. During the constitutional negotiations she and other activists continued their public protest against the apartheid government:

> I remember on the morning of the twenty-sixth of June, which is Freedom Day, I and a number of us, about six of us all together on a nonracial basis, we jumped the walls of Parliament in the early hours of the morning. The regime was, I had told you, continuing with its agenda [of violent oppression]. That period in 1992, there was the massacre in Biopatong. The [constitutional] negotiations were continuing. On the twenty-sixth we jumped. . . . We studied them. We planned it very quietly. There was only one man. We planned and studied: how they moved, where the entrances [were].
>
> We jumped over the walls! . . . And the next thing, people were going to work. It was 7:00. The media was here, the lawyer, monitoring the whole thing. . . . With our placards and our chains, and we tied ourselves around the pillars. We brought paint. We splashed that paint on the walls with our posters: "The Biopatong Massacre." We chained ourselves and threw the key away. People were shouting, "Amandla [Power]! People were shouting. And the police were so shocked. They didn't know what to do. They couldn't touch us because of the media. We were then arrested.

Nobanzi's words relate the complexity of former antiapartheid activists' relationships to the institution of Parliament as a structure of oppression and tyranny. Throughout most of their lives, these activists had seen Parliament as "rubber stamping" the apartheid government's violent and racist policies.

Instead of being an institution based on deliberation, civility, and democracy, Parliament became known to those who were excluded as a place of authoritarianism. Most antiapartheid activists could not enter unless they, like Nobanzi, jumped over the walls. Such actions resulted in imprisonment, torture, or death.

This history makes it remarkable to walk through the halls of Parliament today. The institution is alive with new ethnicities, new leadership, and new ideas. The institution has changed visibly. Even the old pictures of past apartheid leaders were replaced with vibrant art, some of which came from the international Art against Apartheid exhibit. Politically the institution will never be the same, as now two successful democratic elections have filled it with people demographically and ideologically representative of the South Africa population as a whole, not just the white minority.

Although there has been considerable celebration about the new parliament and the new democracy, the activists' path to Parliament has been long and treacherous—and markedly different for men and women. Once inside the halls, activists have had to renegotiate their relationship to an institution they once saw as the agency of oppression. They now hope to utilize the institution as an engine of growth and transformation.

Descriptive Representation and African Democracy

South Africa has suffered many problems of underrepresentation resulting from a tragic history of discrimination and oppression. Questions of race and gender representation have been and will continue to be central to the legitimacy and stability of its democratic system. Descriptive representation—the system in which office holders share their constituents' demographic identities—often becomes a mirror of societal hierarchies and patterns of discrimination (Phillips 1991). This issue of descriptive representation then raises the question of when and how to get women into office. International scholars are finding that women have a key opportunity to move into political office following a revolution or regime change, when there is space open for new ideas and movements (Beckwith 2000). This has not always been the case. The role of "revolutionary" or soldier has not historically ensured women's formal political representation after transitions to democracy (Waylen 1994; Nelson and Chowdhury 1994; Kelly et al. 2001). In Africa the resubordination of women after a revolution has been the norm, not the exception (for Mozambique, see Sheldon 1994; for Zimbabwe, see Ranchod-Nilsson 1994; for Angola, see Scott 1994). This pattern of exclusion is due in part to the fact that women who participate as revolutionaries have two locations of militant engagement. First, they are fighting alongside their male counterparts to gain freedom and democracy for their nation. Second, they are struggling against their male counterparts to gain acceptance and equality and to challenge the restrictive conditions of patriarchy (Beckwith 2000).

This pattern of accepting women as militants and fellow activists during the struggle and then asking them to return to traditional roles in the domestic sphere was quite common in Africa until the mid- to late 1990s. Women across the continent had neither the resources nor the time to consult with their counterparts elsewhere to learn from one another's revolutionary experiences. This was to change in the transitions that occurred in the mid- to late 1990s. Through international women's conferences and new advances in communications technology, women have for the first time been able to create international networks. They are learning from one another's struggles for liberation from colonial oppression and patriarchies. The impact of international networking is seen most strongly in South Africa (G. Seidman 1999), is somewhat apparent in Eritrea (Hale 2001; Connell 1997, 297–302; Connell 1995), and has been found in Uganda (Byanyima 1994; Tripp 2000b). Even if women do not all define feminist struggle in the same way, they often do agree on the strategies and methods for obtaining a voice in the political lives of their countries (Brown et al. 2002).

Again, South African women worked as the "silent strength" behind male leadership, yet they were simultaneously developing a national gender agenda that would ultimately lead to constitutional protection and electoral success (Kadalie 1995). The collective voice of women had power during the transition to democracy specifically because they had been vital members of the struggle as militants, poets, mothers, daughters, unionists, activists, and exiles—even though they were not the visible leaders of the struggle. Their foundation of antiapartheid conservative militancy, discussed in the previous chapter, prepared them for the resistance strategies they would need during the negotiation phase. This power led to the development of a multiparty coalition focused on securing a place for gender equality in the national constitution and ensured the pursuit of affirmative-action measures in the recruitment of women for national office. South Africa's first postapartheid elections, in 1994, saw women gain 26.5 percent of the national offices; the second, in 1999, saw them capture just under 30 percent. No longer the movement's silent strength or the backbone, women in South Africa worked to exert considerable political power and public influence from within their previously limited sphere of influence. To do this, however, they had to negotiate their disparate gender and party identities.

The next subsection will give an overview of South Africa's major political parties, focusing specifically on their agendas and views on gender equality. The subsequent subsections will examine how women worked across party lines to press for representation in a formal political space. The South African case provides a success story showing how women from highly divergent religious, socioeconomic, ethnic, and political backgrounds were able to unify around their gender identity to demand power and recognition within their individual parties and the constitution. Finally, this chapter discusses South African parliamentarians' reactions to the dramatic increase of women in national office.

Gender and Party Identity

During 1990–94 the white minority government and opposition forces negotiated an interim constitution that would guide the creation of the new South African democracy. The 1994 elections were the first free and fully democratic elections to take place in South Africa, and Nelson Mandela's African National Congress (ANC) won an overwhelming majority of seats in the national parliament. The ANC (originally the South African Native National Congress) was formed in 1912 to oppose the increasing segregation and discrimination imposed by the white government, but it did not admit women as members. The purpose of the ANC was to present, through nonracial and nonviolent means, a common African voice seeking redress for discrimination.

The Bantu Women's League, formed in 1931, was considered to be the women's parallel to the ANC, which did not admit women until 1943. The ANC Women's League (ANCWL) replaced the Bantu Women's League at that time, not as a separate organization, but as a branch within the ANC focusing specifically on the needs and issues of women, because the larger organization did not then address gender issues. The ANCWL worked in concert with women's groups from the coloured and white communities to form the Federation of South African Women, or FEDSAW, in 1954 (Ballington 2002). Not until 1956 did the ANC National Executive Council finally have a woman representative, Lilian Ngoyi, who was then the acting president of the ANCWL (African National Congress n.d.).

In 1960 the apartheid government banned both the ANC and the ANCWL; the leaders operated in exile until 1990. During this period women chose to subordinate gender equality to national liberation (Mompati 1991). Nevertheless, the women in exile were learning key lessons and developing an international network of activists with whom they developed a postliberation plan of action. With the end of the ban against the organization and its structures in 1990, it became clear that apartheid was soon to be history. The ANC leaders returned to South Africa and prepared for negotiations and elections. As the primary opposition force, the ANC had a broad election platform focused on reconstruction, development, and reconciliation. The ANC supported a centralized government working toward alleviating poverty, creating jobs, building homes, providing electricity to rural areas and townships, reducing taxes, and reforming the police force.

At the same time the ANCWL was also planning specific steps to increase the presence of women in national office, including a gender quota. Ballington reports that at the first ANC conference within South Africa, the discussion of the quota for women on the ANC party lists was "something of a debacle" given the paltry number of women on the National Executive Committee and the lack of gender consciousness within the male leadership (2002, 76). Women were able to persuade the leadership to reaffirm its commitment to gender equality and women's rights as human rights, but these long-standing rhetorical commitments did not result in any concrete actions. Clearly the ANCWL would have to find its strength to pressure its party from the outside. It would look first to build connections with women from other parties.

These other parties included the six that would later win seats in the 1994 election, including three primarily black parties: the Inkatha Freedom Party, the Pan Africanist Congress of Azania, and the African Christian Democratic Party. The Inkatha Freedom Party (IFP), led by Chief Mongosuthu Buthelezi, draws its primary strength from the KwaZulu-Natal Province, and it supports federalism as an attempt to protect provincial autonomy. Although the vast majority of its members come from the Zulu nation, the IFP is by no means an all-black party. In fact, the IFP has an increasingly diverse representation and has always attracted a core group of white South Africans who are looking for an antiapartheid black party but are ideologically opposed to the ANC's alliance with the South African Communist Party and its policies of a centralized government.

The IFP and ANC have had long and violent conflicts regarding the IFP's suspected collaboration with the apartheid government, which became known as Inkathagate. Inkathagate in part confirmed suspicions that the IFP was complicit in the township violence that took thousands of lives. The Truth and Reconciliation Commission hearings, part of the national reconciliation process, exposed vigilante groups that the apartheid government had paid to foster low-intensity warfare. Deegan (2001) argues this permitted the state to "outsource," or externalize, township violence: the government could appear above reproach and give the impression that the violence in the townships was due to ethnic conflicts. Nevertheless, the government may well have been using individuals, not the IFP itself, to pursue this method of destabilization. The IFP leadership clearly opposes any association with this strategy and vehemently maintains its nonviolent approach in the antiapartheid struggle. Given these long-standing tensions, it is remarkable that women in the ANC and the IFP have come together at key times to collaborate on issues of gender equality, as I will discuss later on.

Its traditionalist, federalist, and classical liberal ideologies have led the IFP leadership to argue against quotas, relying instead on the party's legacy of strong women. The IFP party platform asserts that women's inequality will be redressed through the elimination of economic barriers or social inequality (Albertyn, Hassim, and Meintjes 2002, 36). The IFP opposed the constitutional negotiations and the elections, and it was placed on the ballot only seven days before the 1994 elections, giving it little time to consider or implement any gender quotas. The IFP's manifesto specifically mentions the need for special protection for women and children but often falls short of delineating how gender issues fit into the party's positions on poverty, education, housing, or children (Women'sNet, "Party Manifestos" n.d.). The party asserts that it does not need a quota because it has a rich tradition of female participation (Ballington 2002), especially through organizations such as the IFP's Women's Brigade, the women's branch of the party.

The Pan Africanist Congress of Azania (PAC) began in the 1950s as a militant outgrowth of the ANC. It maintained its devotion to African nationalism throughout the struggle, and its members have generally been distrustful of any association with Western influences. The founders of the PAC were particularly suspicious of the ANC's association with communism and its policy of multiracialism. Throughout the resistance era and the transition to democracy, the PAC retained a position to be left of ANC politics, and party leaders still agitate for greater efforts to alleviate poverty and more emphasis on the needs and strength of black South Africans. The PAC manifesto clearly articulates a gender sensitivity that is informed by the party's commitment to economic and social justice. The manifesto advocates the liberation of women and the rights of all women to education, housing, and employment. While it does not specifically mention women's unique problems with land control and access, the party progressively recognizes unpaid domestic and relational labor (Women'sNet, "Party Manifestos" n.d.).

The African Christian Democratic Party (ACDP) is a fundamentalist Christian party that attempts to appeal to a multiethnic constituency. The ACDP calls for the implementation of biblical principles, the pursuit of a free-market economy, and the creation of a federal system. Its manifesto has been noticeably silent on issues of gender (Women'sNet, "Party Manifestos" n.d.), and the party tends to embrace traditional, conservative interpretations of the role of women in politics.

Three predominately white parties also gained seats in the 1994 elections: the National Party, the Democratic Party, and the Freedom Front. The National Party (NP) is a reformed version of the apartheid-era Nationalist Party; its members are primarily white, mainly Afrikaners but some anglophones, too. The NP supports a free-market economy and a federal system of government that would grant broad powers to provincial governments. The NP, which became the New National Party (NNP) before the 1999 elections, has attempted to move past the highly conservative and patriarchal attitudes of its Afrikaner past. The NP/NNP has historically challenged gender quotas on democratic and equity grounds, arguing that such measures privilege women's rights above men's rights (Ballington 2002), thus replacing one form of discrimination with another. Moving toward classical liberalism, the leaders have advocated a gradualist approach to women's empowerment through developmental assistance and the removal of discriminatory laws and practices (Hassim 2002). Party leaders have tried to recruit women into office instead of using gender quotas, but these strategies have led to very few women in national office.

In an ideologically surprising move, the NNP and the ANC formed a precarious but potentially viable partnership in 2003. As one member of the NNP explained, she felt that her party had come to have much in common with the ANC, especially the experience of governing and having to make unpopular but expedient decisions. This partnership is not a formal voting bloc, but it does represent an increasing collaboration between the parties, especially behind the scenes. The NNP member also stated that this alliance showed that the party was trying to become more progressive and was focusing on the needs of the most disadvantaged, a claim consistent with the party's rhetoric. Given the enormous historical and ideological differences between the parties, however, even this informal partnership is daunting. Others have seen the actions of the NNP as more of an attempt to survive, for it has increasingly lost support since 1994.

The Democratic Party (DP) won several seats in the 1994 election and is the most recent incarnation of the Progressive Party, the Progressive Reform Party, and the Progressive Federal Party. Unwaveringly committed to federalism, it primarily draws its membership from the English-speaking white population and espouses a classical liberal philosophy. The party's official manifesto, reflecting this devotion to classical liberalism, never mentions any special treatment or status of women. Like the IFP and the NP, the DP believes in the equality of opportunity, not the equality of outcome, regardless of demographic characteristics (Women'sNet, "Party Manifestos" n.d.).

The NNP's newfound level of collaboration with the ANC has led several of its members to defect to the Democratic Party, which is now called the Democratic Alliance. Their defection may be viewed as an attempt to remain in a party opposing the ANC, an attempt to escape a sinking party, or an attempt to disassociate themselves with any level of progressive politics—even the limited rhetoric of the NNP. Since it has consistently gained defectors from the NP/NNP, the Democratic Alliance is now the ANC's main opposition in Parliament.

The Freedom Front (FF) is a far-right party promoting Afrikaner nationalism. The party's central electoral platform in 1994 was to demonstrate that a substantial number of Afrikaners supported the idea of a *volkstaat*, an Afrikaner homeland. Much further to the right than the National Party, the FF embodies traditional Afrikaner views of gender relations. Its manifesto asserts that women's participation in government should be based on merit and not through any affirmative-action measures or special treatment (Women'sNet, "Party Manifestos" n.d.).

The 1994 election results alone do not indicate the depths of contention in the negotiations, the role that women played in the negotiations and elections, and the continued struggles that the new government faces. Many of the themes found throughout the liberation struggle recurred during the transition to democracy, including political polarization versus political reconciliation, multiethnic coalitions versus ethnic confrontations, and mass-based protests versus institutionalized reform. Despite these tensions, which challenged the constitutional negotiations, women began to forge a multiparty coalition that worked both publicly and behind the scenes to secure a national platform for gender equality and women's rights.

The Women's National Coalition

Despite the historical and developing political ideologies, early in the 1990s women began to work with one another across party lines to find a voice in the process of creating a constitution. Women of the ANC who had been in political exile during the antiapartheid movement spearheaded this cooperation. While in exile many of these women had been able to secure military training, political experience, and educational degrees that would have been denied them inside South Africa. Many, too, had enjoyed the opportunity to travel to international conferences and to network with women who had participated in similar liberation struggles. One of the key goals of these women was to create a broad-based national women's movement when they returned to South Africa. Women were informed by the examples of failed posttransition gender movements in Zimbabwe, Mozambique, and Angola and by successful women's movements in Europe and the Americas. South Africa women saw again and again the limitations placed on their African sisters after wars of liberation were won.

South African women, especially members of the ANC in exile, sought to avoid these limitations after the transition. They were at the cusp of a new international women's movement and had been exposed to Western feminism. Moreover, the new women's groups received sustenance from Western donor agencies that supported their work for women's advancement (G. Seidman 1999). Several women I interviewed discussed their meetings with activists and academicians at international conferences sponsored by organizations such as the United Nations. They were then able to use their global conference experiences to agitate for domestic political power, a tactic employed by women in the Zimbabwe African National Liberation Army (Cock 1991), in Uganda (Tripp 2000b), and across Africa (Gordon 1996).

The women I interviewed also described discussions with women from other liberation struggles while living in exile camps and military training camps.[1] These stories, as well as the stories of women in Mozambique and Namibia, were etched into the minds of South African women. As Steyn asserts, "South African activist women were determined that the women's movement in South Africa should not meet the fate of so many other women's movements in nationalist struggles, namely, that once liberation had been won, women's issues would once again be relegated to a subordinate role" (1998, 41–42), as had been the case throughout Africa.

The first goal of the women returning from exile was to create a national women's movement with one coalition organization focusing on the goals and needs of women, thus providing a forum for cross-party and cross-race discussion on gender issues. The women knew the dangers of postponing the pursuit of women's liberation until a democratic government was in place. As they had witnessed in similar cases, such hesitation could result in significant delays for women's issues.

The Women's National Coalition (WNC) became the main venue for women's collective action (Meintjes 2001). Women leaders from across South Africa came together in 1991–92 to create the WNC. The coalition comprised over ninety women's organizations that sought to gain a place for women in the new democracy (Ginwala 1992; Schwartz 1994). Although many of the WNC leaders came from the ANCWL, women from all parties, especially the IFP, the NP, and the DP, contributed vitally as both members and leaders.

The WNC was formed to create a national women's movement and to draft an inclusive platform of action, much like the Ugandan women's movement's memorandum of nationwide demands for that nation's 1995 constitution (Tripp 2000b, 77; Goetz 1998, 245). Never before had South African women come together for a common cause as publicly and intentionally as they did when researching and writing the national platform, now know as the Women's Charter.

Tripp (2000a, 655) argues that the WNC may have been the only interest group in South Africa that could work across party, ethnic, and class interests. The WNC maintained unity and a narrow focus. This unity was based in women's exclusion from the constitutional negotiations, a shared pattern of resistance to subordination, and an exclusive focus on gender issues.[2] Unlike Codesa (the Convention for a Democratic South Africa), which regularly disbanded because of interparty conflict, the diverse members of the WNC worked through their differences and maintained a collective force throughout the election process.[3]

With respect to the unity forged within it, the WNC bears a striking resemblance to the women's movement in Uganda, a country that ranks sixth in terms of women's political representation across Africa nations.[4] Parallel to developments in South Africa, the unity of women in Uganda was linked to their exclusion and their "culturally and politically prescribed marginalization," which "may have turned out to be fortuitous," because it granted them the autonomy to control their movement rather than have it be co-opted by the state (Tripp 2000b, 7). These two models are now also joined by the unity within the Pro-Femmes/Twese Hamwe in Rwanda,[5] and collectively these three cases pose a particularly important challenge to Western feminist studies' tendency to emphasize difference. These groups function in highly fractious contexts resulting from decades of racial, ethnic, and class-based discrimination and violence. Aili Mari Tripp maintains that in countries like these, "the challenge for women's movements has been to find ways to focus on commonalities among women and to minimize difference" (2000a, 649). This is not to say that women's groups in Africa try to erase difference; rather, it is to argue that women's groups in Africa are more likely to look for shared identities than to underscore difference in order to rebuild their nations after war and interethnic strife.

Gay Seidman (1999) argues that the transition to democracy itself enabled the WNC's unity. Although noting that women in the antiapartheid struggle tended to delay pursuing gender equity for national liberation, Seidman maintains that they were able to bring gender issues forward once the path was cleared for a new political dispensation: "During the democratic transition, an increasingly articulate women's movement successfully reversed this trend, so that women [who were] within the anti-apartheid movement now treat gender issues very differently than they might have a decade ago" (289; see also Kemp et al. 1995). Whatever its origins, this well-forged unity came together with a new construction of feminism and a particular historical moment to create the conditions under which women could make new demands on their parties and the state itself.

The WNC's Women's Charter ensured that women's interests would be recognized in the constitution. South Africa's constitution has one of the broadest and most inclusive antidiscrimination clauses in the world. Its equality clause (ch. 2, sect. 9) establishes that neither the state nor a person may "unfairly discriminate directly or indirectly against anyone on one or more grounds, including race, gender, sex, pregnancy, marital status, ethnic or social origin, colour, sexual orientation, age, disability, religion, conscience, belief, culture, language and birth." This clause reflects the work of South Africa's progressive movements. The inclusion of sexual orientation, which made South Africa the first nation to specifically prohibit such discrimination, resulted directly from efforts by the gay liberation movement, which had quietly grown in South Africa since the 1980s and had won the support of several high-profile allies in the antiapartheid movement (Croucher 2002). Similarly, women's contributions to the writing and negotiation of the constitution were essential for the entrenchment of women's rights and needs in the formal political language and ideology of the new South Africa.

Women were also able to pressure their parties from the inside based on the growing power of the WNC. Women from the coalition envisioned Codesa's Gender Advisory Committee, which evaluated the constitutional negotiations' gender implications. But this step was not enough to ensure women's representation. In fact, the Negotiating Council of the MultiParty Negotiating Process (MPNP) was completely male dominated at the outset. Codesa established the MPNP to develop and implement structures for the transition to democracy. The negotiating council was responsible for creating the transitional structures, including the Independent Electoral Commission, and negotiating the interim constitution and the bill of rights. Through their collective action, women forced the leadership to permit each party's negotiating team one additional member—provided she was a woman. Women from the NP, the DP, and most notably the IFP worked with the ANC on initiative.[6]

Many political analysts in South Africa see the negotiating council's decision as the women activists' first major tactical win in the transition period, symbolizing the culmination of their years of multiparty collaboration

(Ballington 1999b; Goetz 1998; Geisler 2000). Women had to continue to use their cross-party bargaining techniques and to rely on outside legal experts throughout the negotiations. The DP chairperson, Martheanne Finnemore, served as her organization's female representative at the negotiations. She reflected on her participation in the negotiations in 1994:

> But I did not envisage the tough battle that lay ahead or the barriers that would have to be hurdled if the women were to achieve their aims. Many of us had little formal preparation for the task ahead and took a while to find our feet. During the first phase, the gender oppression directed towards some of the women delegates was quite awesome. Unbelievably, one male delegate would get up and walk out every time the female counterpart spoke. We also suffered from the token appointment of some women delegates who were seen as nothing more than window dressing. The media did nothing to encourage us but almost seemed to hope we would fail. Coordination between the women delegates was also loose and unstructured at the beginning. But the women were to move forward from this first phase of uncertainty to enter a second phase of positive mobilization and claim their victories. Through all the oppression we eventually realised that we would have to stand together and be seen to make a contribution or sink under the criticism. (Finnemore 1994, 20)

Even though ANC women are often given all the credit for the addition of women to the negotiating table (G. Seidman 1999), the successes of women during the negotiations resulted from strategic interparty collaboration and collective pressure.

Such collaboration may in fact be a model for African women's movements, for it closely parallels the Ugandan case. Once Ugandan women mobilized for collective action, as described previously, the impact of their movement was felt almost immediately. Political leaders were forced to recognize the power and influence of the women's movement because of its autonomy from the state (Tripp 2000b, 233). The Ugandan movement rapidly secured the appointment of women ministers and involvement in the debates for the 1995 constitution;[7] its efforts paid off with women winning 19 percent of the seats in Parliament and the vice presidency by 1996 (Tripp 2000b, 67–71).

In both the Ugandan and South African cases, women learned from other failed women's movements and began to envision their own national women's movements growing out of yet distinct from their participation in liberation struggles. Women in the two nations were working almost simultaneously to force their way into their constituent assemblies so they could ensure the protection of gender equality. In both cases a pattern of exclusion and marginalization cleared the way for a unified movement with high levels of associational autonomy. This associational autonomy afforded the women's movements considerable influence to pressure their states for political representation. Their first move was to focus quickly and sharply on building a strong, unified movement to influence their new constitutional frameworks. Their next move was to influence selection of election rules.

Fortunately, South African women were not alone during the creation of election rules, and they could draw on decades of international research to build their case. Duverger (1955, 125–27) posited three broad explanations for the gender gap in office holding: male opposition, female apathy and inertia, and disadvantageous electoral arrangements. Darcy, Welch, and Clark (1994) disputed Duverger's theory of male hostility, finding more significant obstacles to be incumbency power, occupational segregation, and women's domestic responsibilities. At the same time, they supported Duverger's theory of electoral rules, finding that women gain office more readily in systems using multimember districts than in those using single-member districts. The current literature focusing on women's political participation and office holding generally concurs that election rules are the most significant factors determining women's access to office (Reynolds 1999; Norris 1985, 1987; Rule 1981, 1987; Rule and Zimmerman 1994; Matland and Studlar 1996). Also especially important are gender quotas, either mandated or voluntary (Caul 2001). Three central factors of electoral systems influence women's representation: ballot structure (such as a party-list vs. a single-candidate system), district magnitude (number of seats in a district),[8] and the degree of proportionality (allocation of votes to seats).[9] Other research, however, suggests that the congruence of institutional and cultural-ideological factors, as well as the timing of women's suffrage, influences women's electoral success (Kenworthy and Malami 1999).

South African women learned of this research through their connections to women's movements internationally and to the international consultants involved in the constitutional negotiations. South Africa adopted a multi-member-district electoral system that utilizes party-list proportional representation (Ballington 1999b), the system found most likely to enhance women's representation (Duverger 1955; Lakeman 1970; Castles 1981; Rule 1981, 1987; Norris 1985, 1987; Matland 1993; Lovenduski and Norris 1993; Staudt 1998). Although the main impetus for the proportional representation (PR) system was to ensure minority parties a voice in government and to work against ethnic-bloc voting and political polarization (Reynolds 1995), women activists and negotiators were aware of data linking it to women's increased representation worldwide. They actively involved international feminist academicians in crafting the most beneficial electoral system possible (Britton 2002a; Ballington 1999b).

Only recently have women in South Africa started to recognize some of the shortcomings of the PR system and examine electoral reforms (Ballington 1999a; Hassim 1999a). Hassim (2003) evaluates its three main problems for women, especially within South Africa. First, proportional representation gives enormous power and control to the political parties and therefore constitutes a much more centralized form of government than does the system of single-member districts. Although this centrism can be beneficial for women with progressive parties such as the ANC, Hassim cautions that it limits widespread democratic culture within parties and elections. Second, because party leaders have great power—or even complete control—over the selection of women on party lists, they often privilege women who are more moderate and less controversial. Third, legislators will be more accountable to their parties than to their constituencies. This can force women to expend a great deal of energy trying to climb the party ladder instead of working to help their constituents. It is too early to assess whether these problems will undermine women's effectiveness, but women activists should remain cognizant of these important issues.

Affirmative-Action Measures

Having secured election rules that would likely produce more women candidates and office holders, women then turned their attention to internal party politics. The ANC Women's League is the most widely celebrated example of advancing women candidates within a party. By using the power of the WNC to challenge ANC dominance, the ANCWL secured a commitment to have a third of the ANC seats in Parliament reserved for women.

The implementation of the quota was not won overnight, and the foundation for it started during the antiapartheid struggle. To the contrary, ANC women proceeded slowly. First, they placed gender issues on the party agenda by emphasizing the universal nature of women's rights as human rights. This led to the ANC leadership's rhetorical commitment to support the liberation of women. Kanisha of the ANC explained this link between women's rights and human rights:

> We started pushing for the two struggles [of national liberation and women's liberation] to go together, to say that you cannot obtain national liberation without women's liberation. And that started taking root, especially first among the leadership of the ANC itself. The leadership of that time, Oliver Tambo, . . . started articulating the same position, and [so did] other leaders, the president [Nelson Mandela] and the deputy president, Thabo Mbeki, and the present minister of public service—who later on actually headed the Constitutional Committee of the ANC. So all this had been conceptualized. Then we were able

to push issues affecting women, even to make sure that whatever constitutional issues were being considered are taken on board.

Kanisha's words indicate how carefully and intentionally ANC women were working behind the scenes to secure a foundation of women's rights within their party's agenda. By ideologically linking the struggles for racial equality and for gender equality, these women managed to push their leaders to publicly express support for women's liberation.

After several years of the ANC leadership's support for women's rights, ANC women worked within parties and external networks simultaneously. Without this collaboration, the ANC's statements about women's equality might have remained just that, statements. As was previously demonstrated, the WNC's growing national power and influence enabled the ANC's women to assert their gender-based agenda. They then pushed to alter the formal party rules or practices to increase their participation, representation, and influence—namely, by securing the 30 percent quota for women on the party's national election list.

Women from all parties were conversant with the literature on and results of gender quotas. Quotas are seen as the most direct and immediate means for addressing the significant gender imbalance within national legislatures and parliaments (Caul 2001; Rule and Zimmerman 1994; Jones 1996, 1998; Steininger 2000; Phillips 1991). Implementing quotas and targets is much less difficult than transforming society at the level of political, cultural, or socioeconomic structures (Norris 1996; Jones 1998).

The quota was immediately successful, accounting for the majority of the seats held by women in the 1994 election. The symbolic importance of this influx of women into national office was felt immediately. Maria, a member of a primarily white opposition party, discussed the influx within the context of quotas internationally:

> It was a quota, [a] simple matter of a quota system. Been to lots of international conferences, women's conference, where this has been addressed, what works. And the conclusion across the board, whether it is Christian Democrat or Tory type, or whether it is social democrat, socialist-type parties. The socialists are the ones who implement quota systems, and the Tory party bosses appear quite critical of it. But the women in those parties say it is the only thing that works. Because they have been asking for better deals and promised the world, and there has been no delivery or very little delivery, and in the end concluded that quotas work and nothing else much does. And I think you have seen that in other countries. We have 25 percent women because [of] the ANC [commitment for] 33 ⅓ percent.

The ANC was the only party to implement a gender quota It achieved 30 percent representation of women at the national level and thereby raised the ratio of women in Parliament to over 25 percent in 1994. Women in other parties fought similar struggles to achieve gender equity within their organizations, however, and such actions were greatly motivated by the pressure of the ANC's quota. As Dene Smuts,[10] the DP's only female MP in 1994–99, relates, her party boasts a unique history of gender representation. Helen Suzman was its sole parliamentary representative during the apartheid years. Despite Suzman's strong and outspoken leadership, the battle to achieve women's equity in her party as a whole has been considerable. Nevertheless, once women were able to link the need for gender representation to the party's philosophy of sound democratic governance, the party leaders were supportive. Further, now that all parties are working to gain a larger percentage of seats in Parliament, there is even more reason to have women on the lists, as Smuts states:

This party in its previous incarnation as the PFP [Progressive Federal Party], for a long stretch of its existence, it had a single member of Parliament, Ms. Suzman. And she was very famous because she was the lone voice against apartheid and so on. So, by no stretch of the imagination can it be accused of being a party either in this or previous incarnations that was antagonistic to women or didn't see them as MPs. I always make the crack that at one time 100 percent of our party representation was female.

Having said that, the idea of being women in numbers, because to me until I see numbers, and they certainly don't have to be fifty percent or thirty percent—in fact, I eschew the idea of percentages altogether—until I see the numbers, I am still looking at an exception that makes a rule. So I worked quite hard from the time that I came in to establish the idea that on good democratic grounds, there ought to be more women in Parliament and in the party. Let's be frank; the party at that stage was still in the pattern of thinking that applies everywhere in the world: that an MP was unconsciously thought of as someone who was male, in a suit, a breadwinner.

Together with women in the party . . . we plugged away at this idea for a few years. At every congress we did our best. And certainly there was resistance. There was even one congress where someone snickered. You see, we have all been there. . . . Within a few years flat, the idea was fully accepted, and no one would dream of dissenting now. And the way we approach it as a party, since we don't believe in lists and quotas and so forth, we take it upon ourselves to make sure that good women candidates are encouraged to come forward. . . . I think it was in '93 the other parties in Parliament had also gotten the message. There were women out there with votes who took women's issues seriously. And, when you argue it like that, *votes*, boy, do they fall in line fast. They were making feminist speeches in here like you wouldn't believe it. So, formally, the battle was long won, and the only question was whether informally discrimination still operates.

The women I interviewed who were central to the constitutional negotiations repeatedly maintained that obtaining the quota would not have been possible without the external threat and pressure of the emerging women's movement and the WNC. Moreover, both the coalition's power and the previously described internal party politics happened at a unique historical moment. Two members of the South African parliament echoed this sentiment, stating the gains they made during these societal shifts would have been impossible in a normal system. A member of an opposition party remarked: "One of the good things about a society in a complete transition, it is turmoil, but you make strides that it would take decades in the States, in [the] UK, in France, because the whole society is reinventing itself. It is exhilarating." Sarah of the ANC indicated how much they were able to achieve during this transition period, not just for race and gender, but also for sexual preference:

> I always say the one nice thing about being in politics now is that the carpet was pretty much pulled out from under everybody in this country. So everything is up for grabs; everything is being changed. Even the Americans who have this incredibly long history of human rights and fundamental rights—but, for example, gay marriages, which is now the big fuss in America; when people come here and argue about it, we look at them. I think we are going to have it. It is now in the Bill of Rights. I was surprised, because inherently this is a conservative country, not this major liberal left wing. And it is not even that the ANC is that, it is a fairly conservative organization, religious. But I think of this thing: when you change, you change your whole paradigm, not a gradual thing, whole thing happening in two years. You take basically the whole framework out and you put a basically whole new one in. That is what is so exciting about being here—not that rigid old process.

Sarah is aware that the transition was momentous in terms of both racial power shifts and opportunities for women's issues and gay rights. She is also aware this would not have been possible under normal governmental reforms and legislation. The nation was and remains highly conservative and religious. For these women, the goal may be to see not how much more they can achieve but rather how much they can maintain once the transition is complete.

In summary, then, South African women were able to implement the lessons they had learned from international women's movements. The groundwork for an effective movement had been created during the antiapartheid struggle and was utilized during the constitutional negotiation period. Once it was clear the nation would be addressing issues of racial inequality, the women seized the unique and fleeting opportunity to pressure their leaders to actualize their parties' rhetorical commitments to gender equality. Had they waited until after the 1994 election, similar gains would have taken decades, if not longer.

The power and success of the ANCWL were to be deeply tested, if not permanently altered, because of internal conflicts over its leadership and direction during the 1990s. Initially, in 1991, this conflict involved two factions: those supporting the leadership of Winnie Madikizela-Mandela and those supporting leadership by the nationally recognized activists and matriarchs Gertrude Shope and Albertina Sisulu. Shope and Sisulu were elected leaders of the ANCWL in 1991, and Geisler (2000) explains that the opposition to Madikizela-Mandela was concerned that electing her would reduce the ANCWL to an organization led by a soon-to-be president's wife. This, they felt, would strip the organization of its independence.

Tensions continued within the group as its main leaders were elected to Parliament and their roles as MPs became more demanding than their leadership of the ANCWL. Madikizela-Mandela was reelected president of the ANCWL in 1993 and brought with her national controversy. She was now embroiled in conflicts with the ANC given her estrangement from the party and divorce from Nelson Mandela, and there were regular inquiries into her financial practices as well as continued legal action concerning her involvement in the township violence during apartheid. By 1997 most of the key leaders of the ANCWL left the organization because of their opposition to Madikizela-Mandela's leadership and what they viewed as misuse of the league. Geisler (2000) argues that this factionalization of the league "was neither surprising nor bad" given that the league had played an important role in the struggle and subsequent transition to democracy. As the ANC assumed massive power within the government, however, the ANCWL would have to undergo massive reorientation or disband.

Candidate Recruitment and Voting

The ANC, then, led the way in implementing a gender quota for the creation of party lists. Still, although the party committed to having 30 percent of the individuals on its list be women, it failed to specify their placement on the list. As such, only a handful of women appeared at the top of the list. This fact is often overlooked in respect to the ANC because it won so many seats. Thus, many women won office because the ANC won a large number of seats. Having a low rank on the list was not as detrimental as it was in other parties merely because of the ANC's popularity.

Although the ANC was the only party to adopt a quota in 1994, most parties did encourage female representation in some form. The Democratic Party, for example, opposes affirmative-action measures such as quotas but remains committed to nonsexism. The party has had more success with recruiting women into office at the lower levels. During the 1994 elections approximately 30 percent of the individuals on the DP's list were women; their low ranks on the list, however, gave them little chance of being elected.

The Inkatha Freedom Party, much like the DP, asserted that a quota was unnecessary given the party's commitment to nonsexism. The IFP Women's Brigade is a powerful force within the party, and there are several prominent women in the IFP. Nevertheless, only 10 percent of the candidates on the national list were women, which suggests that the IFP's overall commitment to female leadership was more rhetorical than real. Similarly, the African Christian Democratic Party did not have a specific gender policy for its party list, and it, too, relegated women to low ranks—the first woman listed was fifteenth (Ballington 1999b, 12). The same can be said for the Pan Africanist Congress, which asserted a policy of equality even though only 12 percent of its list were women.

The Freedom Front presents an interesting example of party politics. Although the FF was created during the transition period, this far-right Afrikaner party was initially opposed to participating in the 1994 elections and was determined to pursue the Afrikaner *volkstaat* as a first priority. By the time it decided to participate in the election, its leaders did not have sufficient time to consult on the creation of a national list; instead, "those individuals who had already held seats in Parliament were placed at the top of the list" (Ballington 1999b, 14). They had more time to create lists for the lower levels of government, where the party, because of its dedication to federalism and denationalization of politics, places most of its focus.

The National Party matches the DP in its opposition to the quota system. The NP did not compile a national list for the 1994 elections and used only regional lists. Ballington asserts that an "examination of the candidates' lists submitted by the party reveals that women did not feature prominently . . . (averaging only 11%) . . . It is clear that the NP was not committed to a policy of gender inclusivity in Parliament" (1999b, 15). The National Party, now the New National Party, resisted the implementation of an official gender quota despite the insistence of female MPs within their party:

> It was the NNP's insistence against the accommodation of more women that prompted the recent defection to the DP of Western Cape politician Pauline Cupido. She was among the key coloured members of the party supposed to comprise the "new" in the NNP. "The NNP is a male chauvinist party!" says

Cupido, a measured and God-fearing woman not usually given to such outbursts. "The final straw came in December. We asked them to consider that at least one in five places be reserved for women. They booed me! Whenever female members stood up, they were clearly not interested. The [male MPs] were talking on their own." (Haffajee 1999, 1–2)

The women of the NNP maintain that the pressure applied by the ANC quota is substantial for all parties, even if they do not adopt similar quotas, a position held by Martha Olckers, the NNP legislator from Western Cape Province: "If it weren't for the ANC ladies and the pressure they put on the government, females would have been much worse off" (qtd. in Haffajee 1999, 2).

The efforts to recruit women to run for office and then get them elected generally increased with the 1999 elections, although with varied success. The ANC, for example, improved the chances of electing women by having every third candidate on its list be a woman (Ballington 1999d). This new ranking system and an increase in the ANC's percentage of the overall vote led to a slight increase in the percentage of ANC women who won office in 1999. More important, it suggests that women have solidified their position in the party at the national level. The pre-1994 election promises by ANC leaders— promises that had strategically been secured by the ANCWL—are now clearly entrenched in the electoral process.

The United Democratic Movement, too, considered gender when preparing its candidate lists for the 1999 elections. The United Democratic Movement is the only new party to have gained seats in that election. The UDM was founded in 1997 by Bantu Holomisa, a high-ranking and popular ANC member until he was expelled from the party following his public criticism of ANC corruption. Interestingly, the UDM's party manifesto is second only to the ANC's in terms of progressive positions on gender rights. The manifesto argues for women's advancement politically, economically, socially, and educationally (Women'sNet, "Party Manifestos" n.d.).

Several other smaller parties gained representation for the first time in 1999, but none of them had any overt affirmative-action mechanisms or allegiances to gender equality. After winning only one seat in Parliament, the Minority Front dropped its original representative and substituted the longtime union activist Sunklavathy Rajbelly, making women 100 percent of its parliamentary representation. The other parties are ideologically to the right and have disproportionately small percentages of women representatives (Ballington 2002). In almost all these cases, however, the women being recruited into these positions have high levels of experience and skills that make them visible within their parties and Parliament (I discuss this more fully in chapter 7).

All the parties publishing national lists for both elections—the ACDP, ANC, FF, IFP, and PAC—increased the percentage of women on them. The ACDP increased its percentage from 13 percent to 29 percent; the ANC, from 32 to 39 percent; the FF, from 12 to 16 percent; the IFP, from 10 to 22 percent; and the PAC, from 12 percent to 22 percent. The NNP and the DP party did not create national lists for the 1999 elections, but the percentage of women among all the parties' MPs rose from 14 percent to 16 percent. The corresponding figure for the NNP decreased slightly from 1994 to 1999, perhaps reflecting their loss of overall seats more than any intentional decision to have fewer women in office. Indeed, its regional lists reveal an increase of women, from 11.4 percent in 1994 to 18.4 percent in 1999.

But even the progressive ANC adopted some questionable practices in placing women on its list, and South African women's-rights advocates have made important observations about the composition of the ANC list for the 1999 elections. In several cases women who had a history of gender-based activism received a ranking lower than their national political profiles indicated they deserved. Noting that an exclusive focus on gender quotas may obscure the quality of women's commitment to gender issues, Alice Coetzee relates the fears of many women's-rights advocates: although women increased their number of parliamentary seats in 1999, a "central concern was that MPs who do take up gender issues, like Pregs Govender (46) and Nozizwe Madlala Routledge (79), were far too low down" on the list. She adds, quoting Shireen Hassim of Wits University, "What is clear, is that taking up gender issues is not the best way for a woman to increase mobility within the party" (Coetzee 1999). The ANC seems to have heard and responded to this challenge for the 2004 elections, as I will discuss in chapter 7.

Women faced further issues during the two elections—specifically, women's participation in the voting process in 1994. Ballington's (1999b) analysis of the 1994 elections found several key ways women were either excluded from voting or under-represented by electioneering practices. For example, Ballington found that in the 1994 election officials struggled to meet logistical challenges, including the remote locations of rural women, illiteracy, and lack of identity documents. Additionally, threats of violence intimidated many women and men from going to the polls; women further faced intimidation from male family members who tried to control their votes. Several studies have also reported that the election coverage was not equitable in its presentation of women's issues or women's candidacies, and the media tended to focus on the same female leaders time and again (Ballington 1999b, 3–11). These observations parallel others in the literature concerning the media's impact on women's campaigns in the U.S. state legislatures, which consistently argues that women candidates receive less media coverage than men do and that the coverage they receive is gendered and discriminatory (Swers 2001, 171).[11]

Similar media constraints and lack of gender focus during the election process were again observed in 1999. Despite the increase in the number of women registered to vote in that election (1 ½ million more women than men), parties and the media continued to campaign to the male voter. As Shireen Motara, from the Commission on Gender Equality, stated: "One major trend that has emerged from current electioneering is that very little, if any, electioneering has been aimed specifically at women. If political parties are naïve enough to think that women do not notice this, they are mistaken. . . . It is a reminder of how invisible women really are in the political arena—as leaders and as voters. It also indicates that political parties are not recognising women as a specific component of the electorate" (1999, 1). Overwhelmingly, however, most reports indicate that several of the obstacles to voter recruitment and participation found in 1994 had been addressed or somehow taken into account by the 1999 elections. The results of the 2004 elections are discussed in full in chapter 7.

Gender Representation and Party Politics

The ANC's commitment to filling one-third of its seats with women has accomplished two notable objectives. First, it has greatly increased the number of women in national government, which has brought and will continue to bring international support and approval. Vasha, a high-ranking member of the ANC, explained the logic behind the quota:

> Essentially what we have managed to do is begun to make women visible. I think that is an important thing. It's not that there have never been competent women. It's just that they were invisible. And by making a conscious effort by way of the ANC quota—that was at a political level. But perhaps more importantly, by the way women organized, the way they impinged on the negotiations, the way they conducted themselves. All these made an impact. Women put themselves on the national agenda. No one could deny them that.

Phyllis, a member of a predominately white opposition party, agreed with the positive change in atmosphere following the transition, although she was concerned about the dangers of quotas on institutional capacity:

> I must say I have a concern that empowerment has tended to take the form of visible affirmative action of the decorative kind. I have been a proponent of affirmative action—as we have chosen to call it, "positive action," [which] is

really a better way of describing it. But I have been a proponent of it at some cost to myself politically, because inside this kind of philosophy that I come from, interventionism isn't the natural departing point. And so I have been really worried to see people brought in on the wrong sort of affirmative action, and I think it is such an easy way for a new government in a society like this to demonstrate change. You put a lot of new faces in various places. And it is too easy if you are not following the proper route of making sure the people you put in have whatever training of skills you need to do their jobs. Otherwise it becomes counterproductive, and they always end up with a greater sense of inadequacy, which compounds the problem. . . . Take the case of the women, for example, where the ANC decided before the election to have 30 percent of the women on its list—a quota, in effect—which we warned them against the dangers. And now that we are seventh in the world, about a quarter female, and that is fine and dandy. And it does have a certain critical-mass-type effect on the atmosphere in a place, which I think must have implications for how well we will function or not.

This trend has further manifested itself in Uganda, where, Tripp reports, reserving parliamentary seats for women has since 1989 "generally been positive" for women's symbolic and substantive representation (2000b, 71), even though both she and Tamale (1999) have noted the resistance and marginalization facing Ugandan women who gained seats though affirmative action. The practice, which was designed to be temporary, allowed women to gain a significant portion of the seats, which in turn let them challenge the masculinist perceptions of political officials. As of October 2004 Uganda ranked twenty-sixth worldwide in the number of women in national office, with 24.7 percent of the seats occupied by women.

The second and more lasting impact of the quota is the pressure it placed on other political parties to increase the number of women on their party lists. This result conditionally supports Matland and Studlar's (1996) theory of "party contagion." Matland and Studlar postulate that levels of women's representation increase more rapidly within multimember proportional-representation systems because parties within PR systems respond more quickly to the pressure of a rival party's nomination of women. Their work has been provisionally supported by events elsewhere, including Austria (Steiniger 2000).

Although women in South African opposition parties would not directly say they supported the quota, most agreed with the ANC's position on gender equality and would like to see the number of women in office increased. Women in the opposition parties have been advocating for increased numbers, and the ANC's success has assisted this call. One male delegate from an opposition party stated that his party would have more women in the future. He admitted that the ANC had strategically and effectively criticized his party's low numbers and merit policy: "When we said, 'We decide on merit,' they said, 'Oh, so you haven't got women who are capable.' It is window dressing, but under the circumstances, we must do it." Women from the ANC found the pressure points for members of the opposition.

This was a frequent exchange between members of the ANC and members of opposition parties such as the NP, the IFP, the FF, the ACDP, and the DP. Women were also redefining merit. During a debate on an appropriations bill for the Ministry of Water Affairs and Forestry, N. R. Shope criticized the ministry for its lack of diversity. A member of the opposition who opposes affirmative action countered her critiques:

> Mrs. N. R. Shope: The reality [is] that women in rural areas still walk many kilometres to fetch water and carry water on their heads. This has a direct effect on the health of women in South Africa. The weight that they carry has implications for later life, when they develop backache and all sorts of diseases related to that strain. . . . [There are] places where water supply is still something that is being talked about, but is far from a reality. . . . Of the large number of staff members that we have there, there are only two Black chief directors. With water being a problem that directly faces women, in particular African women, I would expect, in that department, to see more faces of African women who are supposed to take decisions on the problems facing them. I hope that when we come to the next appointments, this department will consider women, African women in particular.
>
> Mr. C. M. George: On merit!
>
> Mrs. N. R. Shope: Yes on merit. We have merit. We have managed, without all the things that others have had, to bring our children up without easy access to water. We are still doing it today and we can decide our fate. (National Assembly 1996b, 1760)

Shope asserts that African women's lives, their experiences as caregivers and laborers, are the credentials they bring to office. She goes even further to assert that these credentials are more meritorious than white South African men's experiences. Black South African women, in Shope's estimation, should have a central role in making decisions affecting water policy for rural African women.

Women in opposition parties recognized that the ANC's quota was helping change the gender imbalances in their own parties. A woman from a predominantly white party stated that the increase in the number of women within her party was due to pressure from the ANC numbers:

We realized there was competition here. [My party], I am afraid, hasn't really taken the initiative on pushing women into positions because part of our position has always been against affirmative action, for merit. But I said to our leader the other day, "Is it our view that there are very few women of merit or what?" So it cuts both ways. Women are coming on tremendously in our party as far as local government . . . and provincial legislatures. . . . It has had an impact. I suppose I am a bit of a pioneer of this in our party because I have always spoken up, and I have always gotten a lot of flack for it. But our leader has always supported me . . . and encouraged me to make a big thing of it, which is fine. I think he knows what the political realities are. And particularly in the black community, pushing for women is important. My perception is that black women have been more oppressed in everything—the domestic context—[have] had a double whammy discrimination on basis of gender and color. . . . We are against the quota system, but it does seem to be the only thing that really works.

Members of the FF and the ACDP also insist that they will have more women on their lists in the future. They asserted that the absence of women in the initial party list for the 1994 election was due to the speed of party formation before the elections.

Beyond the rhetorical promises of women's increased representation, the results of the 1999 elections give marginal support to Matland and Studlar's (1996) party contagion theory. In terms of women as a percentage of the parties' MPs, the ANC continued to lead the parties with 36.5 percent, an increase from 34.3 percent in 1994. Several parties increased their representation of women, including the ACDP, the DP, and the PAC. Notably, the ACDP, which had no women in office after the 1994 elections, now has 33.3 percent women (Ballington 1999b, 1999c).

Nevertheless, two parties—the IFP and the NNP—notably fell in their representation of women, despite their verbal commitments to increase the number of women in office. These decreases may be related to the significant drop in the number of seats these parties won as much as to a lack of substantive commitment to their rhetorical pledges of gender equity. The attempts to have more women on the lists clearly improved, as stated earlier. The number of women on the IFP list increased from 10 percent to 12 percent, and that on the NP regional lists increased from 11.4 percent to 18.4 percent. Removing the ANC representatives from consideration, this also contributes to an absolute decrease in the number of women in Parliament in opposition parties, from 27 of 149 (18.1 percent in 1994) to 22 of 134 (16.4 percent in 1999). Therefore, the proliferation of minor parties in the 1999 elections, parties that took a smaller number of seats and filled them with men, contributed to an overall decline in the number of women in opposition parties. These mixed results will need to be examined again after the next election. Clearly, the impact of contagion may be seen in several parties, especially those that held their ground or increased their seats in Parliament, such as the DP and the ACDP. Similarly, the fact that all the parties increased the number of women on the party lists also supports the idea of contagion. The problem is that these opposition parties either took fewer seats in 1998 than in 1994 or they had women ranked in unwinnable positions on the list.

Once a full acceptance of women in office has been achieved, the question must again shift to ensuring that they have an equal voice within the parliamentary structure. The process of making women visible in the formal political sphere is simply one piece of the complex story of gender politics in South Africa.

3. Women's Integration in Parliament

In the previous chapters I have discussed the roles women played in the antiapartheid struggle and the obstacles they faced—and to some extent surmounted—in achieving not only a voice but actual presence in their own parties and in Parliament. Most South African parties have by now expressed commitments to increasing the number of women in the parties themselves and in political offices, whether local, provincial, or national. But how will these commitments be manifested in post-1999 elections? As this book goes to press, the current election rules are up for review; they may be left alone, revised, or even scrapped. The main critics of the current pure proportional-representation (PR) system argue that it removes MPs from direct accountability to their constituents because they are elected at large. Many smaller parties propose instead a mixed PR system, where some seats are elected at large, through lists, and some through specific constituency areas. Still, the electoral review may end up retaining the current system, which has had led to the continued, visible representation of women.

A more auspicious indicator of the future may be the way that South African women have continued to use their mobilization strategies and informal networks to influence parties. Just as women had done in forcing their representation in the constitutional negotiations and the 1994 elections, individual activists and groups again worked collectively to put women on the national agenda in 1999, and they are building a coalition to join the international "50/50 campaign." Although not without its tensions, this cross-party effort to achieve gender parity in government indicates that unity continues to be an important way for women to make their voices heard and to secure their rights. Women's branches of political parties, women's advocates, and women's organizations have been able to extend their tradition of cooperation at particular political moments, implementing lessons they learned in the antiapartheid struggle, building on the success of the 1994 elections, and continuing on through the post-1999 consolidation phase. Although their goals have not been fully achieved, they have developed key methods to propel their actions forward.

Unlike much of the literature on women and parliaments, which focuses on women gaining seats (e.g., Duverger 1955; Lakeman 1970; Castles 1981; Norris 1985, 1987; Rule 1981, 1987; Rule and Zimmerman 1992; Matland 1993; Lovenduski and Norris 1993), I want to examine what happens to women once they take office. Much in the tradition of Gertzog (1995), Thomas (1997), and Considine and Deutchman (1996), in this chapter I study how women are integrated and behave within political office. Unlike previous studies, however, mine examines women's integration and behavior inside an institution and a nation experiencing massive political, cultural, and social upheaval. Before the 1994 elections black South Africans with grievances had no recourse even to legal channels, let alone the halls of Parliament. Women have had to continue to challenge the processes and norms of the institution so that they could find a place there.

What is remarkable about South Africa's transition to democracy is that it was not a revolution in the sense that comparative politics uses the term. Rather, it was a "great reform," a massive society-wide reform negotiated by party and labor leaders. As such, significant gaps separated the goals, beliefs, and experiences of negotiating party leaders from those of grassroots party members. Party, union, and women leaders actively worked with their old enemies to draft a constitution for a new system of nonracial governance. The rank-and-file members, however, were confused and ambivalent about the very idea of negotiations, during which process many women continued to push their parties toward mass action and public protest. For some, the struggle was their only source of political education and training. They feared, reviled, and protested against Parliament. To then be elected to Parliament and asked to serve with life-long enemies was alienating and disorienting.

The complex processes of national and institutional democratization must be seen in terms of an extended process of political learning, both for individuals and for groups within South African society. In this chapter I investigate that process of political learning by examining women's "first-day stories," that is, tales of their early encounters with Parliament. Whereas some women remembered jumping over Parliament's walls in protest, others had long been members of the old regime. Whatever their backgrounds, however, South African women have struggled to integrate themselves in parliamentary life and have worked tirelessly to incorporate their issues and their voices in the democratization of Parliament, legislation, and society.

Old Enemies Become Legislative Allies

> Democracies do not emerge or reemerge as if propelled by some natural process. . . . They are recreated piece by piece, institution by institution, and the creators are usually old enemies.
>
> —Nancy Bermeo, "Rethinking Regime Change" (1990)

The South African negotiations over governance required compromise among parties and forces that had been locked into a bloody, decades-long civil war. As the preceding epigraph suggests, members of the 1994 parliament were old enemies working toward compromise and mutual understanding. Granted, the negotiations succeeded in limiting the potential for bloodshed that accompanies revolutions. With compromise, however, comes concession. Members of more progressive parties feel their agendas and priorities have been slowed and hindered by vestiges of the old regime. Nomuula, a member of a primarily black and coloured opposition party, indicates how the delivery of services has been slowed by the nature of the transition:

> In terms of delivery, most unfortunately, we didn't have a revolution where there was a coup and we took over. It wasn't [as if] we actually needed to amend the present laws and work with the civil service and all the garbage we inherited. [But] we accept the criticism. We know this period has been a painful one. Grappling with issue legislation and everything. And it has slowed down the process of delivery. But we are determined to deliver. That is what we came here for, and that is what we shall do: deliver to our people. And this is one thing that actually kept us going. We want to see how people's lives change and see our communities changing and see integrated residence areas. . . . [But] it cannot be done overnight.

The negotiation process also created a sense of disorientation among party members and antiapartheid activists. Since party and union leadership conducted much of the negotiations, many decisions were made at the top; members were simply informed of the decisions. Thandi, who had been a part of several successful resistance campaigns during the antiapartheid movement, related the sense of confusion and dislocation she and other activists felt during the negotiation period. They were surprised by the very idea of negotiations, yet they were expected to convince the rest of the country to accept the constitutional talks:

> We said, "Negotiation period? Negotiations? What is happening?" That is when the focus started changing. Our leaders left from prison, and the period cre-

ated confusion of what we were to be doing. But the state repression continued, and we had to resist that until eventually we managed to grapple with issue[s], and we were forced to change our focus.

We were forced at the same time to reeducate the masses of this country to the new direction. . . . We were supposed to move slowly away from consumer boycotts, the destruction of white-owned institutions or trucks going into the townships, all such things. And the police! Enemy number one! That had been policy—anything in uniform. We just got very jittery. We had to reeducate on those lines: "The leadership is negotiating." It was a very difficult period. . . .

Those were the kinds of campaigns we embarked on. You know, the passive resistance, not the violent resistance that we used to do, even though the regime was still applying violent means against our people. That was the kind of resistance we embarked upon during the negotiations.

The period towards the elections . . . [she took an extended, deliberative pause] it was too big for us, but we made it because we are activists. We are soldiers on the ground, and we managed it: "We mustn't lose." The enemy has had such experience in dividing our people.

Simply because the leadership had embarked on a period of negotiations did not mean that South Africa's culture of violence had ceased. As Thandi's remarks recount, party leaders handed down orders to stop any active resistance, yet decades of violence from the apartheid state, directly via security officials or indirectly via provocation of township fighting, had made hostility and aggression part of the political culture. Thandi and other activists saw themselves as soldiers on the ground, not in the traditional military sense, but in the sense of those who directly confront defense officials or engage in acts of sabotage. Yet there were other men and women in the resistance who had received military training in exile and employed that training in the conflicts in Namibia or when they returned to South Africa as insurgents. To suddenly have the leadership call for a change in method without any visible or immediate change in the structure of the white government was mystifying.

The militant resistance to state violence did foster violence in the youth culture of the townships, however, where frustration and fear led to gangs that had no other way to express anger (Eades 1999, 70). The ANC leadership tried to control this violence, but its activities and energies were focused on the negotiations, not on township politics: "The ANC faced the problems of an army of frustrated youths who ignored the calls of discipline from party leadership, a conflict between returning exiles and local leaders, [and] dissension within ANC-led community based 'defense units' that were taken over by criminal elements" (Eades 1999, 71).

Brutality and bloodshed continued to rule life across the nation, while leaders of all parties were faced with the challenging yet heady business of writing a constitution. Yet the distance between the leadership and the rank and file was not too vast. Constitutional negotiations initially fell apart after the Boipatong massacre of ANC supporters in 1992. Despite continued efforts within the negotiations and the peace process, the incessant political violence left South Africans living in a state of fear. Conservative estimates suggest that KwaZulu-Natal alone saw over 1,600 political deaths in 1994— the year of the first democratic election (Manby 1995).[1]

The period building up to the elections was brief, confusing, and emotional for the entire country. The activist and consultant Debbie Budlender gave me a larger context for understanding why the negotiations were confusing: "There was certainly discomfort at the time, with people not knowing what was going on. I think this was to do with new players as much as anything else, i.e., the local people did not know exiles, ex-jailed, and vice versa. So there were not the same flows of information, gossip, etc. as before. Then, it was a new ball game, so [it] took time to understand. Thirdly, the complaint has to be seen against the South African obsession with participation, consultation, forums, etc." Whereas the activists had previously enjoyed informal and often underground ties to one another, several new groups had now been brought into the picture. Activists who remained in the country were supposed to accept and trust exiles who had been working for the movement outside the country, and vice versa, yet neither group knew the other. Both groups had been working in highly secretive conditions and had learned not to trust unknown or untested persons.

ANC and PAC members had been treated as insidious terrorists and violent criminals. Now they were exalted as political leaders and dignified visionaries. Many had been separated from their families for years, yet they had to rapidly reenter the nation and begin to create a new society. Moreover, ANC, IFP, and NP leaders had been in constant conflict for decades. Now they were supposed to sit down and craft a plan that could allow all political parties and ethnic groups to coexist.

Following this disconcerting negotiation period, many of these former enemies were brought into the same chambers and were charged with running government under the interim constitution. Given their lack of experience, both in governing and in working with enemies, it may be one of the most notable achievements of this century that the first days of the new South African government went as smoothly as they did. Unlike party leaders, who had extensive face-to-face interaction with their enemies during the negotiations, these soldiers were brought into Parliament having had little or no direct contact with their opposing forces.

The confusion and subsequent reorientation of attitudes reached even the

Afrikaners, a group traditionally thought to contain the most conservative element of the apartheid era. One woman spoke quite specifically about the transition's effect on Afrikaner psychology:

> [When you] read thing[s] written after [election] day, [they say things like] "I had to stand in that queue for five hours. And my maid and my gardener were there, and we shared drinks." And it happened: I was there, and people had to stand for five, six, seven hours, and they did. That was the amazing thing. To go and vote, and that did it. Something happened on that day.
>
> It will be difficult; I am not denying that. We have a painful history. The truth commission is the one thing which is the most necessary, but it is also the most dangerous thing. If anything, this is playing into Afrikaner psychology very much, and I want to keep an eye on that. Don't know what I mean by that, but what can one do?
>
> It is very interesting what is happening to Afrikaners now. It is disturbing them. One shouldn't talk about a group too much, but . . . it is hard for them, and they actually have to realize that the people they supported really did awful things. People quickly say, "We didn't know," but people are also saying, "Why didn't we know?" and "We should have known."
>
> Then having to live with it. People will have to realize . . . the ease with which they [used] to say, "[The ANC] were the bad guys" and now say, "Okay, so we admit we were bad guys. But the ANC were also bad guys, and that made us bad guys." That is still what they believe. The deKock trial—more [of] these things will come up, and maybe [they will see] it wasn't only in response to other bad guys. Maybe [the ANC] weren't as bad as we thought they were. Germany has had to live with having supported a system which was so incredibly bad. . . . Now one has to see how [Afrikaners] react on that feeling of guilt and anger. Seeing people getting very mad at the National Party [and] saying, "I feel so cheated. I trusted you. I never knew you did this. You said you were Christian." It is a difficult phase, and let's hope it can be challenged.

So the transition period involved a redefinition of the apartheid-era conflict and the enemies within it. No longer could whites consider themselves innocent victims or proponents of democracy and freedom. They had to ask whether their archenemies might have been on the side of truth. The period of reflection and reconciliation continues today as elements in the white population begin to identify the enemy within themselves and their previous loyalties. The extent of this conversion remains to be seen, but the period leading up to the elections provided enough confusion to loosen long-held allegiances and ideologies and to open a path toward a new system of governance.

The negotiations period, replete with these experiences of dislocation and alienation, created a shaky foundation for the newly elected MPs' assumption of power, whatever their race. Members of the resistance movement faced internal and often unspoken questions concerning the legitimacy of the negotiations, the constitution, and the electoral process. Some had been trained as insurgents, all had lived in a culture of violence and struggle, and a great many had been victimized by the apartheid state in unthinkable ways. Many members of the Pan African Congress, the South African Communist Party, the African National Congress, and the Congress of South African Trade Unions who were not directly involved in the negotiations—and most were not—found the notions of elections, reconciliation, and cooperation not just dissatisfying but philosophically intolerable.

Moreover, new patterns and new players emerged within these antiapartheid parties themselves, which further confused and undermined the stability of the new parliament and pitted factions against one another: exiles versus local leaders, prisoners versus underground activists, and elites versus the rank and file. The resistance movement was about to take control of Parliament and become the leading political voice for the nation as a whole. Trust, then, was essential for a unified voice and agenda. Yet developing trust requires extended contact, and that was in short supply. Nevertheless, those who had remained in South Africa, working in the underground, were expected to collaborate unquestionably with those coming back from exile.

Then, too, the parties distrusted one another. The Inkatha Freedom Party and ANC had been involved in countless ideological and numerous physical skirmishes over several decades. The ANC and the PAC saw the National Party, the controlling party of the apartheid state at the time of the transition, as the enemy. The NP and the IFP forged short-lived alliances before and during the negotiations but by the 1994 elections found themselves on opposing sides of the constitutional debate (Eades 1999). The Freedom Front was forged out of distrust for the conciliatory moves of the NP, and most members of the FF advocated a complete physical, social, and economic separation from the new South Africa. Elections and negotiations were seen as ideologically and politically abhorrent.

Finally, the negotiation process bore gender-related implications. As I discussed in the previous chapter, women had to force their ideas as well as their physical presence into the negotiation process, for all the original members of the negotiating council were men. It took a fight, but they succeeded. Ultimately this struggle to make themselves and their issues visible in the negotiating body, Codesa (Convention for a Democratic South Africa), ensured a framework for gender issues in the new South Africa. But the methods of securing such a framework required cross-party coalitions and consistent pressure on party leaders.

This quest to actualize the prenegotiation promises for gender inclusiveness and equality made by all party leaders raised even more questions for women who became MPs. During the negotiations party leaders sent women a strong signal that any advances they made would have to be made on their own time and using their own resources. Their goals were far from secure and often put them in direct conflict with members of their own parties. Just as calls for unity during the antiapartheid movement served, intentionally or unintentionally, to silence or subordinate gender issues, so too did calls for intraparty unity; women were asked to delay their own goals for the "greater good."

From Negotiations to Governance

This disjointed and disruptive negotiation period was the backdrop for many of my discussions with women about their rapid transitions from activists to policy makers. Perhaps the most memorable account comes from Nhlahla, a former antiapartheid activist who related in intimate terms the volatile emotions she felt when entering the chambers for the first time. Nhlahla's story encapsulates the feelings of many resistance fighters who were forced to work with old enemies and indicates how miraculous it was that the transition went as smoothly as it did:

> The first day we had a joint sitting with National Assembly and Senate. I looked at some of the people. I mean, some of them had appeared on TV, and they were implicated in all the violence. I looked and said there is [a leader of a rival party]! I just felt like wringing his neck. And we didn't know one another from the ANC. We came from all over. And I said to the person next to me, "Why are we not killing these people? They are here! What is all this about reconciliation?" I mean, I hate reconciliation; my two brothers were killed. So I was saying, "We can't work with people who have killed our people." So I was saying, "We must kill them. No, man; I can't sit here." I don't know what the others think about this reconciliation that the ANC is preaching. But to tell you the honest fact, when I came here and saw some of the people, I wanted to forget reconciliation. But things were happening so quickly. . . .
>
> President Mandela would say, "We must give these positions to the NP" and say "reconciliation," and people went mad. But I want to say that I have changed from that, and many others have changed from that. . . . So I want to say that President Mandela brought about a lot of change, which was rather painful for many of us. After many, many months he came to us and said, "When I made certain changes, when I was president and things were happening so quickly, I didn't know I was hurting any of you. I said you must give certain positions to the NP because they have been in power for many years,

and it would be difficult for them to accept that they were no longer in power. And I have given a number of positions to the IFP because we have had a lot of trouble with the IFP."

As months went by, we had released our anger, and we started to work. I think it was difficult for me because I was from a background—let me say we, as the ANC, were from a background where there was lots of music at the rallies, that we sing, lot of poetry, lots of toyi toying,[2] which is not here. Parliament is like a dead place. When you stand up, people just heckle. They don't know what you are going to say, but because you are ANC, the NP just shout at you. It was difficult for me to adjust. I spent a lot of time crying. Because, I mean, that sudden change. You know, all that time you spent in a shack area, and then all of the sudden you are in Parliament. You are flying all over the place, and when you leave—my place was a place of lots of violence. . . .

But I think the changes that were initiated by President Mandela, they were for the good of us all. I no longer have that anger. Some of my best friends are in the IFP. Some of them are in the NP.

Nhlahla relates in painful detail how the transition affected her individually and as a member of the ANC. Her first-day account relates experiences remarkably similar to those many activists underwent during the negotiations. Policies and dictates came from above, and personal feelings of anger and distrust had to be dealt with privately and quickly. Her sense of dislocation resulted not only from the class identities she encountered but also from the costs of reconciliation. While she personally would have preferred justice or retribution, her only options were acceptance and cool collegiality. Similarly, her identity as a political actor was tied to a particular methodology—one alive with vibrant energy and immediacy. She now found herself in an institution that demanded a new type of political participation, one she found distant, cold, and ethereal.

As Nhlahla's story illustrates, the transition to democracy in South Africa produced an initial legislature composed of individuals most of whom had never before been a part of a formal government, certainly not one governed by Westminster's parliamentary procedures. This disconnection presented a striking irony: former insurgents were learning how to govern within the old system. The rules and norms of Parliament were foreign to most antiapartheid activists. Thandi, too, talked about this culture shock and assimilation period:

I remember the first day in the chamber. And here came these other people in the parties. And they were coming in here with motions and motions and one after the other. And the way we were quiet! We didn't like this, but what does one do? How could we stop it? The air was tension. We all looked around,

"What is this? What is happening?" But when we left the chamber, we said, "This must never happen again!" Because I saw [members of parties within the previous government] enjoying it. They had caught us. We didn't know the rules of Parliament, the procedures of all that.

Thandi continued by discussing the actions she and other members had to take to be part of Parliament and learn the policy-making process:

> We then told ourselves this must never happen again. Then we were forced and said that the rules and regulations must be read by everyone, [to see] what needs to be done. And we were on top of things. It was so quick! We had to do it for our people, and what we came into Parliament for was to learn really fast. . . . We knew some of the procedures would take us by surprise, but we knew our homework was to read, read, and read. And we are on top of things. It is through hard work: reading at home, discussion amongst ourselves, and such things. We are still learning. Not saying that we know everything 100 percent, but we are determined not to let our people down.

The members of the resistance parties worked at a tremendous pace to learn parliamentary rules and procedures. In Thandi's estimation, the process of self-imposed assimilation took only a few weeks. As my interviews clearly showed, however, many women were still trying to learn how to govern in accordance to their beliefs and goals, even though many of the rules and procedures were becoming routine.

When I asked the women how they had learned about the participation process, what steps they had taken to educate themselves, they mentioned several different ways. First, one ANC member talked about the weekly and sometimes semiweekly study circles. Members of a committee would gather in the evenings to read through the bills, research background material, formulate party policy, and discuss committee strategies. These groups began, as Thandi indicated, during the first weeks of Parliament, when members were trying to learn the institution's processes and procedures. They appear reminiscent of Marxist reading circles in format, so such learning groups have a long tradition, especially within the ANC.

Second, these study circles were facilitated and supported by researchers and party staffers. These researchers were often young, college-educated party members who had not been elected into office or had only recently joined. Most often, they were white, colored, or Indian. Many of these staffers were women, and they often described themselves as feminists. During the negotiation period most parties had relied heavily on such staffers and consultants to research and draft the constitution. Several of the gender consultants[3] were academicians who were part of "a relatively visible and powerful feminist lobby" (G. Seidman 1999, 289). This layer of intellectual and academic support was invaluable in helping new members and delegates understand issues, debate policy, and draft speeches and legislation.

Broad legislative training exercises and workshops run by external nongovernmental organizations or international agencies appeared consistently less effective to the women. Most women agreed that they did not have enough time even for their regular committee work, so they were loath to waste it on these overly general training sessions. Once they had learned the basics of parliamentary procedures, women moved from bill to bill, debate to debate, and needed research, education, and assistance for those specific items. The urgent matter of reforming government took precedence.

In 1996–97 women had been in Parliament for over two years. Having had time to adjust to life as legislators, they were beginning to question the processes and norms of the system they had worked so diligently to master. Their critiques fell into three groups depending on predictions: transformation, assimilation, or integration. First, some women were still closely connected to the grass roots and to the antiapartheid struggle's ideals; they sought transformation. These women were aware of the great disparities between what they were currently doing as legislators and what they were attempting to achieve as activists. Nonetheless, their backgrounds and values left them convinced that Parliament's agendas and processes could be transformed. Siphiwe talked about how her background changed the way she approached the transition:

> Coming from a struggle background, and activist background, very easy to demand and demand and demand. Coming to an institution which historically you had a very negative attitude towards, I mean, I never dreamed of it. Never tried to find out how this institution worked because I had such a negative feeling against it. And then coming here and finding yourself to be part of the institution. So transformation, that you have to deal with. It is a period of transition from the old order to the new order. It sounds [like] a lot, you know, but it is also very exciting to be a part of that change.

A second group of women asserted that such transformation would be impossible, primarily because of the seductive economic benefits, influence, and power that accompanies elected office. One MP maintained that, lacking knowledge of or respect for the moral foundation and strategic experience of the resistance movement, the next generation of parliamentarians would be co-opted by parliamentary life. Such blind assimilation would threaten any progress made by the current MPs, as Keorapetse of the ANC stated:

> The liberation movement is changing into a political party. This period still you are finding the people who came into politics not because they needed a job or

wanted a big car or prestige. Not to say that is what all politicians do, but I think that it often plays a big role—they wanted power or whatever. [For the first wave] it was because they fundamentally felt there was an injustice happening, and they somehow fight against that. They knew they were going to do that at a great cost, and they knew that there was a big chance they may not probably be alive. And I think the majority of them did not even know they would get into politics. I mean politics was such a remote thing. They were just trying to stay alive through the next year and not get killed by the security forces. So that is a different reason for going into politics. It will now change. The next election, already, we have seen all the young ones—every single person wants to be in Parliament. The other issue is the people who came in with a very specific idea of wanting to change what was wrong and they had a very clear idea of what was wrong.

As Keorapetse relates, those MPs who never aspired to national political office are being joined—if not replaced—by "young ones," new party members who want to be in Parliament for the prestige and status it brings. In Keorapetse's estimation, those currently in office have earned their place not through a lifetime of electoral politics but through a selfless dedication to the struggle that imperiled themselves and their families. They hold together the center of the movement and the philosophy of a new South Africa, yet those who would define the nation in terms of personal wealth, individualism, and gratification are challenging them.

In between these two groups were MPs who believed that policy makers need certain skills, knowledge, and experience. Although not as idealistic as those supporting broad institutional transformation, neither were they as pessimistic as those who assumed that elected office would co-opt political agendas. According to these women, the parties should seek skilled individuals and put them forward for office. Hanli of the ANC contextualized the problems of this transitional parliament by speaking about the lack of skills most women there face:

> I always think that this particular parliament is the transitional parliament. I hope when we come to the 1999 elections and the drawing up of lists—because this is proportional representation and it is all lists—I hope that the ANC will then take much greater account of skills. People have got to accept that there are certain basic skills required to function in a place like this. Unless we do radically transform [Parliament]. To me there is no sign at the moment that we are going to do that. . . . We have sort of taken over the Parliament as it has existed. [For example,] there really hasn't been a serious attempt to find ways in which she [an MP who organized in the rural areas] can actually contribute. She knows what is happening, knows what the problems of women are, and knows about rural areas—which should be informing what is happening here, but we don't have the mechanisms. We don't have the scope.

Hanli speaks for those who believe political parties should choose individuals who fit Parliament's ethos and not expect radical transformation. Hanli is willing to acknowledge the value of all women, regardless of formal education or political skills training, but she is concerned that such women are not always well matched to the job as currently defined. Women unfamiliar with the dictates of parliamentary procedure will find their contributions underutilized if not dismissed. Coming from a white opposition party, Phyllis voiced strong objections to any suggestion of institutional transformation:

> You can transform institutions to fit the people present in them really only up to a certain point. Parliament is here to do certain things. Only certain kinds of personalities are going to function well as parliamentarians. And, incidentally, no one can tell before you get here if you are going to be an effective MP or not. It is a funny job, a funny life, male or female. . . . I think that Parliament is a certain kind of animal. A lot of it is adversarial by definition, because you are dealing with governing parties and oppositional parties, which could be quite gladiatorial in the past in the very authoritarian type of structure. I am glad some of that is gone. It is far more relaxed now. It fits this country better, and it suits women better too. . . . But a parliament is a parliament. And there are certain things to do, and certain personalities will fit in, and some of them will be men and some will be women.

Phyllis called for a reprofessionalization of the institution, perhaps even a partial return to the norms and identities of the pre-1994 parliament. Although she did not advocate a return of the apartheid rule, she did recommend a return to some of the earlier standards and norms of parliamentary life.

The MPs' first-day stories communicated several notable themes. First, most individuals had not been part of the negotiations or the pre-1994 government. Their initial introduction to Parliament was both rapid and jarring. They were called on not simply to suppress feelings of vengeance against old enemies but to work with them. Many confronted an entirely new reality in Parliament. This new culture had little to no space for their previous lives as activists and demanded an alternative set of skills and rules. Women felt as though "they were parachuted into positions of power, often by civil society organizations, and once they got there they were left behind" (Van Donk and Maceba 1999, 20). Second, many parties had only recently become recognized as legitimate national political entities, and most of their members had little day-to-day experience with one another. They were expected to work together and to present a unified front, even though they barely knew one another and had little basis for trust. Third, the MPs' transition to Westminster parliamentary procedure was not only fast but self-imposed. This was not a revolution; it was a reform. The faces and parties had changed in the chambers, but the rules and processes had not. Rather than question the existing system, new members shouldered their feelings of dislocation or embarrassment to assimilate into the system. The case was similar in Uganda, where, Tamale found, women legislators "expressed a sense of frustration . . . that their participation in mainstream politics was limited by existing norms and the infrastructure of legislative activity" (1999, 143).

Fourth, those who had been a part of the pre-1994 government or were familiar with parliamentary procedure and norms were in the numerical and often racial minority, yet they were able to use their procedural knowledge to capture positions of power at the beginning of the 1994 term. This power has not necessarily diminished as time has passed, because new MPs have joined their system and learned their rules. Fifth, now that everyone is using the same political language and operating within the same political space, some inequalities and differences among MPs are becoming apparent. The pre-1994 system functioned in a way that fit the lifestyle of a completely different set of individuals—primarily elite, white, formally educated, married men. These old expectations came with the old rules. Because new MPs have adopted a new system that implies different expectations, they will continue in a disempowered and dislocated position unless they meet these expectations.

Perhaps the most salient point contained in these narratives is that by the time their first terms ended, these women were just beginning to articulate how the institution of Parliament was biased and, especially, gendered, which presented obstacles to their full participation. The women I discuss in this section questioned how much and in what ways institutional transformation will take place. Because all parties have promised to increase the number of women in government—and most did increase the numbers on their party lists—they are faced with a critical decision. Parties must decide whether they will (1) choose women who already have the skills and capacities to fully participate in Parliament, (2) train and develop the women who enter so that they may fully participate, or (3) transform Parliament to create space for women's voices and knowledge.

The Gendered Institution

Research concerning the gendered nature of institutions, especially bureaucracies and legislatures, is now well established. To consider an institution "gendered" is to "recognized that constructions of masculinity and femininity are intertwined in the daily culture of an institution" (Kenney qtd. in Rosenthal 2000, 23). Beyond examining the number of men and women in such institutions, these studies investigate how institutional norms and practices themselves are gendered and how they in turn enhance or inhibit women's participation. Rosenthal argues that conforming to institutional norms leads to institutional power, and she asserts that, since most institutions have been "peopled by men and [have] featured competitive male behavior," legislatures will privilege women who have masculinized their behavior (2000, 26, 40). Thus, institutions themselves carry specific messages to women about how to behave and how to succeed or fail. This has been the case internationally, and it is now widely recognized within the African context as well. Aili Mari Tripp's analysis of the Ugandan state found that "female parliamentary candidates face a myriad of cultural prohibitions on political activity not experienced by their male counterparts" (2000b, 229). Shireen Hassim (2003) supports these findings within the South African parliament, asserting that the institutional norms and rules of procedure have served to limit women's political effectiveness.[4]

Despite the significant victories won by South African women, several recurring obstacles continue to limit their full participation in Parliament. Admittedly not all these obstacles are gender specific; men, too, lack support staff and researchers, as well as training in policy, English, and management and finance. These challenges faced all incoming parliamentarians from previously disadvantaged groups, regardless of gender. One incoming MP stated she desperately needed "backup staff and . . . to know who to go to and get help," adding that she "wouldn't know where to start" if she had to draft legislation. All the women listed skills necessary to function within the current parliamentary structure: proficiency in English, high competency in reading and speaking, training in management and finances, and familiarity with parliamentary procedures. Most women I interviewed felt they lacked most or all of these skills before they came to Parliament.[5]

At the same time, society's expectations of the MPs have been high. As one ANC MP stated, "[You are] faced with thousands and thousands of papers to read, so many committees, and you concentrate on three and you don't know what happens in the others. But when you go to the people, they expect you to know everything. To them it is your duty to know everything and answer all their questions." Most women stated they did not have the time to attend skills-training workshops once they started work in Parliament. If such training is to be effective, it needs to occur before the women enter.

Again, not all these problems are gender specific. Nevertheless, men in most parties, even those from highly disadvantaged backgrounds, have more knowledge of and experience with public speaking, management, and finances based on their positions within social hierarchies. Ever since colonization and the imposition of European gender systems, men from all racial group have been positioned higher than women from the same social groups. Black South African men have been oppressed compared to white men, but they have been given a higher status and more experience in formal political space than black women have. For example, I met one woman who could not be paid for her first month in Parliament because she had no bank account in her name. Even though women were most often in charge of managing the household, formal financial matters such as bank accounts were often the responsibilities of the men. Accordingly, even these neutral, nongendered obstacles may in fact have a gendered component based on mens' positions in society as a whole. Geisler (2000) observed precisely this phenomenon in her work on women in the South African parliament. Lawless and Fox acknowledge a similar bias that starts before women enter office: "The primary barrier to electoral success of women in Kenya [is] the sociocultural training to which men and women are exposed from childhood" (1999, 53). Furthermore, they argue that once women take office, these gender roles and this political socialization shape political activity and public perception.

As the interviews revealed, however, many obstacles to participation in government are more narrowly gender specific. All but one of the MPs in the study discussed how their gender imposed an additional layer of responsibility. These gendered obstacles fit into five broad categories: double workload, male resistance, backsliding of party or institutional support, indirect sexism, and domestic obligations.

Workload

Women have their traditional committee work, but unlike their male colleagues, they must also serve on "gender" committees or meet with gender-related groups such as the Parliamentary Women's Group or their parties' women's caucuses. Women thus carry a disproportionate burden, and many feel that they are doing twice the work of men. They are also pulled into interest groups and legislative debates that deal with gender issues falling outside their official committees. Mafuane, an ANC MP who is active in the women's structures, talked about this double burden women carry: "I must say that it hasn't been an easy task. As I say, most of us are involved in many other hundred and one things. We haven't yet formalized ourselves within the ANC, and the multiparty caucus isn't formalized yet, so both of them are at their embryo. We are still mostly struggling with programs to empower most of those women in Parliament, since not all of us are at the same par. Most women don't have the skills to deal with the present challenges." So women struggle to develop the skills and abilities necessary to be policy makers, as do many of their male counterparts, but they must also spend time and energy to forward gender equality.

Women from smaller parties face even more difficult constraints. Since they do not have enough MPs to cover the committees, any additional expectations of women often hinder their effectiveness. I interviewed one woman in a smaller opposition party who served on over ten committees. And again, almost all parties, regardless of size, have some form of a women's caucus. Men and women are to be judged equally based on their work within Parliament and the extent to which they serve their constituents, yet these extra gender-related responsibilities are not taken into account. This may be an additional causative factor in Coetzee's (1999) discovery that women with active gender portfolios were not given high rankings in the 1999 party lists. Coetzee related the comments of Rebecca Holmes, a gender consultant who worked with the multiparty Parliamentary Women's Group; Holmes "observed that women were generally more active than their male counterparts in Parliament, yet that proportion was not reflected in the list" for the 1999 elections (1999, 1).

With respect to such double workloads, the women MPs bear a striking similarity to women in the ANC during the early 1990s. As Gay Seidman reports, the ANC leadership decided that women should sit on key committees, yet the party did not have enough women to realize this goal. As a result, "the policy meant that leading women activists were stretched thin, running from meeting to meeting, but the principle [of women's representation] was increasingly accepted within the national headquarters of the ANC" (G. Seidman 1999, 293). So, although a commitment to gender representation has pre-1994 roots, so too does the pattern of overworking women. The image thus presented suggests that women have been doubly burdened not just during their terms of office but for their entire lives as political actors. Whether they were early participants in party politics or in resistance politics, they have almost always had an additional layer of responsibility.

Resistance from Men in Parliament

Women from all parties stated that men in Parliament express support for women's roles and goals in politics, but most interviewees believed that the majority of men are neither genuine in their approval nor active in their support. As an MP of an opposition party stated, "I think that men will say they are for affirmative action and speak to it, but down deep they are really not all that concerned." A member of the ANC stated, "There is a resistance of men to accept and acknowledge that women can be leaders." Another MP of an opposition party stated that "male chauvinism is a major problem. Definitely." And this resistance appears in many areas, from committee assignment to leadership positions. The resistance is widespread throughout the parties, and at the very least there is a recognition that most political parties "remain male-dominated at all levels and have embraced gender equity concerns with reluctance" (Goetz and Hassim 2003, 3).

Such resistance can be overt. According to Meintjes (2001, 75), women MPs have been ignored by the ANC caucus when they wished to speak, blocked from meeting rooms, and denied access to computers. One MP from the NP recalled that the first time she walked into a committee meeting, two men left the room because they felt women did not belong in politics. Tana, an ANC MP from a rural constituency, stated that the men in her party are not supportive: "I wish the men in our party would move faster and help with the process. One male friend has told me that even our very best comrades won't say it, but they are not and will not be ready for this change. They are not at all behind us." Several women told me they had heard discriminatory comments or jokes made by their male colleagues, and women from every party except the PAC could identify instances where men resisted women's participation or where women were marginalized into particular jobs and roles. My findings here were very similar to those of Tamale, who observed that, although women did not name sexual harassment or discuss it directly, carefully posed questions revealed that most female legislators had to deal with sexism and sexual comments often on a daily basis (1999, 132).

Another interviewee examined how female MPs from South Africa are marginalized into gender-specific committees, as their counterparts have been internationally. For example, women were often assigned to committees dealing with education, social welfare, or gender issues. This has not been entirely negative, however; women's work on these committees has helped advance programs to meet women's basic needs, and Hassim (2003) asserts that these committees deal with the policy areas to which the ANC is most committed. Nonetheless, initially there were relatively few women sitting on what Hassim calls "hard" committees, such as the Land Affairs, Mineral and Energy, Transportation, Foreign Affairs, and Labor Commissions. Such marginalization seems clearly related to the depth of male resistance, as Dziko of the ANC discussed:

> Oh, I still think we have to go a long way. . . . You know I think that I, [in] my own personal experience with South African men—I think we need to do much more with men, their attitudes. Not just their attitudes. It is a deep, cultural, religious, customary—[a] combination of all of those—impacting so deeply. But those attitudes have become crystallized now, and you've got to penetrate those deep-seated roots where the attitude comes from. And it is very, very difficult. And you speak to very learned, educated men, but somewhere they will

give themselves away. You know, in my activist days, I was on a platform with [a high-ranking ANC man] when he came out of prison . . . and said, "We must be eternally grateful for the women who have cooked for us and looked after us." I was absolutely disgusted. I think he has come a long way. But even then he was a very liberated person, an activist, highly intelligent. I think we have a long way to go in terms of men, and I think we are going to have tremendous problems with the constitutional rights for women when it comes to religious and indigenous laws and customary and traditional practices. I don't know how the courts are going to resolve this.

Dziko also told me that even the most progressive men have contributed to locking women into domestic and subordinate positions. This problem may be indicative of the transition, which was based on liberal legislative reforms and broad constitutional protections even though the society remains conservative and traditional.

This continued male chauvinism was a concern of women involved in the 1998 Women at the Crossroads: Women in Governance conference hosted in Cape Town.[6] Conference participants listed various strategies some men used to ensure that women are excluded and marginalized (Van Donk and Maceba 1999). Not only do South African women feel unwelcome in political office; they also have to combat some of their male colleagues's active attempts to undermine their legitimacy.

My research supports Swers's (2001) and Rosenthal's (2000) work, which found that women are often seen as intruders in male institutions. Africa, too, demonstrates this widespread pattern of male resistance, if not overt hostility, to women's participation. Tripp relates that men in office advised women not to run for election because politics is a "male domain in which women [have] no business" (2000b, 19). Tripp presents one case where the husband of a female candidate in the 1996 Ugandan election publicly supported her opposition (ibid., 230). Within the Ugandan parliament, Goetz reports, women who are interested in and actively promote a gender-equity agenda "have faced considerable opposition to efforts to promote women's interests" (1998, 249). Tamale's (1999, 2000) work on the Uganda parliament also carefully details the resistance women have experienced in office there, many times related to the very affirmative-action measures taken to ensure women's participation. Men became the gatekeepers for those seats in Parliament, choosing the "appropriate" women, because "the space into which women were being pushed was both compositionally and institutionally a male one" (Tamale 1999, 91). Despite all the significant accomplishments, constitutionally and numerically, public space continues to be seen as a men's sphere of influence.

Party Backslide

Toward the end of my fieldwork in 1996–97, women stated that they sensed an incipient general backslide of support, which could soon become a backlash against women's participation. ANC women gave several examples of backsliding from their own party, including the initially low percentage of women in the cabinet, the decision that members could abstain from voting on the Termination of Pregnancy Act,[7] the appointment of the chief whip,[8] and the low percentage of women in local government. One member of the executive stated:

> We know that by 1999 there will be a consolidation by more—I don't want to say conservative elements; that is a bit unfair—but where men will try to consolidate their position. If you look at the difference in quotas between national and provincial and local, it is 18.5 percent. This is still high according to international standards of local representatives, but for South Africa we should have had much higher representation now. That is an indication that we are going to have to regroup and recapture various sectors, spheres of power.

An ANC MP stated, "We have a reverse trend in comparison to the world. We have more women at national and provincial level[s] than at the local, which has to do a bit with ANC backtracking a bit on its commitment."

This pattern manifested itself in Uganda, too, where 24.7 percent of parliamentary seats are held by women, making it twenty-sixth worldwide in terms of women in national office. South Africa ranks fifteenth, with 29.8 percent. The women of Uganda followed a path to office that was similar to, if not simultaneous with, that of their South African sisters. They used autonomous women's movements, which developed in response to their marginalization from formal political space, to make demands on the state and the party system. Although party leaders had promised to advance the cause of women, this commitment has become more tenuous with passing time. Tamale has found that women's roles in the Ugandan parliament are limited by the masculinity of the institutions (1999, 120–21), and Goetz further contends that "women who are in affirmative action district seats are selected through an all-male electoral college . . . which can favour the selection of fairly conservative women" (1998, 249). Holding party leaders accountable becomes even more difficult when the system is designed to limit progressive women's voices.

Invisible Structures of Sexism

Because of its preexisting practices and norms, parliamentary culture fosters institutionalized sexism as well as racism and classism. Women's exclusion from male-only groups and activities provides one limited example. These informal groups are often locations of networking and collegiality that boost the advancement of cross-party collaboration.[9] One woman discussed the double standard she experienced with male members of her party who were opposed to a women-only multiparty caucus yet frequently participated in multiparty, multiethnic men-only rugby clubs: "There has never been an eyebrow raised that the men have a rugby club together. And they don't just play against one another. They have, like, these little rugby parties. And I don't object to that. [Pause] Maybe I do. It is the difference when we are putting up a political structure [such as a women's caucus] and there are these queries as to 'Well, why?' Whereas, if it is a sports structure, it is a national psychosis; they have no problem." While outward expressions of sexism grow more infrequent with each passing day, the informal, institutionalized sexism within the South African parliament continues to limit women's political identity formation and access to spheres of influence and power.

Women are faced with pressures to adopt "Western" models of femininity, which are billed as professionalism. Women found this version of femininity confining, for it created a distraction from the issues they had been elected to address:

> I must confess I didn't want to come to Parliament. [I said,] "Don't want to be there. What am I going to do there?" I wasn't excited at all. "What does one do there?" I had this fear: "Parliament, me a member of Parliament." And it came; no way to avoid it. And I came in still an optimist. And the worst thing, it was such a cultural shock. This building and all these officials and all this bureaucracy in this place. I didn't like it at all. And I still sort of spoke like an activist. I remember one workshop where this lady ran this workshop: "The way you dress, stockings and shoes." I said, "This is bullshit! It is not in my clothes. It is in my heart!" But all of us, all of us in the ANC were in this identity crisis of "I am here but my mind is there [in the grass roots]."

Many of the women came from severely disadvantaged backgrounds and were struggling to develop a political profile and a professional persona. Political education and training then became conflated with clothing and makeup, but many women tried to resist confusing legislation and the delivery of services with the need to "dress for success."

Double Workday

The women I interviewed stated that the most debilitating challenges they faced were personal problems created by balancing the demands of the job and their traditional domestic obligations. Marriages are ending; friends express feelings of abandonment; children voice concerns of neglect. Nonyameko, a former antiapartheid activist and now an ANC MP, talked about the job's impact on her family when I asked her to describe her biggest challenge:

> Our family lives. The rate of divorces among parliamentarians are not available due to the organization—we are not to make it public—but it is more from the woman's side. . . . Once a woman becomes a politician or becomes active—and she is a married woman—then the man will start accusing her of having affairs outside because she is most of the time busy with the community. . . . When on recess, I used to go down [to visit family], but now they say, "It is useless you coming down here anymore. When you come for recess, we thought for one day maybe you would be with us, but if you leave in the morning at seven, we see you tonight at eight or nine, or maybe we are already in bed. What is the point?"

Many women moved to Cape Town, away from their support structures, often with husbands remaining behind, leaving the women to become essentially single parents. Katherine, an MP from the NP, talked about the challenges of motherhood within the parliamentary context: "The support structures aren't really there. Of the divorces last year, 90 percent were women parliamentarians. They were initiated mainly by their husbands, not because they wanted them. It is hard. Most of the women have children, small children. Most of them are single parents now." Women feel they are ready to take charge of the government, but the reality of their lives and of society demands that they must remain in charge of the household as well. One politician who is also the mother of four asked, "What am I supposed to do with the demands from both sides—not both sides, three sides? Your house life, political life, as well as government life—it is more than we can give." Abongile, a senior member of the ANC, stated that her husband and children lived in a different province but that the domestic responsibilities still fell mostly to her: "I need to ensure the house is run, 100 percent! I make up a schedule that there is always someone there, someone taking charge of kids and monitoring homework. . . . Actually, there are two levels of planning and programming: you need to program the house and you need to program whatever you do in Parliament."

Two other parliamentarians also spoke of the different expectations men and women face in politics, society, and the home. Several women I interviewed discussed the fact that men had a much easier time in Parliament because they had wives at home to take care of their domestic and personal lives. One ANC MP stated that women parliamentarians needed "wives" to care for the emotional labor of families and friends.

This situation is not unique to South Africa, of course. Sawer (2000) describes the historical assumption that members of legislatures have a built-in support system—their wives—to carry domestic responsibilities and even constituency work. This pattern surfaces elsewhere in Africa, too. Tripp found that "women candidates have to project an image of absolute devotion to their husbands and families and of being good wives and mothers to a degree not required of men" (2000b, 229). Tripp relates the media impact on the gender roles of women candidates. Interviews of candidates focused on women's marital status and children; moreover, women in Uganda's 1996 electoral campaign "faced greater public ridicule than men, were labeled 'unfeminine[,]' and some even risked their marriages and public discrediting by their husbands" (Tripp 2000b, 230). This double standard carries a lasting impact for women who do win seats and sends a particular message to potential future female candidates.

This especially intractable problem may result from placing women in high governmental positions within a society that continues to expect women to carry the bulk of domestic responsibilities and that has historically disadvantaged women educationally, economically, and politically. Several women I interviewed in South Africa commented that it would take at least two generations to have society "catch up" to the national government.

Implications of the South African Case for the Critical-Mass Literature

The women MPs I interviewed were aware that the legislative changes they had made were significant, but they now know that national power and leadership do not directly translate into status and influence within their personal lives. The cycle of exclusion reinforces itself because the societal constraints they face as women in turn limit their full participation in public office. These women explicitly called for reform in the politics of the domestic sphere to match their legislative advances and for a societal revolution to match their institutional and electoral successes. Full institutional transformation cannot be complete without attention to the politics of the domestic sphere or a revision of the societal perceptions of power, leadership, and labor. A critical mass alone was not enough to counteract the patriarchal structure women faced in society and in office.

Several women discussed ways to implement this reform nationally, through educational initiatives and social-welfare programs. Most striking, however, were the women who challenged patriarchy within their own lives. Because the private sphere exists outside the social contract, they argued, legislative solutions will inevitably fail. Public tools cannot adequately address private problems. This resonates with Tickner's beliefs: "Although women may suffer from particular forms of repression under capitalism, the liberation of women through class struggle cannot be assumed. It will only come about when women are equal to men in both the public and the private spheres, a condition that would not necessarily obtain in a postcapitalist world" (1992, 90). That is, Marxism is simply not the antidote to patriarchal domination. In fact, Marxism has served to reinforce women's subjugation in much less visible ways.

The women I interviewed are focused on trying to change the patriarchal culture that limits them in all aspects of their lives. They link that personal struggle to the national search for gender equality. One ANC MP specifically tied the problems with gender equality in Parliament to patriarchal culture and male socialization. Sasha believes that women have been raising boys to be adult children who are incapable of addressing their most basic needs. She believes that to be a successful MP or delegate, one must have a domestic partner willing and able to raise children, to maintain the home, and to sustain relations with family and friends:

> We don't look at how we as mothers failed to socialize our male children in a way that they become independent. We find later on that men can't do it without a helper, you know. And it has been sort of an amusing antidote amongst us that "we all need wives." You know, it has become quite a popular story. But by saying that, what we are saying is the message—you find that all the men that have wives at home are able to work without tensions. What is happening to us, then? So what do we really need? . . .
>
> This is a major area of contention. Unpaid work of women at home, and men are not liberated. Because the minute [a man's wife] walks out of the door, what will happen to him? He will look around for another one. That is why I say men need to be liberated. They are not independent. They are very dependent.
>
> It isn't transforming Parliament alone. You need a much bigger transformation of the society that we live in at every level. I feel sorry for men, that macho image they want to project. They can't express their feelings. They can't cry, and there are a lot of things like that they can't do because of the image they are brought up to project. . . . Their whole personality changes, and they become hardened and uncaring and sometimes go too far. . . .
>
> Why do women have to be more caring? We are not born with that. We are born equal: a man and a woman. A woman learns to care because she is encouraged to express her feelings, and, you know, she becomes more caring. Man becomes more hardened because of the socialization. So those are some of the things that I feel we need to address and train our entire community to look at things different. That is a huge task.

According to Sasha, then, either the public or the private sphere must change. Either men and women should both be able to occupy a full range of roles in their professional and personal lives, or the private sphere must change so that women have partners who perform the duties traditionally assigned to a wife, mother, or lover. The women MPs and delegates were keenly aware that they were at a significant disadvantage to their male counterparts who had supportive, constant partners caring for the private space. Men may lead the nation politically, but they are socialized to be incapable of running the home properly. Moreover, Sasha suggested that men cannot express their feelings. Their emotional intelligence and knowledge are truncated, she said, which may lead to distorted policy decisions. She thus unequivocally called for societal transformation, far beyond the institutional changes made to Parliament. Sasha asserted that public discrimination against women will end only when men and women are equally responsible for domestic duties and mutually dependent on one another for maintaining the private sphere.

Sasha's words, as well as this chapter, call into question the ideas of the critical-mass literature—the idea that legislators from an underrepresented group cannot effect change until they control some specific percentage of government. How many women does it take to transform policy and institutional culture? Kanter (1977) claims that women cannot affect their status in government unless they constitute at least 15 percent of it. Thomas (1989, 1994) asserts that women need at least a 30 percent share of the government to affect policy as well as institutional structure. Similarly O'Regan (1998) concludes that women must control 30 percent of the government to influence employment and wage policies and 40 percent to affect social policies.[10]

But might greater numbers of women or any other identity group never have an impact? An equally rich body of research suggests that women need more than mere presence in office to influence either policy or legislative behavior. Bashevkin (1985) found that preserving party loyalty within proportional-representation systems hindered women's parliamentary mobilization in Canada. Whip (1991) has identified several obstacles to female mobilization and solidarity—most significantly, the strength of the party system and party discipline. McAllister and Studlar (1992), in work supporting that of Whip, found that party affiliation influences behavior more than gender does.

Newer research suggests that the number of women in office does not directly or immediately affect the institutional culture. Considine and Deutchman (1996) found that greater numbers of women did not correlate to a shift in the culture of legislatures. Examining women in U.S. state legislatures and Australian state parliaments, they found that women were able to change the structure of the governmental institution but not its gendered culture—the habits, norms, perceptions, and daily experiences of legislators—which continue to be male identified. Instead, they found that the institutional culture is often stronger than changes in institutional culture. In fact, they found that "both men and women adopt a subtle and pervasive gender schema which denies to women full equality within the legislature" (Considine and Deutchman 1996, 7). This affects all aspects of women's legislative lives, including the creation of identity, mobilization for gender-based issues, and the manipulation of policy. In many ways, the institutions themselves are structured so that there is no "magic number" for women in office, and "the dominant norms might stay in place long after numeric changes have removed the most visible forms of inequality if internal barriers . . . are not addressed" (ibid., 18). Rosenthal makes a similar case for U.S. state legislatures, arguing that "women may be disadvantaged in leadership roles and face unique pressures to alter their behavior" to match the preexisting masculinized norms and rules (2000, 40).

Tremblay and Pelletier distinguish symbolic from descriptive representation to examine the impact of women on the Canadian parliament. Their findings, too, may challenge the critical-mass theory, in that they advocate electing feminist men rather than nonfeminist women in certain instances (Tremblay and Pelletier 2000, 397–98). Mexico further challenges the critical-mass literature. Roderic Camp (1998) questions attempts to rapidly increase the number of women in political office. Because Mexican women have been acquiring political office slowly, they have had time to develop the skills and capacities necessary to challenge the institution, at least to a limited degree, once they arrive. At this point any push toward increased electoral presence would require an acceptance of or assimilation into masculinized norms and practices. Thus, Camp argues, "the short-term achievement of greater numbers might sacrifice a level of diversity that female politicians, with a different set of experiences, might bring to that same leadership" (1998, 177).

Whatever the truth about numbers, other institutional factors, too, may affect women's success in office; these factors include patronage politics, patriarchal social norms, and semiauthoritarianism. Lawless and Fox argue that the critical-mass literature ignores the reality of Kenyan society: "The nation has a strong patriarchal tradition with a firm adherence to traditionally stereotypical gender roles" (1999, 52). Kenya is far from a 30–50 percent benchmark, with women constituting only 7.1 percent of its national parliament (Inter-parliamentary Union 2003). Despite this abysmal number, Lawless and Fox assert that increases by themselves will not suffice to counteract Kenya's social norms and hierarchies. The Ugandan case casts further doubt on the impact of a critical mass of women in office. Tripp's comprehensive analysis of the Ugandan women's movement found that its effect on the gendered institutions of the state was limited at best: "Expanding female representation is insufficient to serve women's interests adequately as long as institutions are configured in ways that continue to suppress the expression of those interests" (2000b, 216). Tamale's work within the Uganda parliament similarly indicates that culture was used "as a tool for preserving the male power structure" and inhibiting women's full acceptance in the institution (1999, 125). The institutional norms and benefits threaten the cohesiveness of women's collective action and delegitimize women's participation. Even with a greater number of women, institutions deeply entrenched in patriarchal culture are often highly resistant to change.

These cases suggest that the critical-mass literature may overlook deeply important case-specific factors that limit women's success in office. Drawing on the work of the Africanist Amina Mama, the South African gender expert Shireen Hassim (1999b) argues that women in African parliaments frequently do not represent women's issues. This situation contrasts with that in Nordic and other European nations, where the number of women in office correlates somewhat to the representation of women's issues in policy making. Hassim's more recent work notes very clearly that getting women into political office in South Africa was "only one part of the task of representation" and that representation in and of itself is not sufficient (2003, 89). Political effectiveness depends on several factors, as Goetz and Hassim argue, including the nature of civil society, the political system, and the state (2003, 5–7).

My work in South Africa clearly supports this notion. South African women underwent rapid integration and in some instances involuntary assimilation into the national parliament. Following the disorienting negotiation period, women were brought into Parliament in great numbers and charged to work with old enemies to create a nonracial form of government. They were also expected to alleviate the problems of national gender inequality. A mere two years into the new system, women were able to evaluate Parliament and discuss with vivid detail the multiple ways the institutional culture reproduces the white, upper-class, patriarchal system they were trying to overthrow during the antiapartheid movement and the negotiation period.

These observations may indicate that the very foundations of critical-mass theory and research are flawed by their apolitical, idealistic, and perhaps even utopian assumptions. The critical-mass literature presumes that larger numbers of women in office will automatically alter institutional culture and policy making. These studies provide one explanation why, when women fall below some magic threshold, they are unable to affect agendas as they may have promised and planned to do. Yet the critical-mass studies do not explain why women are often unable to change much even when their numbers surpass the threshold. Quantity is simply not enough; demographic representation is not the entire question. Issues such as the nature of the regime itself are essential for determining how successful women can be in office. Obviously, authoritarian and semiauthoritarian regimes will greatly diminish the autonomy of MPs. Hassim (2003, 83–84) argues that dominance even by a progressive party such as the ANC is problematic in the long term, because women's interests are best served by a broadly established democracy that supports the development of engaged participants and opponents as well as a strong voice for women in civil society.

Also important are culturally specific issues, such as the levels of patriarchy inside and outside governing institutions. The number of women incumbents matters as well, for it takes several years to be fully acclimated to the role of MP. If there is a constant turnover of women, then it does not matter that a state consistently has women making up 30 percent or more of its legislature, because many of those women will still be within their first few years of the job. It also takes time for new legislators or MPs to ascend through the party system and gain seniority within committees.

Physical representation is crucial, of course, especially in terms of the essential issues of justice and equity, as well as basic human rights. But as the South African case and others indicate, physical representation alone is not a panacea. Coetzee (1999) indicates that women activists and gender consultants in South Africa are increasingly concerned not only with the number of women in office but also with the type of women there, regardless of the party. Drawing on interviews with women activists, Coetzee found that, "while supporting the quota system and the gains it has brought, the group also highlighted a downside to a purely quantitative approach and its underlying assumption that by putting a woman on a party list or in executive office, one had a champion for gender equality" (1999, 1). Following the surge of women into the British parliament after the 1997 elections, which was due primarily to the Labour Party's women-only short lists now under scrutiny, women MPs voiced similar concerns. Their activities and advances were often inhibited by "male dominance" in the House of Commons (BBC News 2001). Women had assumed that the influx of women into Parliament would change the climate, but they actually lost ground in the 2001 election. Feminists and activists voice concerns that, despite the changes in electoral rules, the institutional norms of Parliament, the Labour Party, and labor unions continue to be less welcoming to women than party rhetoric would suggest (Bashevkin 2000).

The critical-mass studies assume that finding the threshold level will give women a benchmark toward which to work as well as a means to explain their collective impact. These are noble and important goals. Additionally, most critical-mass studies are careful to note the limitations of the research: the critical-mass theory alone cannot explain the impact of women in office. Yet these studies have increasingly become the point of reference for research focusing on women in office, especially cross-national studies examining national office. Because most of these studies are quantitative, they are finding increasing acceptance in leading journals in the discipline, which are predisposed to such methodology.

These studies lack both a deep understanding of the preexisting culture of formal party politics and legislative behavior and, more important, an understanding of the cultural and societal issues within each specific case. In the South African case, those issues mattered more to women's initial participation in Parliament than did the number of women. It would be easy, if one were adhering strictly to the critical-mass literature, to look at the South African case and explain away any missteps or unattained goals during the 1994–99 term as merely a problem of numbers. If the critical threshold is 30 percent, as O'Regan (1998) has asserted, then the 1994 parliament fell below that mark, with only 27 percent of MPs being women. Arguably even the 1999 parliament misses the mark, with only 29.5 percent. Yet clearly the picture is much more complex. Women MPs faced vast challenges that potentially limited their effectiveness, including the disorienting negotiation period, the alienating transition to Parliament, and the gender-specific obstacles of political office. Moreover, as the next several chapters indicate, duration in office is crucial for women's eventual success and mastery of their jobs as MPs.

Awareness is the first step toward institutional transformation. The similarity of experience across racial and party lines indicates how women may unify for collective change, much as they did in their pretransition mobilization for representation. We need to do more than just recognize the gendered parliamentary culture, however, so in subsequent chapters I will show how women attempted to change the system and to redefine politics, participation, and feminism. The next chapter relates how women asserted this transformation as individual actors in Parliament; the following one examines the same issues by investigating how women as a group managed to effect change despite the obstacles they faced.

4. Class Structure, Role Differentiation, and Gender Identities

Gaining formal political representation for women may be seen as the most significant accomplishment of the women's movement in South Africa to date. Utilizing collective bargaining and cross-party mobilization, women obtained a remarkable presence in national office. Yet the negotiation period and the transition phase were as rocky and disorienting as the struggle against apartheid had been. This challenging road to Parliament sent a clear message to women: they would have to continue to struggle if they were to become a viable, consistent voice for all South Africa. Gaining office was only the next step in their ongoing quest for liberation.

My interviews in 1996–97 quickly showed that, despite the often inhospitable chambers of Parliament, women were coping and operating quite differently within their new roles as MPs than they had as activists. In fact, over one-half the women I interviewed did not plan to return to Parliament, because they believed that the institution did not have a place for their voices and that they could be more effective as activists. In fact, the attrition rate within the ANC was quite high. Over one-third of their representatives chose not to seek election again in 1999 (Ballington 2002), and several other women MPs had left before the 1999 election period. Although Parliament has shifted to reflect some of the needs of women, the capacities required to be an MP or delegate remain fundamentally unchanged from the previous regime. Most significantly, I found that the parliamentarians who most closely resembled the majority of South African women in terms of educational, economic, racial, and occupational backgrounds were the most likely not only to be alienated from the processes of policy making and dissatisfied with their roles as politicians, but also to leave Parliament before, during, or soon after the next elections.

Since the women in Parliament do not constitute a monolithic category, I found it necessary to disentangle how their backgrounds influenced their participation strategies and views on gender politics. Several women have adapted well to the institution; again, however, they are not the most representative in terms of socioeconomic, educational, or ethnic backgrounds.

Women in the South African parliament have created numerous ways to participate in the political process, from leading the national movement for gender equality, to legislating against gender and racial discrimination, to working with grassroots women on community development projects. Following the transition women have demonstrated a similarly wide range of responses to feminism and gender politics, ranging from a complete acceptance of women's issues to an avoidance of any association with gender politics. The women's strategies and identities are directly linked to their widely divergent educational, socioeconomic, political, and ethnic backgrounds.

I found that those most likely to adapt to life as a legislator and remain in Parliament were primarily white women from affluent or privileged socioeconomic backgrounds working in "traditionally nonfemale" occupations, such as the law, journalism, or academia. This tendency has been observed as well by Geisler (2000), who found that those leaving Parliament in 1999 were often women from activist and grassroots backgrounds, not the affluent and politically confident women MPs. Of course, this trend mirrors the socioeconomic composition of parliaments internationally, but it is emerging in South African with remarkable rapidity. My research thus examines whether parties and governments can ensure a demographically representative democracy, especially given the institutional constraints of formal parliamentary political systems.

I also found that women in the new Parliament faced challenges that threatened their incumbency. Their reasons for leaving after the 1994 term or the 1999 term may differ, but women have tended to leave office less because they lost their seats than because they chose not to run for reelection; indeed, over one-third of women legislators within the ANC chose not to run again in 1999.[1] Again, the South African parliament is not unique in seeing its women leave office after relatively brief legislative tenures; a similar pattern has been observed in many other nations, including the United States (Darcy, Welch, and Clark 1994; Darcy and Choike 1986; Whicker and Whitaker 1999). The larger issue for governments and parties committed to diversity becomes not simply getting women into office but rather keeping them there.

This chapter reflects three specific objectives. The first objective is to map how well their prior experiences prepared these women for life as a legislator. Race, socioeconomic class, and professional backgrounds proved to be the most significant factors determining how women participated in Parliament and how they viewed gender issues. The second objective is to delineate how women currently participate in Parliament. Women face disproportionate burdens because of their gender, but—perhaps as a result—they have crafted distinct and useful roles for their political activities. Understanding these distinct modes of participation is essential for a comprehensive understanding of how women are shaping and are being shaped by parliamentary life. The third objective is to analyze how the background factors are linked to policy positions and approaches to women's issues. Although a politician's ideology cannot always be inferred from identity factors, certain groups of women clearly lean toward a rights-based equity approach to women's issues, while other groups gravitate toward a socioeconomic-development approach to improve the status of women and help meet their needs.

Identity Affects Participation

The South African case differs distinctly from those previously examined in studies of women's integration and behavior within a political institution. With the 1994 elections the South African parliament began a massive upheaval in its composition and culture, as well as its policy initiatives and legislative outcomes. Unlike the legislators discussed in Gertzog's (1995) and Thomas's (1997) studies, South African MPs were developing new models of participation within a highly unstable environment.[2] Previous studies also focused on legislators who were career politicians, who had sought and received appropriate political training and experience.

Unlike the legislators in those studies, most women in the South African parliament never expected to enter office, had no formal legislative training, and had little prior knowledge of the duties or requirements of being an MP. The women I interviewed were experiencing two levels of uncertainty with this regime change. They were individually shifting from a politics of resistance to a politics of governance, while their parties were attempting to reform Parliament's institutional culture, structure, and purpose.

This chapter identifies several key roles women occupied in South Africa's first democratically elected parliament.[3] Going beyond the studies of Gertzog and Thomas, it demonstrates how political roles and gender attitudes were determined by women's educational and socioeconomic backgrounds. Although I do attempt to identify specific characteristics and modes of women's political participation, this should not be seen as a static typology of women's lives. Rather, it is an attempt to outline women's multiple roles against a backdrop of the forces that shaped their identities.

Even though no one factor in their backgrounds sufficed to indicate where women would situate themselves in the new parliament, a combination of factors consistently did so. These factors included ethnic identity, educational status, and occupational experiences before entering Parliament, as well as former and current economic status. When taken together, these factors, broadly construed, provide a composite profile of different groups of women. The women parliamentarians in each group had similar participation patterns, political viewpoints, and gender attitudes. Identity, therefore, affected the modes and goals of their political participation.

In many ways these composites are based broadly on what most would recognize as class distinctions. Class is a widely contested concept, yet it is also particularly instructive, if not determinant, of what these women have been doing and what they believe. Class indeed matters, helping shape these women's effectiveness in Parliament, their political agendas and goals, and their views of women's issues. In the following analysis the idea of class comprises a broad set of characteristics, including not only socioeconomic status but also educational achievement and occupational background. Also, given the country's history of colonization and apartheid, race is perhaps more enmeshed with class in South Africa than in many other nations. Although black South Africans have enjoyed some mobility since the 1994 transition, it will take several generations to see broader changes in those patterns.

Within the African context, the structures of colonial oppression created a system that conflated ethnicity, social class, and gender to marginalize the indigenous population. Postcolonial systems have often served to extend and reproduce this oppression, and parliamentary politics is not immune from such patterns. Not only did I find this in my work in South Africa, but class has been a major factor in determining the types of women recruited via affirmative-action policies for seats in the Ugandan parliament. Tamale indicates that these policies, which were supposed to benefit the vast majority of Uganda's impoverished population, have in fact benefited "a minority of an educated, elite group of Ugandan women . . . perpetuating mainstream post-colonial politics" (1999, 197). Class affects which women are chosen and which women survive.

Exile status, too, influenced women's positions in the new parliament and with respect to their constituents. Steyn found that women returning from exile initially had difficulty connecting with the average South African woman or representing her issues: "Exiles returning in the early 1990s, who were more aware of women's movements elsewhere, were sometimes accused of being out of touch with the grassroots needs of South African women who had participated in the struggle at home" (1998, 43). This gap is shrinking, but it played an important role in the 1994 parliament, and it established patterns that continued within subsequent terms. As will be discussed, their international experiences gave women who had been in exile different conceptions of women's issues and needs.

Using these distinctions of class, I have characterized several groups of women, each with its distinct notions of the issues women should espouse and the role they should play in Parliament. Gertzog's (1995) notion of role differentiation can be instructive concerning these South African women MPs. Gertzog linked the gender-role orientations of U.S. congresswomen to their legislative interests and career goals. I seek to extend this approach, however, by describing the ways women participate in Parliament and specifying their spheres of influence. In the first stage of political learning, Gertzog found, individuals have undifferentiated role behaviors; they are only "dimly aware of the role requirements or expectations of others, and they proceed either to neglect their responsibilities or fulfill them in a diffuse and unspecialized fashion" (1995, 250). They often have negligible career goals and superficial policy concerns.

In the second stage legislators begin to display differentiated behavior, meaning that they are now aware of the legislative role and its duties, expectations, and norms. Individuals' differentiated behavior and participation strategies "conform to expectations about what constitutes appropriate behavior for persons holding such a position" (Gertzog 1995, 250). Although these legislators have developed career goals, Gertzog found their policy concerns to be truncated, because they often avoided being associated with legislation that could place them "in a position of representing women's interests" (ibid.). In Gertzog's third stage the role becomes dedifferentiated, meaning some pieces of the traditionally defined role are abandoned or pieces of another role become absorbed. Women at this stage were fully integrated into congressional life but sought to transform their traditional legislative roles and often worked openly on women's issues.

The following subsections discuss in turn four groups of women in the 1994 parliament, with these groups based on class as I have defined it. (I discuss the second generation, those entering in 1999, in chapter 7.)

The Elites: Affluent, Highly Educated Women from Traditionally Nonfemale Occupations

Educational Status:	High educational achievement, often a postgraduate degree
Professions:	Knowledge-based occupations, such as attorney, journalist, or professor
Race:	All races (most black women had been in exile)

Exile Status: Former political exiles (blacks); nonexiled
                                 women who were prominent in the apartheid
                                 government (whites)
Parties: ANC, IFP, NP, and DP
Participation Mode: Detachment from constituents
Level of Influence: National
Lawmaking Orientation: Dedifferentiated mode
Women's Issues
    Orientation: Self-described feminists and those comfort-
                                 able with the term; women's issues listed as
                                 one of top two political goals
Gender Policy Agenda: Abortion rights, antipornography, imple-
                                 menting the Beijing Platform of Action and
                                 the UN's Convention on the Elimination of
                                 Discrimination Against Women, establishing
                                 national institutions for gender equality

The elite group comprised affluent, highly educated women from traditionally nonfemale occupations. Women in this category represented about 20
percent of the women I interviewed in 1996–97. These high-profile women
occupied key decision-making positions within Parliament and their parties.
They were less connected to their constituencies and spoke in terms of representing broad national issues of gender and racial equity through economic
empowerment and community development. They were centrally concerned
with the creation of structures and institutions for gender equity at the national level that they felt would alter societal imbalances. All of them ranked
gender and race as equally important issues, although a few ranked gender
as their primary concern.

Women in this group were able to recognize the utility of Parliament and
use it to achieve their goals. For example, one ANC MP, Hananke, stated, "Parliament is a tool, something that we actually use to transform society. And one
of the things that we want to achieve in society is to change the power relations
such that in fact the equality that we have institutionalized becomes a reality
to women, not only it being words in the constitution and it being something
that is raised in court." Aware of the structures and institutions of power,
Hananke was willing and able to use them to further women's equality.

These highly educated women are found in every ethnic group and most
closely align with Hirschmann's (1991) category of "key women," who are
well placed to control, direct, and influence national policy and agenda.
South Africa has several such women. One ANC leader discussed her continuing pressure on all parties to appoint women to cabinet positions and

national commissions. Such pressure has met resistance, to which she has responded: "I said, 'Well, sorry, go to the Rules Committee and change the rules and take away my power. But when I've got the power, you have to live with it.'" In addition, these women know how to use the media and nongovernmental lobbying groups to apply pressure. In relating her reaction to political resistance, one such woman stated: "I told them I would go on national television. . . . I think that is part of the kind of pressure you have to apply."

These nationally recognized politicians are often highly trained professionals with previous careers as lawyers, journalists, writers, or academicians. Many have already fought long battles to gain entry to and acceptance within their professional fields, often being part of the first generation of women to do so. As one member of an opposition party stated, "My generation of women, we were pioneers. In my law firm . . . I was the first woman they ever took on. . . . In my law class, there were two blacks and two women; now [there are] 30 to 40 percent. . . . We were pioneers in this country, even though perhaps we were ten to twenty years behind the U.S. But we have overtaken [the United States] as far as Congress goes."

Within the ANC these national politicians were most often exiles who often received extensive training and education outside the country. Some women attended classes in European institutions, learning about economic development, international feminism, and parliamentary politics. Others were involved in military training in Africa and Europe. Still others discussed working abroad in their chosen fields and raising funds and support for the antiapartheid struggle. This training prepared them for lives as national politicians and afforded them the opportunity to work closely with the party's top leadership. Further, it provided sources of political learning, for these women could make comparisons with similar struggles in southern Africa. For example, Abongile, an ANC member, talked about what she learned while in exile:

> I was not in exile in Europe. I was in exile in Africa, and I think that makes a difference. . . . As much as I traveled abroad, I was based in southern Africa, and my travels were on very specific issues. Part of it was studying the realities of international struggles, looking at Mozambique, Angola, and Zimbabwe. I think I learned in the instance that women will be on the agenda [during] the national struggle, but the minute you get involved in parliamentary struggle, [women] very easily get moved out. It doesn't always happen the first time around, with the dynamism that goes with transition—a greater window of opportunity. That is why we are trying to push as much as possible during these first few years in government. . . . So, yes, we have learned from international struggles and have learned what the lessons are. But I don't think you only needed to be in exile. Exile was quite an opportunity for many of us, and there

was the international experience where we could look more discerningly at various approaches to feminism and say, "Is this going to work on the African continent and in South Africa?" We have a strongly patriarchal environment, but we can move quite a way ahead depending on how we try to influence issues.

Because these national politicians were outside the country for much of the struggle, however, they have had a difficult time connecting to any particular constituency or location since their return. They initially did not have concrete knowledge about daily life for the average citizen, and they did not have well-established grassroots support within the country. Steyn (1998) reported a similar phenomenon: women who stayed in South Africa felt a distance from, if not distrust of, those who had spent time in exile during the struggle and vice versa. Although many viewed this disconnection negatively during the 1994 term, there were some positive aspects to this detachment. It allowed these women a national vision with which they could see the larger structures of gender oppression within their society. They are thus often better situated to address national inequities.

Some national politicians belong to traditionally white parties or opposition parties that stayed within the country during apartheid. Interestingly, they and the women who were in exile share many of the same background characteristics, career goals, and policy aspirations. Many of these national politicians have worked their ways up through their parties' ranks or made lateral moves from their professions into their parties based on family power, professional prestige, or ethnic patronage.

Women in this group tended to possess the clearest understanding of existing government structures and institutions for women's empowerment. They also had a coherent vision for developing new institutional structures' functions, memberships, and agendas. Although these women were aware of the steps necessary to establish governmental structures, they were similarly aware that little had been done to deliver services to ordinary people.

These women were experienced with interviews and comfortable with the gendered nature of my project, more so than women in any other category. Most had experience with various forms of feminism, understood the complexities of feminist dialogue within the nation, and were working against a feminist backlash within their parties. Mafuane of the ANC discussed the notion of feminism within the South African context:

> But I must say in South Africa [feminism] has had a negative connotation. During the process, this is one of the issues we had to deal with. We had to decide what feminism is. We found that it is not only women who can call themselves

feminists, but also there were some men who thought they were feminists. . . . This issue of saying that those people have been educated, I find it very destructive and divisive to women. We never do that with men. Every time a woman stands up and talks about issues affecting women, you are branded a feminist and are classified as those educated women who are the only ones who have problems. We have worked with rural women, and I have found them more radical than women who call themselves feminists. . . . I find it divisive, and it is a way of putting down those women who have been able to articulate the issues of women to try and remove them from the rest of the women to make sure they don't have any influence. So I usually reject vehemently the issue of saying that it is only educated women who are feminists. We agree that women are not homogeneous. But [that is the] same as men. They are not homogeneous. You never hear any man being questioned as to whom do you actually represent. But every time a woman stands up, people ask that question. I have a serious problem with it, and so we think it is a backlash that we must deal with right away.

As a whole, these women were the most comfortable in their roles in Parliament, although each one could also provide specific examples of male resistance to women's activities there. They were also the most likely to say they would stay in Parliament through the next election. Nonetheless, even though they were the most powerful and best-acclimated group of women in the institution, they were not immune to isolation and alienation. One MP who was a member of the resistance commented on the difficulties of moving from exile and the struggle to Parliament and the executive office: "You know the fundamental difference . . . between the struggle and now is that in the struggle it didn't matter where you came from, where you are going to. You were part of one big family. . . . We have now come home and [to] the differentiated structure in society. And we somehow have fallen into a continuous conflict. . . . The communal spirit is gone. . . . Parliamentary politics is not about that." As she continued, she evoked the well-recognized idea that it is lonely at the top, especially for women: "I thought that was the end of my loneliness when I became a member of the executive. . . . From the very day I was sworn in . . . [I was] alone. . . . So I think that every step of the way it gets lonelier and lonelier. The higher up you go, it is very cold."

When asked about women's rights and issues, the women in this group mentioned broad national agendas, such as implementing governmental structures for women's empowerment, working on legislation for abortion or against pornography, or furthering women's political equity. They were often active with or aware of the Beijing conference's Platform for Action and the UN's Convention on the Elimination of Discrimination Against Women.

The Middle Class: Women from Labor Backgrounds with Moderate Education

Educational Status:	Moderate education, occasionally including some university training
Professions:	Nurses, teachers, clerical workers or industrial workers, often with union backgrounds
Race:	Indian, coloured, or white
Exile Status:	Exiles and nonexiles
Parties:	ANC, PAC, IFP, NP
Participation Mode:	Focus on drafting legislation; capacity for excellent committee work
Level of Influence:	Parliamentary (leaders within committees and strong voices within party caucuses)
Lawmaking Orientation:	Dedifferentiated mode
Women's Issues Orientation:	Women's issues among important political issues; caution about and resistance to the term *feminism*
Gender Policy Agenda:	Focus on community development legislation to ensure equality in terms of race, class, and gender; implementation of national gender institutions, CEDAW, the Beijing Platform; creation of a "women-friendly" climate in Parliament

About 35 percent of the women I interviewed fell into this group. These women were actively involved in the daily activity of Parliament. They were most visible and effective working in committee, and they often led the work of Parliament on a wide range of issues within them. Haffajee (1999) similarly found that women in the South African parliament were finding their voices within committees, where certain women have been most able to influence the channels of government. One member of an opposition party was an active member of fourteen committees. Women in this group were able to integrate national vision and local knowledge into policy debates. This has been a trend internationally as well; Sawer found that women MPs "feel more 'at home' in more intimate forums" like committee work (2000, 370). And Tamale's research, too, clearly demonstrates the success women have within committees, much more than they have enjoyed in the formal debates in chambers (1991, 131).

This group included exiles and nonexiles. Although education and privilege were two key factors in their success as parliamentarians, many also had backgrounds in labor unions or other mass-based organizations that provided them with useful parliamentary skills. They had learned skills ideal for committee work, such as negotiation, management, consensus building, networking, and lobbying. Several others had media experience that provided them extensive training in communication skills, such as reading, writing, and speaking English. Nomuula directly linked her success in politics to her experiences in the trade unions:

> I was in the trade unions since 1970s, and that is where I got groomed in politics. . . . When it came time for the negotiations, for the interim constitution, your whole negotiation skills and ways [you'd] picked up of negotiating was of great benefit to you. You know because already at plant level, when negotiating with employers, once you walk into negotiations, you are equal with them. You know they've got the money and the jobs. We've got our hands. We are the workers. And there was always a power play, you know. It helped tremendously in [the] negotiations at the World Trade Center.

These women focused their energy on legislative change. Both the national and local levels of politics informed them. Nonetheless, they focused primarily on passing legislation that would assist general development and democratization programs rather than on creating specific programs or institutions for women's empowerment. One MP, Nombeko, articulated her legislative role in a particularly interesting way, within gendered terms: "It is like coming into a dirty house with children who need to be fed in that same house. You've got to clean and cook at the same time. And that process has to go on at the same time because we have to clean up the old legislation and also make [new] legislation for life to go on." In South Africa women find their experience with multitasking to be especially useful in the legislative process.

These women were also active in the life of Parliament, creating or participating in party or women's caucuses. They were working toward the transformation of the institution itself, seeking to create an entity that can accommodate women's needs by, for example, supporting the creation of a day-care center, increasing the number of women's toilets, and restructuring Parliament's hours and calendar to fit child-care needs. While it was obvious that they were still connected to women in the grass roots, it was equally obvious that their lives were so filled by their parliamentary duties that they could become detached from the grass roots and their constituencies in a few years.

Women's issues were a central concern to these women, although rarely did such issues take precedence over their other committees or interests. Several women tried to incorporate women's concerns into their other committees, but limited time and energy often forced them to choose one or the other; either they focused on committees specifically concerned with gender, such as the Joint Monitoring Committee on the Improvement of the Quality of Life and Status of Women, or they devoted themselves to other committee work.

One parliamentary leader's view of feminism blended ideas held by national politicians and those common among community workers. She cautioned against an exclusive focus on feminism and argued for a unity of race, class, and gender:

> You know, I have never been actively involved in clearly only gender issues. The gender issues surface everywhere. It overlaps with race and everything. . . . I have also tried to point out that the kind of gender, the kind of feminism, that took root in this country, especially from 1990 onwards, was more sort of an imported model, more west European based, some of the American feminists. You find with gender approaches today a sort of mixing of all that. And, of course, women's problems are the same all over the world. In any case, we just have different approaches. . . . We don't need to reinvent the wheel. Women's problems are the same all over the world. We need to link up with international groups and learn from their experience.

These women were generally willing to stay in Parliament through the next election, although most expressed concern that the institution was alienating, male dominated, and exhausting. These women did not stress attaining the status of national politician, but most stated they were increasingly comfortable in their political roles. Some, however, voiced concerns that they had been more effective in community or union organizations and were contemplating a return to that life.

The Working Class: Women from Lower Socioeconomic and Educational Backgrounds

Educational Status:	Low education, often not above grade 9 or 10
Professions:	Domestic workers, teachers, social workers, nurses, farmers
Race:	Black or coloured
Exile Status:	Nonexiles
Parties:	ANC, IFP
Participation Mode:	Focus on solving local problems; activist and caseworker approach
Level of Influence:	Primarily local
Lawmaking Orientation:	Undifferentiated mode

Women's Issues
   Orientation: Rejection of the label *feminist;* promotion of
                                          programs for women's socioeconomic gains
   Gender Policy Agenda: Clean water, land rights, microenterprises,
                                          education, electrification, reduction of gen-
                                          der violence

About 30 percent of the women I interviewed fell into this class. These women sought applied solutions to local problems in their home communities instead of working to initiate policy. In many ways their work in Parliament was a natural extension of the work they did before coming there. These women were community activists, and one woman characterized her work in Parliament as identical to her efforts as a social worker. She said that she responds as a caseworker to the problems of individual constituents. Women in this group thus focused on helping individuals, whereas the elites and middle class were working to transform national institutions and societal structures.

These women came from disadvantaged and working-class backgrounds, and they never anticipated or prepared for lives as a national politician. Often their lack of social power conflicted with the expectations and norms of parliamentary life, as Serafina of the ANC stated:

> I am please[d] that I am from the poorest of the poor. I was able to come to Parliament. I then said one day I wish my parents were alive to see this. All my sisters and those in my family cried. None in my family had ever had a car. My father died never having a bank account. When I came to Parliament, I had no bank account. When I get form to fill for the bank account, mine went empty. What happened on the day we were supposed to go and get our salaries, he said "Senator, I didn't give you a salary," because I have got no bank account, and I said to him, "A poor woman like myself." I knew nothing about banking. Even in my family nobody had a bank account. It was just from hand to mouth, you understand.

Most of those in this group were black women who had been involved in the antiapartheid movement in some form. In many ways these women formed the backbone not only of the struggle but also of their families, churches, and communities. In addition, this category included a handful of women in traditionally white parties. These women were often community volunteers, church workers, or philanthropists who decided to pursue a career in politics so they could help people. In some instances a party would recruit these women in an attempt to diversify its gender balance. Again, these women were concerned with concrete, direct, specific solutions to individual or local problems. One MP worked with women to develop sound farming practices that would minimize water loss in her constituency's dry climate. Another was pushing her community to develop an agenda to eradicate violence against women.

These women were not exiles. In part because of this, they were much more connected to their particular communities than national politicians were to theirs. They often had broad-based support and extensive political networks within their areas of origin. These support structures, political networks, and local knowledge made them invaluable to the new government in terms of policy initiation, formation, and implementation. Unlike the national politicians, however, these women often felt detached and isolated from the institution; as one MP stated: "I am not a politician. I am a community person and a people person. I am too honest to be a politician and in fact find most of this frustrating. I never thought I would be in Parliament. . . . I wasn't ready for this level of politics."

Two factors inhibit the translation of this local knowledge into national policy. First, women from working-class backgrounds who are community workers or grassroots activists are not necessarily skilled or experienced policy makers and have difficulty communicating their knowledge within the current parliamentary structure. Second, Parliament is not designed to hear their specific voices, as Grace reveals:

> It is not easy. It isn't easy. It's like you need different kinds of skills. You need management skills. You can't depend on mass mobilization and those kinds of things, and our management skills were not well developed in the liberation movement. . . . And we find our leading members are suddenly in charge of ministries and huge departments and vast staffs—and the departments are not terribly sympathetic. . . . We didn't really understand what was required. . . . Particularly women don't actually have the background and education to be able to really take advantage of those skills.

All these women expressed intense dissatisfaction with their lives in Parliament. Aside from the alienated members, whom I discuss later, they were the most likely to express desires to leave the institution before or during the next election period. Siphiwe of the ANC, for example, stated that she hoped to return to grassroots activism: "In 1999 I will be at home with my children. I think it will be much better because then I will work with the people on the ground. . . . So in 1999 I will step down, but in fact I am tired, but I will work with the people."

The women in this group resisted the term *feminism,* but they were all interested in the socioeconomic advancement of women. They were not interested in debates about abortion or pornography; they were interested in clean water, land rights, electrification, basic education and skills training, small-business initiatives, job creation, youth programs, and environmental preservation.[4] Violence against women was second only to these socioeconomic issues, however, although it was not discussed by all members. They described in great detail a number of applied projects to assist women in their areas, including bread-baking projects, nutrition programs, water initiatives, and job creation, as well as assistance in both plant and animal agriculture. One woman linked women's empowerment to water access: "We could so empower women if we could have water close to their homes."

The Poor: Women from Significantly Disadvantaged Educational and Occupational Backgrounds

Educational Status:	Very little education
Professions:	Domestic workers, farmers, informal traders, community activists
Race:	Black
Exile Status:	Nonexiles
Parties:	ANC, IFP
Participation Mode:	Voting
Level of Influence:	Local; little power to effect significant changes for constituents
Lawmaking Orientation:	Undifferentiated mode
Women's Issues Orientation:	Lack of understanding of women's rights or feminism; belief in and promotion of women's equality
Gender Policy Agenda:	Little articulation of specifics; general concern with development and equality for all people

About 15 percent of the women I interviewed were in this significantly disadvantaged group. Caught at the far end of the class spectrum, these women were not prepared for life in Parliament, have not found a place for their voice or skills in there, and have now left or are preparing to leave the institution. I spoke with one woman who called these women "sleepers," because they sat in the back rows of the National Assembly and literally fell asleep, no doubt exhausted both by their jobs as MPs and by the continued hardships of economic deprivation at home. These women were loyal party members and reliable party-line voters, which may not have played in their favor; their party's leadership perhaps did not seek to fully develop their capacities as long as they voted the party line.

In some ways this category of largely alienated MPs resembles Thomas's (1997) category of the "resigned and frustrated," since both are groups of women who have stopped attempting to change their situations or reform the institution. The two groups differ markedly, however, as to the reasons for such resignation. Legislators in Thomas's study became inactive after years of attempts to be effective. This group of South African women never had the opportunity or capacity to participate because they had been significantly marginalized by apartheid-era discrimination.

Many in the media and academia seem to think that the vast majority of women in Parliament are alienated, but my research suggests otherwise. Nevertheless, about 15 percent of women in my study were baffled by the confines of formal government. Most often these were former activists who were denied both the education and training necessary to be active members of this type of institution. They continually tried to find ways to participate as parliamentarians, however, either through committee work or community work. I did interview one woman who was explicit in her inability to function:

> I came into Parliament . . . , and everyone is on their feet. Nobody is showing you around. You have to struggle to find your way. When I came here somebody said, "Let's go to a committee meeting," [and] then I went to the sitting. I didn't know the procedures. I didn't realize you had to read the order papers and the weekly diary. I still haven't read all the rules. We get a lot of papers, and frankly I don't go through all the stuff, and sometimes the service officers come in and clean it up [pointing to the waste bin].

The critical question, then, is how certain women managed to move through such isolation and dislocation while others did not. The institutional expectations and norms hindered women from disadvantaged or struggle backgrounds more than it did other women. Even with the attempts by leaders, such as Speaker Ginwala, to assist these women to advance professionally, the neglect, discrimination, and oppression wrought by apartheid has left them with skills completely unmatched to formal parliamentary politics.

Class and Role Differentiation

Again, class broadly defined has influenced not only how women have participated in the new South African parliament but also how they have viewed women's issues and crafted their legislative agendas. Moreover, the first major lesson to be drawn here is that women from disadvantaged backgrounds—the working-class and poor women—most closely resemble the majority of the South African population in terms of race, class, occupation, and education. These women are primarily black and coloured; are found within "traditionally female" occupations, including domestic service, farming, education, and nursing; and have limited formal education, consistently lacking higher education and often failing to have completed secondary education. Although these women know quite a bit about their constituents' needs, they have found the process of making policy tedious and alienating. Increasingly they focus their time, energy, and attention on working with individual problems of their constituencies. Many planned to cut short their careers in Parliament because they felt that they could be more effective in grassroots politics in their home communities. The women from affluent backgrounds—the elites and middle-class women—have had a smoother transition from their lives under apartheid to their lives as legislators. They, too, experienced dislocation, but they have found ways to exert pressure and wield influence to accomplish several significant gains for women, including constitutional protection and guaranteed representation.

This situation reflects Geisler's (2000) categories of "honorary men," who assimilated into parliamentary life; "movers," who were elites and national leaders; and "older women," who had been activists in South Africa's struggle for democracy but had not managed to secure power or influence. Geisler indicates that these older activist women, who were most closely attached to the grassroots struggle, were the first to leave their roles as MPs (2000, 621). I found similar "matriarchs" within my study, although I use term *matriarch* to mean women who played well-established roles in the antiapartheid struggle. (Age itself cut across all the categories.) These women also possessed some of the most prominent political profiles of all those in the study. On one level, matriarchs embody the history of the struggle. Interviews with these women were often filled with personal accounts of their parties or movements. In addition to chronicling the past, these women serve important ceremonial roles, such as delivering key speeches on national holidays. They closely monitor their parties and are often well known internationally, serving as unofficial ambassadors abroad and continuing to raise funds for their parties. They are aware that their high-profile names make their stories well known. A few of the women's reputations derived from their husbands' careers or profiles, much as did those of women in Hirschmann's (1991) "key women" category.

These distinctions among women, linked most often to class, have implications for the future of women in Parliament. Despite the constitutional mandates for gender and class equality and despite the parties' commitments for representational diversity, I found that Parliament's institutional structure and the experience and training necessary to be a legislator discouraged specific groups of women, leading them to leave national office. Regardless of political leaders' intentions, therefore, institutional structure can block a nation's path toward a truly representative democracy. Sawer's (2000) work on the Australian parliament discussed how the increasing "professionalization of politics" determines the type of women who obtain or stay in office. As politics became more professionalized, there was "the reduced likelihood of community activism as a pathway to parliament for women and an increased likelihood of a background in law and paid party work" (Sawer 2000, 374). A similar pattern has been found in Mexico, too (Camp 1998). As time passes, this trend could easily become the norm in South Africa as well.

This circumstance implies critical questions about the social power necessary to foster institutional reform and the impact of collective social learning on the agenda and tactics of reform movements. It also calls into question Molyneux's (1985) division of strategic needs and practical needs. Women need strategic power to meet the practical needs of other women, as the South African case demonstrates. Yet being granted strategic power in and of itself is clearly not sufficient. Women from lower socioeconomic classes have not had their own practical needs met, but they currently occupy positions of national power. Since they do not have the personal economic resources to facilitate their new professional lives, these women have not been able to use the strategic power they possess as MPs. If the goal is to keep South Africa's national parliament as representative as it currently is in terms of race, class, gender, and occupational and educational backgrounds, then dramatic steps are needed to ensure that women from all backgrounds and experiences find a place there for their voices and avenues through which to participate. The skills training that could facilitate this is currently in its infancy and most often occurs only after women have assumed their new positions.

International activists and academicians concerned with securing women's electoral success face serious new challenges. As the South African case demonstrates, such electoral success alone may not ensure women's sustained multivocality in government. The women who will stay in office for an extended period may be women who do not fully represent all South African women either formally or ideologically. As feminist academicians have asserted for decades, gender diversity alone cannot ensure a progressive gender agenda. The South Africa case strongly supports such a belief. Indeed, my research demonstrates that there are vastly different policy agendas among women and specifically among different groups of women. It underlines the danger in assuming that descriptive representation (where each group is represented by members of that group) will lend itself naturally and easily to certain policies.

The lessons for international gender activists are fairly complex. Centrally, any quest for electoral success must be combined with skills training for new legislators or some measure of institutional reform to accommodate new members' abilities. As the South African case demonstrates, these efforts should be accomplished before the MPs take office. Otherwise, either their preexisting patterns of political participation will serve to disfranchise certain women, or Parliament's preexisting institutional norms will empower women of privilege. Unfortunately, the financial and logistical costs of such training or reforms are often prohibitive.

Class and Feminism

The second major lesson to be drawn here is that class significantly determines how an MP will define and pursue women's issues and feminism. Many studies have examined the distinction between substantive and descriptive representation for women (Pitkin 1967; Thomas 1991; Tremblay and Pelletier 2000) or the difference between the legislative priorities of men and those of women (Little, Dunn, and Deen 2001). I have gone a step further, however, in trying to differentiate among groups of women concerned with women's needs and issues.

The South African women MPs from affluent backgrounds—the elites and the middle class—talk about gender in terms of a rights-based equity movement. Women from more disadvantaged backgrounds—the working class and the poor—do not talk specifically about gender or women's rights, but they are centrally concerned with the socioeconomic development of women. Several conclusions can be drawn from this situation. First, adding this difference to the chapter's other observations and conclusions indicates that women advocating a rights-based equity movement were more likely to remain in Parliament and function well there. Conversely, those espousing a socioeconomic and needs-based development strategy were most likely to leave Parliament or, lacking the necessary training and experience, to never rise above invisibility there.

These differences and ideological disparities were often apparent to the women legislators I interviewed. Sasha, an ANC MP and community worker, discussed the class differences in the feminisms she had witnessed:

> Two kinds of women's organizations: . . . The one is where you are looking at employment equity and equity at that level, education and so on. The other is

looking at the more grassroots issue. You find that the multiparty, with the other parties, you are talking about those rights and they don't understand the social issue. So it has become like a class issue. . . . Because we are in a grassroots party, we look at it from a grassroots level, whereas the other parties will look at it from their point of view—which is from the higher class. And that point of view is totally different. They are able to go and do things because they have a nanny at home and don't ever look at the life of the nanny at home and what is happening to her. We are concerned about that nanny. In a nutshell, that is the difference.[5]

As Sasha indicated, South African women have a wide range of views on how feminism should be constructed, how women's rights should be pursued, and how women can or cannot unify across race and class lines.

In many ways some of the "movers"—the elites—and the "honorary men" have become gatekeepers. The gatekeepers deny that there are any structural imbalances that inhibit women, and some even indirectly support class and race hierarchies that oppress other women so that they can remain on top. I estimate that 5–8 percent of the women I interviewed could be described as gatekeepers. These women were focused primarily on achieving individual political gains or preserving their political prominence. Many enjoyed places within the inner circle of national politics, and they planned to maintain their status by preventing other women from entering, chiefly by denying that gender is a factor in political life, by reinforcing gender obstacles in political life, and by dismissing women's movements. For example, at least four women in the study agreed that mothers with "baby babies" (a South African term for infants) or toddlers should not consider being an MP; all were white women from opposition parties, with both the means and the inclination to hire domestic workers and child-care workers. They resisted attempts to change Parliament to accommodate mothers, and they denied the societal structures that enabled them to hire a staff. Rather than work to eradicate obstacles based on race, class, and gender, their efforts often reinforced barriers between women.

For example, one white MP from an opposition party stated, "To say Parliament isn't women friendly is rubbish"; she applied the same term to the need for child-care facilities there. She stated that she didn't take a position in politics until her children were old enough for school, and she added, "If husbands can't accommodate them, then they shouldn't run. I took on a female boarder who was a teacher for my kids, and also got a domestic servant—you just have to stay organized."[6] When pressed about the class differences that provided her with the resources to hire a household staff, she insisted that she had no income besides her parliamentary salary, so that all

MPs of whatever race and class could do the same. She further stated that she was not involved in women's groups in Parliament: "We've got to work ourselves into it, support one another, not do this one man/one woman thing. If women can't cope, they should get out." She was not alone in her critique that women with children and unsupportive husbands should not enter parliamentary life. Another MP presented strong objections to establishing parliamentary child care, asserting that women should instead employ domestic workers: "I think it is much better to put them [children] in . . . a home environment with the wonderful nannies that we have in this country. Don't tell me it is a white thing. There are wonderful mamas around, all of whom need employment, need jobs and are unqualified to do other kinds of work." These statements show how class shapes women's political agendas as well as their personal politics.

What does this say about gender politics in Parliament and the prospects for gender issues nationally? Because the rights-based equity feminists, falling within the elite and middle class, are more likely to remain in Parliament, legislation and resources will match their emphases, focusing on issues such as abortion and pornography. What may be less emphasized, however, are socioeconomic women's issues, such as access to clean water and land. This does not bode well for the majority of South African women, who are black, rural, and lower or working class. If those representing their needs and interests leave Parliament or remain alienated and distant from the legislative process, a continued lack of access to economic and political resources will threaten the social development of most South African women. The needs-based agenda may remain invisible because the women most committed to it lack the training and experience to do much.

The disparity in gender agendas among women points to another important conclusion. As I have indicated, divisions among women may threaten future collective action. During the apartheid era women were able to join together for specific issues at critical moments. The success of such collective action has been documented in the previous chapters, but, as this chapter has shown, characteristics within each group can undermine such cross-party collaboration.

The gatekeepers provide the clearest example of the potential pitfalls. These women have found ways to propel themselves forward while impeding other women. They often gained their positions because of their gender, yet they are among the first to dismiss the importance of gender identity. They reinscribe hierarchies of power to stall the advancement of other women. Poor women, in contrast, lack the capacity to further collective action by women or to advance women's unity. Elites are setting the national gender-policy agenda, yet their national focus and international training often place them too far from average women. The middle-class MPs have found an effective niche, yet they may rapidly become policy experts who lose touch with constituents and focus on the heady business of legislation.

This potentially dangerous lack of unity was a principal concern of women involved in the 1998 Women at the Crossroads: Women in Governance conference, held in Cape Town. Women there recognized that, as they headed in the 1999 elections, the partisan nature of Parliament had weakened the unity they had shared before the 1994 elections. The then ANC MP and outspoken women's rights advocate Pregs Govender "called upon women Parliamentarians to jointly subvert the institutions, rather than doing it individually. She argued that unity among women is a critical requirement for the transformation of institutions, but that this unity is often obstructed by party interests" (Van Donk and Maceba 1999, 19). Conference participants, who included women from civil society and from political office, agreed that unity—both among women in Parliament and between MPs and the grass roots—would be necessary if women were to enjoy continued success.

Conclusions on Class Divisions, Incumbency, and the Potential for Unified Action

My data clearly indicate that gender can combine with sociocultural and geographic factors to influence legislative agendas positively, a circumstance hardly unique to South Africa.[7] At critical moments and in important ways, women can overcome if not utilize such divisions to secure collective goals. However, such divisions make collective action even harder in an institution, such as Parliament, that by its very nature inhibits cross-party collaboration. The partisan nature of Parliament powerfully divides women, some would say irrevocably. These fractures are further complicated by differing levels of legislative experience or political training women have received. Such fractionalization is compounded by demographic differences among women, which, as I have shown, often lead to differences in policy agenda and gender ideology.

Aili Mari Tripp came to the same conclusion in her examination of the impact of women on Uganda's gendered state institutions. Certain women were able to maintain their ideological commitments, while others began to play by the rules of the "old boy's game": "Instead of being able to rewrite the rules to meet their own or more gender-balanced aspirations, women are told to play along under the pre-existing rules which have entrenched particular male interests, usually of relatively wealthier elders and patrons. . . .

But rarely can they make the rules or make the rule work on their own time" (2000b, 219). In both South Africa and Uganda, then, the divisions among women inside formal politics are surprisingly greater than those they face outside formal politics.

The South African case raises important questions about female incumbency and legislative turnover. Incumbency has long been a problem for women legislators, even in the United States (Darcy, Welch, and Clark 1994; Whicker and Whitaker 1999) and the United Kingdom (Lane 2001).[8] As I have argued both here and in the preceding chapter, the South African parliament continues to be dominated by men, and women often find themselves fighting an uphill battle against this gender bias at great personal and professional costs. Women differ as to their reasons for leaving, but their choices not to run for reelection, not losses of contested seats, account most for the turnover among women in Parliament. Indeed, the growing evidence about female incumbency bears critical implications for women activists and practitioners internationally. Darcy and Choike (1986) observed that incumbency has often been more important than consistent female electoral success for changing the overall compositions of legislatures. Little, Dunn, and Deen, too, address the impact of legislative turnover on women's political agendas. They found that senior members, male or female, of U.S. state legislatures have been more likely to support women's needs and issues than younger members have. New members are working to gain acceptance, and they will therefore work toward what they view as more moderate of "mainstream" goals (Little, Dunn, and Deen 2001, 43).

More important here, incumbency is increasingly important for women in African parliaments. Tripp (2000b) demonstrated links between incumbency and campaign resources in Uganda. Because women have been marginalized economically, they often lack the funds necessary to run for office. Tripp describes multiple dimensions of this problem; in Uganda candidates traditionally offer monetary tribute or present gifts to their constituents at key times, such as funerals, weddings, community events, and fundraisers. Once women are in office, they are at least able to "use their positions to build roads, bridges, hospitals, clinics, schools and churches" (Tripp 2000b, 230). They can thus demonstrate their service and dedication to their constituency at a larger, sustainable, institutional level, which differs remarkably from the scant personal resources women have before office.

Despite this growing understanding of the importance of incumbency and legislative turnover, research on women in politics has focused almost exclusively on initial electoral success, not on retention of women. In South Africa, moreover, only women of certain types remain in office, with structural forces drastically reducing diversity. Parliament may quickly come to have the features typical to most liberal democracies, including specific candidate eligibility criteria, such as high levels of education or occupational status (Darcy, Welch, and Clark 1994; Lovenduski and Norris 1995). Since these patterns manifest themselves in legislatures as diverse as those of the United States, the United Kingdom, and now South Africa, the importance of incumbency for women's representation and multivocality cannot be overestimated.

The implications are clear if we seek to preserve diversity within South African women's political representation. Rather than try to elect only skilled women adept at the demands and expectations of Parliament, parties should work to uplift and empower each category of women, as only such a diverse spectrum of ideas will match the society's needs and identities. Having diverse women occupy national positions of power serves the interests not just of women but of society at large. Instead of allowing community workers or alienated members to remove themselves from office, parties should attempt to illuminate these women's roles and to elicit their inputs on policy initiation and implementation. These women possess the most direct connection to the grass roots within the national government. South Africa needs women concerned with clean water as well as those focused on equal pay. The problem is not determining which type of interest or participation is necessary. Rather, the problem is trying to balance the interests being voiced, the policies being implemented, and the ideologies being pursued.

5. Institutional and Legislative Transformation

One of the most visible results of our new democracy is the presence of women in key positions in Parliament. Even the establishment of our crèche is a reminder to the Government that unless the sexual division of labour is challenged, and unless men take equal responsibility for parenting, women will remain unequal.

—Ruth Mompati, National Assembly of the South African Parliament, National Women's Day, 1995

The words of Ruth Mompati encapsulate the dichotomy facing women MPs. They clearly made tremendous inroads by gaining national political positions, yet many women were still limited by the inequities they faced in their home lives and their political lives. The goal quickly shifted from getting women into office to changing the system to accommodate and empower women at all levels. In this way the South African case constitutes a critical testing site for the liberal feminist argument that getting women into positions of power and leadership will by itself improve women's lives, status, and opportunities. This argument assumes that women have methods and agendas different from men's. Liberal feminism asserts that the types of policies will change merely because women have been brought into office. It focuses more on gender identity and discounts preexisting inequalities of ethnicity, class, or educational experience.

The South African case does not appear to support this liberal feminist argument. First, the women in the initial postliberation cohort of MPs—those responsible for most of the moves toward gender equality—came from more affluent backgrounds, the elite and the middle class, which were the two groups with the most political experience and formal educational training. Despite direct and indirect gender discrimination, these women made individual and collective advances toward the promotion of women's rights in order to increase women's visibility, power, and voice. Women from more disadvantaged or less experienced political backgrounds did not have the essential political skills or proper training for their positions. They were not, therefore, efficient institutional participants. The initial gains thus came primarily from the work of a limited group of women.

These South African women have continued their active engagement with the structures of economic, social, and legislative power. Just as they labored at the heart of the antiapartheid struggle, women have continued to work for institutional transformation and legislative reform, particularly in terms of gender equity. They have continued to pressure their parties and the government to fulfill rhetorical commitments to women's equality.

Recognizing that the culture and norms of institutions affect women's lives, these women attempted to alter the parliamentary ethos to be more accommodating of all women's needs and responsibilities. They institutionalized structures throughout government, civil society, and Parliament that focus specifically on the needs and interests of women. They were able to make these changes and implement these policies because they had developed the necessary skills and knowledge before taking office. Many of the national leaders also brought ideas for gender structures and legislation from their international exile experiences.

Several women leaders were making institutional improvements specifically to help other women function to their full potential within office. These changes were not, however, implemented quickly enough to prevent alienation that caused several women to leave office before or during the 1999 elections. Nonetheless, these advances in institutional culture and structure will undoubtedly help the next generation of parliamentary women and may be the most sustainable means to prevent a continuous turnover of women in elected office.

This brings me to the second hypothesis, that women MPs in this initial cohort would pursue women's issues that would balance strategic needs with practical needs. The elite women leaders in Parliament have started to incorporate gender issues and priorities into the legislative process, but the policies that they popularized and that first became known as "gender issues" dealt with abortion rights and pornography, which arguably fall into the category of strategic needs. In 1996, two years into the new dispensation, these policy debates were the first to involve the women's caucus as a lobbying body. Abortion and pornography debates divide women, and as my interviews revealed, they are not the most pressing issues for most women in South Africa. In fact, many women were far more interested in meeting their practical needs than in meeting their strategic needs, but this attitude was not reflected in the initial legislative priorities of women as a group. As I discussed in the previous chapter, several of the women I interviewed identified access to clean water, land ownership, health care, education, and occupational opportunities as the most important women's issues in South Africa, but these were not the first issues championed by women MPs. Freedom from violence was second only to these practical needs, but it, too, was much less consistently a priority than either abortion or pornography. The average woman sought solutions to practical problems, whereas Parliament pushed to meet women's strategic needs—a circumstance that reflects the type of woman most active there.

In this chapter I first trace women MPs' attempts to transform the culture of Parliament to accommodate women and then examine the 1994 Parliament's major policy debates with a recognized gender content. Women initially targeted strategic issues, and I analyze the possibility and limitations of women's collective action within the party structure. The chapter concludes with a discussion of the shift in the legislative agenda as the 1994 parliament ended and the 1999 one began, a shift from a focus on strategic needs to a more balanced concern with both strategic and practical needs. I conclude that merely having women fill the seats of Parliament will not solve the crisis of gender equity. Instead, women must develop new ways to participate in the national political forum—as they in fact are doing. South African women are finding ways to mobilize outside the traditional confines of Parliament, working in nonformal groups that concentrate on improving women's lives rather than on merely changing legislation. In this way, women MPs can worry less about uniting women through gender and more about pursuing a radical feminist agenda.

Advances in the Institutional Culture

Frene Ginwala, the then Speaker of the National Assembly and a senior member of the ANC from 1994 to 2004, has made the transformation of parliamentary culture one of her top priorities. She has received widespread praise for making Parliament more welcoming for women, and most women I interviewed agreed that her leadership has helped to make the institution more "women friendly" since they first arrived. The relevant changes fall into two broad categories: first, changes to accommodate the greater number of women in office; second, changes that reflect women's domestic responsibilities.[1]

Increasing Numbers

My interviewees mentioned several adjustments the institution had to make to accommodate the vast influx of women MPs and delegates. For example, the government had to build several women's lavatories. Before the transition Parliament had only two women's lavatories, an appropriate number for the three to five women who managed to win office during each election throughout the apartheid era. With over 120 women holding office following the 1994 elections, there was an immediate need for more women's lavatories.

Women parliamentarians faced a chilly climate in chambers, literally. The chambers were kept considerably colder before the transition because the men wore suits that kept them warm. Women pushed for an increase in the temperature because they wore thinner dresses and often had to add shawls to stay warm. Considine and Deutchman (1996) discovered a similar situation in Australian state legislatures, which they classified as indirect exclusion of women legislators.

Parliamentary forms and contracts were changed from the pretransition days, when it was assumed that members were male heterosexuals. Dziko commented that she felt these changes were in many ways a barometer for the nation:

> I think it has been difficult here. This parliament, one cannot deny that it was a totally male, white male, domain. So much so I am sure you heard about how the temperatures of the air-conditioning were too high. Men wear suits. The toilets! The forms! I can show you the forms [that] say "wives." They have changed it. It used to say "For Members and Wives." And I think the rate of development of this country can be assessed by this form itself. Not only have we changed [it to] "members and spouses," but we have added "companions"—which I think is a tremendous leap ahead.

These changes in the culture of Parliament have affected the institution's processes. As Ruth Rabinowitz of the IFP stated, "Women have brought a different culture to Parliament. It's less of a beer-swilling, let's sort things out in the bar kind of place" (qtd. in Haffajee 1999, 2).

In addition, the public's perception of parliamentarians was changing because of the number of women holding top positions. Women from all parties were pleased that the Speaker and Deputy Speaker were women of color and asserted that Ginwala and Mbete's leadership was redefining old demographic assumptions. With the 1999 parliament, eight women served as cabinet ministers and eight as women deputy ministers (Feris 1999).

When women hold the highest offices in Parliament, it becomes much more difficult to assume that members ought to be white males. A member from an opposition party stated, "I think that if we didn't have Frene as the Speaker, we would be in serious trouble. Everyone worries, 'What happens when Mandela goes?' I say, 'What happens when Frene goes?'" The impact of having women in these offices was felt throughout South Africa, not just Parliament. Feris reported that the Independent Electoral Commission chairperson, Joyce Piliso-Seroke, commented that "it was critical for women to enter Parliament to 'explode' the myth that women did not have the capacity to make decisions" (1999, 1). Piliso-Seroke credited women's new "democratic spirit" for the remarkable change in registered voters for the 1999 elections, with "1.5 million more women than men registered" (qtd. in ibid.).

Domestic Obligations

There have also been limited cultural changes to Parliament to accommodate women's responsibilities outside political office. These changes largely reflect the reality that most women still have primary child-care and domestic responsibilities in their homes. Sawer describes the working conditions in governments worldwide as "indirect discrimination against women," because "parliamentary arrangements assume that . . . representatives are not at the same time primary caretakers for family members" (2000, 370). Brown's discovered a similar situation among Scottish women, whose "role in the family was considered to be a key factor limiting the supply or participation of women in Scottish political life" (1996, 29).

South African MPs have shifted the parliamentary calendar to reflect the school calendar as much as possible. There is also general consensus that debates and committee meetings should end at a reasonable hour so that mothers can be at home with their children. Finally, they have established a childcare facility for the children of MPs. These three changes echoed those in other nations' governments (Brown 1996; Brown et al. 2002; Sawer 2000). As Hananke, a leader in the South African parliament, explained to me during one interview, these changes are an attempt to recognize that the institution must understand and accommodate the everyday realities of its members:

> One of the things we realized when we came here is that this had been structured to fit males or people who don't have children or a home to look after. We started off firstly with facilities here, like the bathrooms, the meeting times, and the very sessions of Parliament. We have tried to make sure that they coincide with the school holidays whenever possible, but it has been a nightmare because we come from different parts of the country, and schools have different schedules. Also . . . Parliament only met for six months, the first six months of the year. It would be closed for the second six months. So those who have got children will be [away from them] for six months. That used to destabilize, I think, the children. We made sure, at least, [that] Parliament meets right through the year, breaks coincide with holiday, and that the sessions themselves

don't go very late so we can be with our families. And we found that when we raised these issues, the men were supporting it, and they actually felt that they also needed to go home and be with their families, but all that time they were not raising it. We make sure that when we raise issues affecting women, it is taken very seriously as part and parcel of the work we have to do.

The goal, therefore, is to allow women to operate simultaneously as law-makers and homemakers. As an indirect benefit, such changes may also encourage men to expand their domestic responsibilities. The changes that are making parliamentary culture more "women friendly" may thus be seen as making the culture more "parent friendly," too. As I discussed earlier, married South African men are typically accompanied by their wives when they join Parliament and move to Cape Town, whereas their female counterparts are usually not accompanied by their husbands. This has created a common scenario of "overnight single moms" who must care for their children while caring for the nation and who face criticism by family members for deserting their husbands, if only temporarily.

The women I interviewed knew that these changes would eventually help women (and, one hopes, men) balance their multiple roles. Most indicated that the changes had not been in place long enough, or soon enough, to offset their disproportionate domestic burdens. Accordingly, there were several key challenges still working against women's leadership and participation.

Integrating Gender into Legislation

Most of the legislation in the first several years following democratization has been geared toward eliminating the vestiges of apartheid. Members also debated several key pieces of legislation affecting women during the transition period, most dealing specifically with women's strategic and not practical needs.[2] For example, early in the first democratically elected parliament, the National Party's Sheila Camerer won a long-fought struggle to change the tax code: "Married women paid more tax than their husbands because their salaries were ostensibly used for luxuries. [The former finance minister] Dereck Keys always said, 'It's just not possible.' The tax tables were rewritten in 1995" (Haffajee 1999, 2).

The National Women's Day Act was and continues to be one of the most visible symbolic measures honoring and promoting women's rights in South Africa. The Choice on the Termination of Pregnancy Act legalizes abortion on demand and greatly reduces the requirements for obtaining an abortion to assist impoverished women. The National Gender Commission Act in-

stitutionalizes a national commission that focuses on locating, document-
ing, and overturning societal gender oppression. The Films and Publications
Act primarily ends apartheid censorship but has been extended to include
protections against the degradation of women and children. Concern with
the issues involved in such legislation, such as abortion and pornography,
did not originate in the grass roots. These debates therefore often proved divisive and threatened the tentative unity of women in Parliament. So women
were struggling not simply against the structures of power but also among
themselves as they sought to define their agenda.

The National Women's Day Act

South Africa declared August 9 to be National Women's Day in commemo-
ration of the 1956 pass laws protests (see chapter 1 for a discussion of these
protests). Approximately twenty thousand women from every racial, ethnic,
and political group in the country converged on the Union Building, the seat
of the executive branch, in Pretoria in 1956 to protest the introduction of pass
books designed to control the movement of women to and from the townships. National Women's Day memorializes and honors the role women have
played in the country's history. The day serves, within Parliament and society, as a rallying point for women's rights and unity.

In parliamentary debates during 1994, the year of the act's ratification, members raised issues surrounding the Reconstruction and Development Programme, a program intended to promote socioeconomic development
nationwide. Speaker Frene Ginwala stated in the 1995 Women's Day com-
memoration, "It is important to note that this is not a day for women, but a
day chosen by our nation for men and women to focus on the challenges that
lie ahead. The responsibility for bringing an end to the subordination of
women in our society . . . rests on all of us, men and women" (National Assembly 1995, 3512). In the 1995 session women spoke frequently about the up-
coming United Nations' Fourth Conference on Women in Beijing and the ratification of the Convention on the Elimination of All Forms of Discrimination
against Women. The day continues to be a critical symbolic moment for the
nation and for women. Beyond the commemorative and community-building
impact of the event, however, National Women's Day does not directly provide any substantive socioeconomic improvements for women's lives.

The Choice on the Termination of Pregnancy Act

Abortion has been legal in South Africa since 1975, but only under special circumstances, such as rape, incest, or risk to the mother's health, whether phys-

ical or mental.[3] Meeting the requirements for obtaining abortions was expensive, for women had to consult three different doctors to document the cause and the need for an abortion. Such financial burdens excluded legal abortions for the majority of South African women. Black South African women were obviously at a great financial disadvantage, but they were also particularly victimized by the gender system of the apartheid era. Black women were disfranchised legally by their race and socially by their subjugation as domestics in customary law and the introduction of cash into the bride-price system of *lobola* (Haroz 1997). Over 70 percent of abortions conducted during the apartheid era were obtained by white women—mainly claiming the mental-heath exception—even though they constituted no more than roughly 12 percent of the female population (ibid.). The 1975 legislation, far from legalizing abortion on demand, did not exempt women financially unable to care for a child. Back-street abortions, estimated to number between 300,000 and 400,000 a year, were thought to have resulted in hundreds of deaths annually (Viall 1997, 8).

The Choice on the Termination of Pregnancy Act, passed on November 22, 1996, eased the requirements for obtaining a legal abortion, recognizing that "the decision to have children is fundamental to women's physical, psychological and social health and that universal access to reproductive health care services includes family planning and contraception, termination of pregnancy, as well as sexuality education and counseling programmes and services" (Republic of South Africa 1996c, 2). The act legalized terminations through the thirteenth week for any reason and terminations through the twentieth week for risk to the mother's health, an abnormal fetus, rape, and incest. Most significantly, abortion may now be granted up to and including the twentieth week if the "continued pregnancy would significantly affect the social or economic circumstances of the women" (ibid., 4), a provision that eased the financial hardships of child rearing for poor women. This act therefore extends both the access and legality of abortions to the majority of women and is considered "one of the most progressive abortion laws in the world" (Viall 1997, 8).

Women voted on this issue almost exclusively along party lines, reflecting the nature of the constitution. Although antiabortion lobbyists pushed for a "free vote," which would have allowed MPs to break party ranks on this issue, the move was resisted throughout South Africa. The editors of the *Johannesburg Mail and Guardian* took this idea's proponents to task, arguing that "the electorate voted for a political party, not for an individual": "We have sympathy for those MPs who might find it impossible to vote for abortion on religious grounds. But if their consciences weigh so heavily on them, they must pay the price demanded by their convictions and bow out of the parliamentary arena" ("No Free Vote" 1996, 1). Most opposition parties allowed a free vote, although many analysts believe that women may have voted according to their parties, not their consciences, for fear of reprisal (Haroz 1997).

In a decision criticized by many of its leading women, the ANC allowed its MPs to be absent from the vote on this particular issue as long as they had informed the chief whip in advance. Only about a dozen ANC MPs chose this option. The ANC MP Jennifer Ferguson created national controversy when she abstained from voting on the bill, thereby violating the ANC's policy. Ferguson, a longtime women's advocate who had a back-street abortion at the age of twenty-one but is now the mother of two children, found herself conflicted about abortion on demand after twelve weeks. Ferguson was criticized by abortion-rights proponents and ANC leaders, most publicly by Pregs Govender in a *Mail and Guardian* op-ed piece. ANC leaders instead extolled the Catholic priests, nuns, and parishioners among their MPs who risked expulsion from the church to vote with the party (Davis 1996, 1–2).

Heralded as a triumph for women's rights by many progressive party leaders, the debates and outcomes of the act did not help unify South African women. One ANC member stated that religious and cultural differences, as well influence from the U.S. antiabortion lobby, had caused the debates to create as many tensions as they had helped to resolve: "The unfortunate thing is that something like abortion doesn't tend to unite women. It tends to divide people, and I think, for what it is worth, [that] we should have handled it differently. . . . We shouldn't have given people a year to mobilize. Very much American right-wing money coming in here, and the religious right came in." Many women felt that abortion was not a top South African women's issue. One former exile interpreted abortion as an issue brought into South Africa from the outside: "Personally, I don't think it is a woman's issue in this country. . . . I think it is the exile women in Parliament who are taking this up. . . . The main women's issues, I think, are unemployment, poverty, landlessness, lack of training and education, teenage birth, violence, domestic violence, rape." This MP feared the long-term impact of legalizing abortion on demand before the national culture was prepared to accept it. Abortion-rights' activists now face the challenging problem of abortion education. Informing women about the option of abortion and finding physicians willing to perform them may prove to be more difficult than enacting the legislation. Further, a growing antiabortion movement, supported in part by lobbyists from the United States, continues to press for legislative reform and to disseminate antiabortion information. The antiabortion lobby in South Africa, however, professes a commitment to nonviolent resistance, having observed the problems of abortion-clinic bombings and physician assassinations in the United States. The South African antiabortion movement intends to oppose abortion through litigation, prayer, education, demonstrations, and lobbying (Salie 1997).

The number of women seeking abortions has grown every year since the 1996 legislation, from approximately 29,000 the first year to over 44,500 in 2001 (Magardie 2001a; Sapa 2002). Yet the number of botched, incomplete, and illegal abortions continues to be dangerously high, averaging close to 44,000 a year (Magardie 2001a). The problem stems partly from women's lack of financial resources but more from a lack of facilities: only one-third of public health facilities are performing abortions, and almost all those facilities are located in urban areas (Altenroxel 2000). Additionally, a great many women lack knowledge about their rights. As late as 2001, in fact, 47 percent of all South African women, 60 percent of women ages fifteen to nineteen, and 61 percent of rural women were unaware that abortion was legal (Magardie 2001a).

The Commission on Gender Equality Act

The Commission on Gender Equality Act created a national commission charged "to promote gender equality and to advise and make recommendations to Parliament or any other legislature with regard to any laws or proposed legislation which affects gender equality and the status of women" (Republic of South Africa 1996a). The Commission on Gender Equality (CGE) has a wide brief, for it is charged with promoting gender equality through educational programs as well as investigating, monitoring, and advising the state, public authorities, private businesses, and systems of indigenous law (ibid., sect. 11). Early on, some MPs debated whether to have a commission for gender equality separate from the South African Human Rights Commission. Such a division was thought to marginalize and ghettoize women's issues. During the debate for the act, however, the ANC and the NP both supported separate commissions. Ruth Mompati presented the ANC position: "An autonomous Commission on Gender Equality is vital to the protection and promotion of women's gender rights at all levels . . . [and] also in educating civil society. . . . The two commissions should complement each other, and duplication of powers and functions should be avoided as this would result in artificial separation between gender rights and other rights" (National Assembly 1996a, 675–76). Dene Smuts voiced the Democratic Party's support for the commission but advocated that it eventually be subsumed into the Human Rights Commission after gender equality had become a reality (ibid., 687). Two parties had interesting but not surprising positions on the CGE. First, the Inkatha Freedom Party supported the creation of the CGE but wanted its powers as limited as possible, in line with the party's belief in decentralization and federalism (ibid., 682). W. A. Botha of the Freedom Front took the debates as an opportunity to reinscribe women as the "weaker sex," as feminine, and as mothers:

> We furthermore believe, however, that women as the weaker sex are entitled to certain protective measures, for the protection of their honor and dignity. I am making reference in this instance specifically to measures protecting her against sexual harassment, particularly in the workplace, but also to measures that would prevent the exploitation of her female body. . . . The FF, as the mouthpiece of the Afrikaner, has great respect for the female sex, and has always in the past treated them as our equal. Because we respect them and accept that God has created them, physically and emotionally, different from we men, we believe, however, that in certain respects they should be handled differently. . . . The commission will have to watch over the interests of women circumspectly and wisely, without implicating their femininity and maternal nature. We should please not allow a desire for equality ever to affect the femininity of the mothers of our children. (In ibid., 686)

A second critical point of divisiveness concerned the commission's power. Although the ANC enthusiastically applauded the commission's broad search and seizure powers, few other parties agreed. Mompati expressed the ANC's support for the commission's broad powers, especially in fighting racism, poverty, rape, and violence and in ensuring access to basic services (ibid., 676–77). The other parties, while all endorsing the commission, tried to limit its power and influence. Sheila Camerer vowed that the NP would support the act but voiced concerns about the search and seizure powers over government and business. Going well beyond such conditional cautionary statements, T. J. Malan of the NP likened these powers to a witch hunt: "The Commission on Gender Equality can make a great contribution to a balanced society, if it does not see its task as a witch-hunt on departments and companies. For that reason the excessive powers of entering, searching and confiscating are unnecessary. . . . [It] may be an essential mechanism at this stage of our democracy, [but] this commission will be doing society a favour by placing less emphasis on prosecution and a greater emphasis on development and reconciliation" (ibid., 696–97). L. M. Green of the African Christian Democratic Party stated his party could not support the bill in a large part because of these search and seizure powers, believing them to be "a gender police force . . . [that] is antifamily, antimale and antitolerance" (ibid., 701). Thus, while voting in favor of the commission, all the opposition parties except the Pan African Congress attempted to limit or circumvent the power of the commission even before its creation. (An evaluation of the CGE's progress to date appears in the following chapter.)

The Films and Publications Act

The 1996 Films and Publications Act attracted extensive public attention and was vigorously debated within parties, Parliament, and women's caucuses. The major intent of the proposed bill was to end decades of state censorship, which had been a cornerstone of the apartheid government's information control (Republic of South Africa 1996b). Prior to the debates in the National Assembly, however, members of the ANC women's caucus realized that such an act would allow the production of pornography, a matter they raised within their party and the assembly. Ironically, the person in charge of piloting the bill was Lindiwe Sisulu, the daughter of Walter and Albertina Sisulu, an active ANC member, and the newly appointed deputy minister of home affairs under Minister Buthelezi of the IFP. When she introduced the bill in the National Assembly, Sisulu stated that she saw it as a balance between two poles, freedom of speech and protection against pornography and hate speech (National Assembly 1996a, 4108–9).

The act now classifies material that depicts bestiality and explicitly violent or degrading sexual conduct and strictly prohibits its distribution. Further restricted is the presentation of minors or those depicted to be under the age of eighteen engaging in sexual conduct (National Assembly 1996a, schedule 1). In their discussion of harm, the bill's supporters relied heavily on research from the United States that linked exposure to aggressive pornography with aggressive behavior toward women (ibid., 4114). Sexually explicit material outside the previously mentioned categories remains free from restriction.

The issue of harm and violence against women is of the utmost importance to South African women, because South Africa's rape rates are continually the highest in the world. The women of the ANC worked diligently to clarify the separation between sexually explicit, nonviolent pornography and material that could incite violence against women or children. Gxowa of the ANC tried to show how she was both deeply dedicated to free speech and deeply committed to the rights and well-being of women and children:

> As mothers of children it is our duty to protect our young from the abuse, exploitation and harm that is done to them through their depiction in child pornography, their exposure to pornography and the acts of harm that adults may commit against them as a result of child pornography. I do not like pornography. I do not agree with pornography. I wish that people did not find it necessary to indulge in pornography. But I accept that in a free and demo-

cratic society, some people will wish to conduct themselves in ways I do not agree [with]. . . . Just as I would defend the freedom of expression of the hon members opposite, who are a minority in this House, I defend the freedom of the minority in society to enjoy pornography in privacy where they do not cause harm to themselves or others. To those opponents of the Bill who warn that a new era of censorship is beginning I ask these questions: Do they believe that children should be used for the sexual gratification of adults? Or do they believe that children should be protected from harm? Do they believe that women should be exposed to harm by people whose attitudes to women have been influenced by violent sexually explicit pornography? Or do they believe that women should be protected from harm? (National Assembly 1996a, 4122)

Members of the FF did not accept her distinction between nonviolent and violent pornography. On the contrary, they saw any legal pornography as a threat to the safety of women and children (ibid., 4127–31). The DP's Dene Smuts summarized the debate's significance for the new constitution and bill of rights. Using her party's classical liberal approach, Smuts discussed the gendered aspects of the bill and its hate-speech language, arguing, "The Films and Publications Bill represents our first practice run, as a rights-based society, with the concept of free speech and expression." Smuts further placed the proposed act in its international context, stating that it went beyond the ambiguities found in U.S. legislation and moved closer to Canadian definitions. Because the act could limit free speech, however, Smuts argued that the DP could not support it.

Smuts alluded to the fact that this debate, like the abortion debate before it, had become internationalized. Several women I interviewed indicated that as the legislation was being drafted, they had studied the relevant laws in the United States and Canada, some of them traveling to those nations to do so. South Africa had the benefit of seeing both the legislation and its impact—or lack thereof—in both contexts.

One of the strongest and most influential voices on the issue of pornography and women's rights was that of Nozizwe Routledge, head of the Parliamentary Women's Caucus but speaking as a member of the ANC Women's Caucus, which the left had widely criticized as pushing proposals that preserved the attitudes and practices of the apartheid era's censorship boards. Routledge resisted this accusation and claimed that the ANC Women's Caucus in fact supported free speech and human sexuality. Nevertheless, she said, "pornography is not about the celebration of human sexuality. It is about the degradation and the dehumanization of women. It is about violence that thrives on the power imbalances that exist in our society. . . . it is the most vulnerable groups such as women, especially Black women, illiterate women and poor women, which are harmed in the production and consumption of pornography" (National Assembly 1996a, 4150–51).

As the women of the ANC saw it, then, the issue involved determining who would hold power over the classification, regulation, and distribution of films and publications. The women believed that this power should reside with a classification board, not with the courts, for, they argued, a board would be more likely to protect women's and children's rights. Ultimately they ensured the adoption of this system, which departs from the U.S. arrangement. In addition, the ANC caucus steered the legislation so that individuals serving on the classification board would be knowledgeable about women's and children's rights and the board would include men and women in equal numbers.

Routledge and the other women from the ANC Women's Caucus made significant alterations to the bill as it moved from the National Assembly to the Senate.[4] No one felt the impact of the caucus activities more than Deputy Home Minister Sisulu, who stated as much when she introduced the act in the Senate:

> Very soon after my appointment as Deputy Minister of Home Affairs I inherited the responsibility for the Bill before us today. I must confess that it has proven to be a baptism of fire. As fate would have it, the parliamentary women's caucus came of age just as I was preparing to pilot the Bill, and I was suddenly confronted with the phenomenon very few Ministers have been confronted with, and that is the power of women. It did not help that I myself am a woman. I have not had a single peaceful night of sleep since then. [Laughter.]
>
> However, through dealing with this Bill I have come to appreciate the gains that women have made in the legislature. We have had to amend the original Bill that was passed in the National Assembly to accommodate some fundamental concerns raised by women. Although the amendments do not sufficiently cover these concerns[,] I would like to think that the compromise position is in some way a concession of women's influence. . . . This amendment will, firstly, ensure that the members of the advisory panel[,] which must be appointed with a view to nominating persons for appointment to the Film and Publication Board[,] shall have experience in or knowledge of gender matters and children's rights. (Senate 1996, 3165–66)

Even though the issue of pornography tends to divide rather than unite women, their input during the debates demonstrated their knowledge and abilities, regardless of their political affiliations. Soggot reported that many saw the revisions to the bill to have been "a collaboration between the National Party and the ANC" (1997, 1). In many ways the debates represent a culmination of the collective social learning that had taken place during women MPs' first two years in office. Women had made significant legislative advances, and they also took great strides in learning how to amend bills. Sisulu's comments also reveal that the debate for the Films and Publications Act was the first time women had successfully altered legislation by injecting a gendered perspective into a bill.

1998 Fast-Track Legislation

Thanks in large part to the highly effective leadership of the ANC MP Pregs Govender, the Joint Monitoring Committee on the Improvement of the Quality of Life and Status of Women pushed through three vitally important pieces of legislation in 1998: the Maintenance Act, the Domestic Violence Act, and the Customary Marriages Act. In 1997 Govender and her committee created a list of priorities to be addressed by Parliament; together, women in both Parliament and civil society exerted enough pressure to get these priorities translated into legislation in 1998. These three acts greatly extended protections for women with respect to poverty, violence, and human rights generally. They reflect some of the most pressing issues facing women in South Africa, and especially in the case of the Domestic Violence Act, they resulted from decades of grassroots mobilization.

The vast majority of South African women have been struggling for the day when there would be enough committed women in Parliament to take their issues forward. The mere influx of women into Parliament in 1994 was cause of hope and celebration, but several years passed before these women legislators gained their feet. As I stated previously, the first recognition of their power was seen in the Films and Publications debate in 1996. Their success with incorporating gender issues in that piece of legislation clearly demonstrated that women had developed the skills and abilities to influence policy. The joint commission then began to set and accomplish legislative goals. There is perhaps no better case for maintaining women's incumbency than the legislative prowess demonstrated by the members of the joint commission during the final years of the first parliament.

Meintjes (2003) details the legislative process for bringing the Domestic Violence Act to life. The legislation is in her estimation an outgrowth of efforts by highly organized civil organizations working with, and sometimes even propelling, the women in Parliament to take the issue to the floor. The groups working to end violence against women often originated during the apartheid era, and several pieces of legislation to end family violence were enacted during that period. Gender violence has been one issue that brought women together across party and ethnic lines.

Both Hassim (2003) and Meintjes (2003) note the fast-track passage of these acts, and Hassim remarks with some poignancy that the legislation was pushed through at the very end of the first parliament "so that the first Parliament would be seen to be concerned with gender equality as a substantive issue" (2003, 102). Hassim's observations are not isolated. Several women, especially in opposition parties, indicated to me that they have seen flurries of legislative activity on hot-button issues right before an election. Speaking to me in mid-2003, these women MPs said that they expected a similar flurry of activity by the ANC before the 2004 elections, especially in terms of HIV/AIDS. The issue of HIV/AIDS has brought international attention to South Africa following President Mbeki's controversial stance questioning HIV as a source of AIDS and his blockage of AIDS drugs from overseas. As predicted, however, the ANC has switched its stance. On November 20, 2003, the South African government announced its decision to distribute free AIDS drugs. This is definitely the result of a long battle fought domestically and internationally, but the timing of the decision—relatively shortly before the 2004 elections—is at least an interesting coincidence.

Balancing Women's Strategic and Practical Needs

As time has progressed, women MPs have started to broaden their focus from women's strategic needs to include more practical needs. Molyneux (1985) first delineated the difference between women's practical needs (e.g., for food, shelter, health care, and employment opportunities) and their strategic needs (e.g., for political and economic rights, an end to domestic violence, and an equitable division of labour between men and women). Again, the initial focus on strategic needs reflected the type of women who were leading the fight for women's equality in legislation—that is, typically elite, well-educated, affluent women, who were the best prepared to function in Parliament. These women prioritized strategic needs above practical needs. As time has passed, however, more women are finding ways of influencing the policy agenda, and the parliamentary leaders among them are beginning to embrace women's practical needs.

There are numerous examples of this shift toward women's practical needs, relating specifically to basic needs such as those for food, shelter, employment, and health care. For example, women legislators are focusing on women's health issues, including the "introduction of a private health system—with major benefits for poor rural women, who are still the most disadvantaged sector of society" (Feris 1999, 2). Women in Parliament are beginning to work on the HIV/AIDS issue as their first priority, recognizing the impact of AIDS especially among South African women. Some MPs have taken this cause to the most personal levels, as MP Patricia de Lille did by adopting an HIV-positive child (Smith 1999). Additionally, the Joint Monitoring Committee on the Improvement of the Quality and Status of Life for Women (originally called the Joint Standing Committee) monitored the government's implementation of microsavings pilot projects and poverty-alleviation programs, as well as social security and welfare services for women and children (Joint Monitoring Committee 1999b). The Commission on Gender Equality launched a national campaign for women's land rights and worked with the joint commission on legislation. Women in Parliament have placed violence against women—the amelioration of which is often seen as both a strategic and a practical need—among their top priorities, holding public hearings, monitoring the Ministry of Justice, and drafting the Domestic Violence Act of 1998.

Regardless of whether women are pursuing strategic or practical needs, they must find ways to actualize their legislation. Their intentions may be thwarted by a lack of resources, an incapacity or resistance among civil servants, and women's lack of awareness about their rights. Even though 51 percent of all civil servants are women, only a handful of those women are in senior management positions (Clayton 1999). Such inequity will affect policy implementation. And the civil service retains powerful bureaucrats from the apartheid era. In an attempt to ensure a smooth transition from the apartheid state to the new democracy, all parties agreed to retain civil servants from the old bureaucracy until the elected officials were functioning properly. However progressive legislation from the new parliament might be, it would be implemented by civil servants who were ideologically a part of the old dispensation—and policy implementation is often more important than policy creation.

Despite women parliamentarians' continued success in passing progressive gender-oriented legislation, women in the greater society are growing restless waiting for the policies' implementation. The South African women's-rights advocate Joanne Fedler vehemently argued during the 1997 Women's Day celebration that legislation is simply not enough (Fedler 1997); implementation requires funding.[5] Fedler's concerns over funding women's initiatives are well grounded. For example, "one-stop" clinics for rape victims, which are to provide medical, legal, and psychological assistance, are either underfunded or unfunded nationally (Magardie 2000b). Nongovernmental organizations have carried the lion's share of the funding and staffing. Then, too, putting laws on the books is a long way from ensuring that women know their rights. Attempting to change the gender system and the patriarchal culture is a much larger project than drafting legislation.[6]

Conclusions

Women in the South African parliament have been most successful at ending indirect discrimination against women through changes in parliamentary culture. The institution's hours, calendar, and climate have all changed to reflect the massive increase of women into the previously male-dominated domain. The assumption that parliamentarians enter office with a wife in tow can no longer be made. As such, the institution itself has been changed, if only moderately, to accommodate women's multiple roles inside and outside political life. The key challenge will be to permanently alter the perception that all parliamentarians need "wives," with men and women being encouraged to share domestic responsibilities.

Within only a few years many women in the South African parliament have been able to find their individual and collective voices on key policy debates. Although too much legislation continues to deal with women's strategic needs, MPs and delegates continue to monitor the administration's implementation of key development initiatives and programs. To date, legislation has proven more effective than implementation. Developing a better balance between policies to meet strategic needs and those aimed at practical needs will require many developments. First, the more vocal women MPs need to broaden their gender platforms. Second, an effort must be made to empower the less vocal women MPs so that they can initiate and pursue their legislative priorities. As I discussed in the previous chapter, the women who are the most silent in Parliament are those who most closely represent the average South African woman. These are the same women who are focused primarily on women's practical needs. As this chapter indicates, their voices and the policies still need to be heard.

This case also presents interesting possibilities for and limitations of cross-party collaboration. Women from opposing parties came together unexpectedly yet successfully to lobby for changes in the Films and Publications Act. Members of the NP and the ANC rarely see eye to eye, but they found a common goal within the context of pornography. Women used networks of personal relationships developed during the constitutional negotiations to pressure their parties for change. Even within this debate, however, the differences among parties may be bigger than their similarities. Parties on the left want to limit pornography because it disempowers women; parties on the right want to limit pornography because it is dangerously immoral.

Such divisiveness can be seen within the debates for the Commission on Gender Equality Act and for the Choice on the Termination of Pregnancy Act. Here again the limitations of cross-party collaboration within the partisan environment of Parliament make themselves apparent. Even when women wish to support a position different from their parties', they remain silent. If they do choose to "cross the floor," they risk public criticism or censure by their parties. Only a few goals will appeal to all women in Parliament; therefore, any movements for collective action need to be decisive and swift.

Fortunately, legislation and cultural transformation are only two ways women can expand their participation and acceptance in Parliament. Women leaders and gender-oriented activists recognized that a much larger structure would be necessary to achieve South African women's equality. The following chapter evaluates the movement toward creating a set of separate yet coordinated governmental agencies and institutions to foster gender equity not limited by the confines of partisan politics.

6. Implementing Gender:
The National Gender Machinery

Changing South Africa's commitment to gender equality from a constitutional mandate to a social reality will take the combined efforts of both governmental and nongovernmental organizations. Activists and leading politicians recognized that getting women into office would be only one piece of the plan to secure their long-term empowerment. Learning to integrate women's issues into legislative debates was yet another piece. The third and most lasting goal of leaders in both Parliament and the women's movement was to create institutions of state feminism. State feminism involves utilizing governmental structures, resources, and institutions to advance and empower women, which contrasts with the antigovernment stance of most mainstream women's movements. The women leaders in Parliament envisioned and implemented state structures that would focus on women's needs and issues, institutions that would outlive individuals in Parliament or the women's movement.

Because of the training, research, and international networking they had done during the antiapartheid struggle, the leading women in the South African parliament were familiar with the numerous women's agencies and feminist institutional strategies found around the world (G. Seidman 1999, 295–96). Most recognized that institutionalizing women's issues within the new democracy would be essential for securing long-term advancements for women. A significant step in achieving that goal has been the creation of several structures and institutions to facilitate, promote, and monitor gender equality, collectively entitled the National Machinery for Advancing Gender Equality in South Africa but more commonly known as the National Gender Machinery, or NGM (see figure 1).

To examine women in the South African parliament in isolation from the overarching structure of the National Gender Machinery would limit the un-

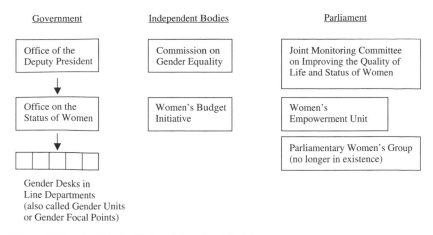

Figure 1. South Africa's National Gender Machinery

derstanding of their role in creating positive change for their country's women generally. Women in Parliament played a crucial part in shaping the NGM and enacting legislation for it. Now that the NGM is in place, women MPs are only one essential part of it. Just as a car would not work without an engine, the NGM would be unable to function without the women in Parliament. Similarly, an engine would be immobile without, for example, a transmission, wheels, and fuel, and the valuable legislation of women MPs would be immobile without the rest of the NGM. In fact, women legislators' most visible successes have been linked to the joint efforts of women from all areas of the NGM. As the South African political scientist and gender commissioner Sheila Meintjes argues, "successful integration of gender policies in the state" requires all levels of society to be engaged in the policy process, from women's groups in civil society, to supportive women in office, and to a bureaucratic framework supportive of these goals (2003, 140–41). Women in Parliament are one cog in the overall gender machinery for South African state feminism.

Women in Parliament work collectively with others in this national framework, but such collaboration has not been without its tensions. Understanding where women MPs and delegates fit in the overall structure of South African feminism is essential for understanding their current role in legislating and implementing gender-based programs and policies.

State Feminism

Interest in state feminism has resurfaced in the last decade, an important contrast to the more common feminist picture of the state as a negative force for women. As Friedman argues, radical feminists have seen the state as an agent of women's oppression, Marxist feminists view state welfare policies as a way to guarantee women's continued complacency with capitalism, and postmodern feminists view the state as a set of processes that are contextually bound and often construct women as outsiders (2000, 48–49). Rather than vilifying the state as an institution to be resisted, however, international feminists and gender advocates are developing ways to utilize state power and state resources to improve women's lives. This trend is perhaps more prevalent in developing nations than in developed nations (see Friedman 2000 for Venezuela and Baldez 2001 for Chile). Beckwith asserts that, contrary to the situation in years past, the "increasing centrality of the state in feminist theory and in feminist movement scholarship underscores the state as an important structural, legal, and discursive venue for women's movements" (2000, 451). Indeed, over 90 percent of nations now have some form of state feminism, most typically in the form of a national agency for women, such as a women's ministry, department, or commission (Friedman 2000).

Although most of the literature on state feminism focuses on developed nations (Stetson and Mazur 1995), there is an increasing interest in the formation, use, and effectiveness of state feminism in developing nations (Staudt 1998; Friedman 2000; Baldez 2001). For example, although the state has been a source of women's disempowerment in Africa (Parpart and Staudt 1989), visible trends indicate that African women are beginning to use state resources and institutions to secure their rights. More generally, women's uses of the state differ between the North and the South. First, developing nations are "more constrained in their national policy-making capacity than developed states" (Friedman 2000, 50). Because of severe financial circumstances and the dictates of international funding agencies or other global superpowers, most developing nations find themselves trying simultaneously to create national agencies for women and to cut government spending and social-welfare projects. Second, national state agencies for women often risk being "captured" by state bureaucrats "to promote partisan or personal ends and to attempt to co-opt nonstate actors" (ibid., 51). In this way, women's agencies are dependent on the whims of parties or bureaucrats. Third, the process of creating national agencies in developing nations differs from that in developed ones. Such agencies are "attributable to the activism of women's rights advocates" in both contexts (ibid.), but women in developing nations cut their political teeth during liberation struggles or democratization movements. Securing state feminism is their next step in creating the democratic society for which they have fought.

Each of these differences is supported in the South African case for state feminism. The goal of South Africa's NGM is to create interrelated and supporting structures that will help to mainstream gender issues in all government processes, thus reducing the chances that the pursuit of gender equality will get marginalized or sidelined in a single ministry or Parliament (Mabandla 1994; G. Seidman 1999). Instead, as Goetz outlines, following "widespread debate amongst women in civil society, . . . a package of mechanisms was favoured to allow for the cross-institutional promotion of gender equity" (1998, 255). So in many ways women were hoping to avoid some of the main problems facing state agencies in other nations—especially the overcentralization of women's issues within a single state agency that leaves them vulnerable to partisan politics. In fact, women in South Africa rejected the UN's standard recommendation to have a single body or ministry devoted to women's issues. As Meinjtes relates, they worked from the wealth of examples of state feminism throughout the world; the movement "drew on . . . comparisons of structures in Australia, Scandinavia, Canada, Bangladesh, and Uganda to suggest a 'package' of institutional mechanisms" (2003, 142).

The South African model demonstrates an integrated machinery involving executive, legislative, and civil institutions. None of these elements would be able to operate in isolation from the others. Unfortunately, the diffusion inherent to South Africa's national machinery exacerbates the funding problems always pressing in developing nations. This diffusion may also create new problems of accountability, fractionalization, and viability: too many structures, too little money.

In another interesting development in South Africa's formation process, women focused on creating institutions for gender equality instead of setting a national gender agenda or solidifying the ever-tenuous women's movement: "Most South African feminist activists seemed more concerned with creating gendered institutions than with outlining specific policies needed to redress gender inequalities" (G. Seidman 1999, 300). Leading women activists intended to use the unique moment created by the democratic transition to secure as many institutional advances as possible within a narrow window of time. Long-term coalition building and unity within the movement would have to wait. This strategy raises questions about unity of vision and direction for these fledgling agencies. Controversial issues were tabled in favor of forging a coalition as rapidly as possible, even though it might not be sustainable. Although the institutions thus created reflect the goals and values of the ANC, the leading party, issues on the far left and far right were typically avoided. Baldez argues that similar compromises by Chilean women across the political spectrum ultimately "worked against the interests of the left" (2001, 10).

In this chapter I briefly outline the key parts of the South African National

Gender Machinery, including those within Parliament, those within the executive that must interface with Parliament, and those within civil society that also cross over to parliamentary activities. It is still too early to assess the NGM's effectiveness or predict its long-term impact, but some commonalities and generalizations are already evident. First, all the institutions within the national machinery have faced challenges to their permanence, their budgets, and their legitimacy. In fact, most of the institutions were formally put in place only in 1996–97, a bit after the 1994 elections. In addition, most of these agencies received severely limited funding; they managed to secure sufficient funding only by 1998–99. As a result, they initially had to rely on international funding sources. Indeed, many governmental agencies and parliamentary committees spent their first several years fighting to secure permanent funding and guaranteed existence. Funding affects salaries, and salaries affect staffing, so the underfunding made it difficult to maintain a regular staff or to fill positions on the relevant parliamentary committees and national commissions. Since most of the NGM came into being two or more years into the new government, many of those working in it had already overcommitted themselves to other committees and organizations. The pool of interested, available, and qualified candidates became increasingly shallow as more and more agencies, committees, and commissions were put into place. These issues raised related questions about the institutions' power and accountability. It is only now, since the issues of permanence and budgeting have been resolved, that the NGM is able to focus on executing its gender portfolios.

Second, all these institutions must now find ways to implement their policies. As one member of an opposition party stated, "All the mechanisms are in place now. We've got the Beijing Platform of Action, the Gender Equity Commission; we signed CEDAW. What remains now is to start implementing. It is very easy to talk about problems, but when it comes to implementation, the scenario changes dramatically." The new democracy's already limited resources and its self-imposed structural adjustment policies complicate matters, however; as Goetz asserts, "a central obstacle has been the limited capacity of the relevant departments to make new resource commitments and create new institutional structures in the environment of strict fiscal discipline" (1998, 256).

A resistant bureaucracy makes policy implementation even more tenuous. As the women in Parliament have discovered, the policies they draft mean little if they are not put into practice. As I discussed in the previous chapter, the apartheid-era civil service was left in place through the South African electoral transformation. Leaders hoped that this tactic would maintain stability, limit interruptions in delivery of services, and foster international confidence in the transitions. All these goals were met, and the decision has widely been regarded as a wise one. Once the new Parliament was up and running and rapidly slashing through apartheid-era legislation, however, civil servants found themselves charged with implementing policies vastly different from those to which they were accustomed. These new laws and policies reflected a political ideology quite different from that of most in the civil service, which had become a stronghold of Afrikaner power during apartheid. Even if bureaucrats did not resist the legislation, most were untrained in the new ideologies and attitudes, especially those concerning gender equality. The transformation of the South African civil service, including gender-sensitivity training, is now underway, but the process will be a long and slow one.

Government

Within the executive, the Office of the Status of Women (OSW) has been charged with developing and implementing a national gender policy. The brainchild of leading women in Parliament, including the Speaker, the OSW was placed directly under the Office of the Deputy President and is charged in part with coordinating gender units in the government's various departments. Since government departments are responsible for implementing policies and delivering services, they often constitute the most direct contact citizens have with the government—more direct even than the contact that constituents have with members of Parliament. The leading women in Parliament asserted that the best way to ensure that gender issues permeate government is to create gender units in each department (G. Seidman 1999, 301). These units are charged with monitoring government, consulting the public, and facilitating gender sensitivity within the departments' staffs. OSW leaders focus more on their office's role as an oversight and visionary body, as Tambika, of the national OSW, stated:

> The office is a kind of institution within the public sector and within the government apparatus. And our role is to really make government work for women. Not the implementation; we are monitoring. The government has put on itself a particular obligation that it firstly in the Constitution states that one of our core values is nonsexism and nonracism. We say we want gender equality, and it is a constitutional obligation. So government has said, "How do we do that technically?" And we very clearly said we don't want a ministry of government affairs. But we want to be able to say, How do we put systems in place in a government to ensure that we better serve the interests of women and men, and how do we monitor that? . . . We are within the policy coordinating unit, which is really supposed to be monitoring what government is doing. So we assist them in developing a set of indicators to do monitoring. There is a whole

infrastructure to monitor. We track the issues such as, Have they built in gender indicators? and so forth.

The OSW thus monitors governmental commitments to gender by tracking spending and policy implementation. Every government department is supposed to have a gender unit; these units differ greatly, however, in terms of structure, location, and power. Certain departments place their gender units in their human resources offices, limiting the focus to ensuring gender equity in employment practices within the relevant department. Other departments have gender units that focus exclusively on the implementation of gender legislation, which is more in line with the original vision within the NGM. Finally, certain gender units are located within ministries; this placement at the top of the hierarchy, in itself an important symbol, provides them real access to power. These units most often combine the human-resources focus with the implementation focus.

This unevenness in power and location has limited the success of the gender units. Several government departments I contacted in 2003 had no one currently representing the gender unit or the gender focal point, and several departments had a difficult time finding the organizational location of the gender unit. Nonetheless, numerous departments had fully functioning and well-located units. The main problem is that departments were given the mandate to construct these units but few stipulations as to how they should be structured, where they should be located, and what they should be doing.

Because South Africa uses a parliamentary system, its MPs are ultimately responsible for the operations of government. The OSW reports to and works with Parliament to fulfill its activities. For example, the OSW has recommended that each of the government departments move its gender unit to the relevant ministry, thus enabling the units to focus both on internal gender issues and on external implementation and service delivery.

Although the OSW is located in the Office of the Deputy President, Tambika described it as "a very small office": "I don't believe that we need to be a huge operation, but I do feel that we do not have sufficient resources to do what we need to do. It becomes quite hard." This lack of human resources and capacity is compounded by inadequate enforcement capabilities. When I asked Tambika about enforcement, she stated, "You see, the office doesn't really have power. That is the point. In real terms, no, we don't. You can put [your recommendation] on the table, but whether anyone takes it or not is another thing. And that is discouraging." Under the parliamentary system, the OSW is charged with creating national gender policy but cannot do so directly (Baden, Hassim, and Meintjes 1999). Its initiatives must go through a committee, typically the Joint Monitoring Committee on the Improvement of the Quality of Life and Status of Women.

Despite these limitations the OSW appears increasingly effective. In addition to monitoring policy implementation and assessing the various governmental gender units, the OSW functions as the focal point for the National Gender Machinery. The OSW recently decided to convene meetings of the NGM every two months. According to Tambika, these NGM meetings are increasingly important: "They get well attended. And they are growing as well, because people are beginning to see the relevance." Women parliamentarians meet regularly with representatives from NGOs, CBOs (community-based organizations), gender units, and the provincial offices on the status of women to set national priorities and goals, providing critical collaboration among the NGM's various bodies, governmental as well as civil.

Parliament

In addition, several bodies within Parliament have been created to sustain widespread gender consciousness and to support the work and goals of women MPs. The Women's Empowerment Unit was most active during the first years of the new government and worked specifically to train women parliamentarians for their new roles as legislators. It used workshops to provide ongoing training for the initial cohort of women, but it also specifically targeted those to come following the 1999 elections. The unit received funding from international agencies, and it is now decreasing its role significantly.

The Parliamentary Women's Group (PWG), which was started after the 1994 elections, was supposed to institutionalize the mission of the grassroots Women's National Coalition within Parliament. The PWG initially worked both to tackle cultural issues blocking women's participation in Parliament and to provide a clearinghouse for cross-party coalitional building on women's issues. At its inception this multiparty caucus was envisioned as linking women in civil society and government, mobilizing women from all parties in government, and monitoring the government's efforts to promote gender equality.

The PWG had not reached these goals by 1996–97, however, for several obstacles, including the difficulties of organizing across party lines, stood in the way. While almost every woman I interviewed agreed that it is important to have multiparty cooperation and mobilization around gender issues, most were not participating in the PWG. Half the women I interviewed in 1996–97 had serious reservations about such an organization's viability in the parliamentary setting, where party loyalty is supreme, and several knew almost nothing about the current gender structures or goals. As a member of an opposition party stated: "The women's caucus here is not really functioning properly at all. One or two women are quite into it, but there is not the kind of consistency or regularity which it needs in order to work."

Women in the study identified two main obstacles facing the PWG. First, it was an informal structure, so that the official parliamentary calendar did not list its meetings. A woman in the ANC complained, "They would be effective if we had the time, but those groups meet at lunch time. That is the only time to run errands and go through stuff and get ready for committees. They organize a lot of workshops, sometime during weekends and at night. It is just a busy schedule." Many women stated that they are already overcommitted with their committee work and in their constituencies. Although the PWG was meant to be a place for women's empowerment, women often see it as yet another responsibility added to their already impossible workload. Many women stated that if the PWG were institutionalized and given a proper space on the calendar, they would be more likely to participate. Such comments echo Hassim's work, which indicates that the PWG "foundered" in part because it was an unofficial parliamentary structure operating without a budget or a place on the official calendar of meetings (2003, 92–93).

The second and perhaps the biggest obstacle facing the PWG is the nature of Parliament itself. Many women feel that the scope of the PWG is limited since women are bound by party decisions. Because MPs and delegates are elected to represent their party, and not their personal or constituents' desires, women from different parties are "allowed" to agree on very few issues. The fear of being "axed" or "finished" puts MPs under great pressure to follow party dictates. Although several women expressed this feeling during my interviews, two MPs voiced specific criticisms about the possibility of cross-party collaboration given the fractious nature of parliamentary politics. The first indicated that such collaboration would necessarily be limited to issues of institutional culture: "What you tend to find, therefore, is that women's caucuses do not become political places. They become like the crèche, maternity leave. It solves fundamental problems for you, but it doesn't give you a power base." In fact, these issues of institutional culture were the main success story coming from the PWG in the first years of its existence. The second MP, from an opposition party, voiced similar objections:

> Look, it has limited scope anyway. We are all members of parties, and we have the opportunity to influence our parties on issues in parties and in caucus. Once the parties make a decision, you are of course bound by that decision. . . . I think that very seldom we will want to unite on some issue where we absolutely see eye to eye and where the party as a whole won't budge. [There are]

plenty of other political issues [where] a body like that could make a difference. The one, for example, is sending of parliamentary delegations [on] overseas tours. Some parties will always control who goes, and you will seldom see a woman. . . . There are certain things we could do, [but] not so many.

These discussions took place in 1996–97, only a few years into the new government, but the partisan nature of Parliament will always limit cross-party collaboration based only on gender. Hassim (2003) similarly finds that the work of the PWG was undermined by tensions among parties, especially the DP, the ANC, and the NNP.

Another tension that undermines the effectiveness of the PWG is the inability to use gender as a unifying identity when issues of race, class, and ideology become more divisive or are forced to be more salient, as is often the case. While layers of these tensions appeared throughout my interviews, two remarks warrant particular attention. First, Sarah, a well-educated white MP from the ANC, had her loyalty to the party and to the struggle questioned by a male counterpart because of her participation in the PWG:

> When I moved in here, . . . [I] started telling [a senior minister] about the women's caucus, and he said "What the hell does an ANC woman have in common with Dene Smuts?"[1] and I said, "Well, there is a lot that we don't have in common and we don't share, but there is a lot that we do share." And he said, "Like what?" And I said, "A lot of things, like being women and how we are being treated, the kind of experiences we are having as parliamentarians having children." And he said, "Yeah, maybe that is because you are a white and middle class."

A male leader in Sarah's party was thus using one identity to disrupt another. He attempted to undermine her participation in cross-party collaboration with other women by diminishing her party loyalty and using her racial classification to question her devotion to the struggle. This is a remarkable move by a member of the ANC, the party committed to nonracism and nonsexism.

Such attempts to disrupt women's mobilization can also spring from internalized racism or fear of reprisal. The second poignant example comes from Wendy, a white MP in a predominantly black opposition party. She told me how black women in her party are silencing themselves on gender issues because they are afraid of political and personal repercussions, whereas, they believe, her racial identity protects her from such reprisals. As a result, they have privately asked her to be a champion for controversial issues, such as abortion:

> The problem is multifaceted. There is a fear factor involved. On abortion, for example, female colleagues came to me, some who are vehemently opposed [to her party's blockage of the abortion bill], and said, "Look, go for it. We can't say anything. We are black. We are rural. We have to go back to communities.

> We can't say anything. But we are right behind you. But we will not vote for [the abortion bill] or be seen speaking for it." So one is out in the trenches, and you look behind you and find there is nobody there.

This dynamic of racial identities being pitted against gender identities is not unique to South Africa, but it is clearly heightened by the legacy of apartheid. The intersection of race, class, and gender combined with the necessity of party loyalty led to insurmountable tensions. The constricting nature of parliamentary politics thus significantly thwarted the PWG's ability to focus on political issues and build coalitions. In fact, during my most recent research trip, in May–July 2003, none of the women I interviewed indicated membership in or specific knowledge of the PWG. All discussions of cross-party collaboration centered on a highly visible legislative body, the Joint Monitoring Committee on the Improvement of the Quality of Life and Status of Women. Officially the ANC leadership and the Speaker's office launched the JMC in 1996 to monitor the government's implementation of the UN's Convention on the Elimination of Discrimination against Women. In truth, however, the JMC was instituted when the PWG became mired in party politics. The JMC was specifically mandated with monitoring legislation for gender sensitivity. Hassim (2003) similarly finds that most progressive parliamentary movements to end gender discrimination have come from an elite group of women within the ANC, not through cross-party coalitions.

The women MPs I interviewed expressed a general sense of support for the committee, but several members indicated that by 1996 they already had pressing commitments to other committees. As one ANC woman stated, "That committee came in far too late. We are already entrenched in our other committees." Initially the JMC was an ad-hoc committee, which further undermined its legitimacy, permanence, and importance to overworked MPs. Each ad-hoc parliamentary committee must jockey for its share of a small pot of funding for all such committees. The concern over the ad-hoc status of the JMC led the committee members to push for permanent status, which it achieved in 1998. The joint committee was then afforded its first research assistant and clerk, but it received independent funding only in 1999 (Joint Monitoring Committee on the Improvement of the Quality of Life and Status of Women 1999a).

Under the leadership of Pregs Govender of the ANC, the JMC was formalized and became a highly visible, consistent, and effective voice for women. Some argue that it became an unrelenting challenge to Parliament, and specifically to the ANC leadership. Under Govender's tenure the JMC addressed key issues facing South African women, including gender-based violence, maintenance (i.e., welfare), rural poverty, gender budgeting, and as MP

Priscilla Themba states, a "whole barrage of legal changes such as the Domestic Violence Act and changes to the labour laws specifically targeting women workers, such as the sexual harassment code, parental rights" (Themba 2001, 1). The JMC established a list of priorities in 1998, and as Govender reported, "Eighty percent of the legislative changes that we prioritised were enacted into law by the end of 1999" (2001, 1). Yet the strongest indictment of the new South African government was the committee's HIV/AIDS report, Govender's last major challenge to the government during her parliamentary career.

Perhaps the biggest challenge the JMC now faces is the departure of its chair. Govender publicly discussed her intentions to leave Parliament to return to a career as a gender activist, consultant, and writer ("Two Top Women" 2002). Members of the JMC indicated to me in May-July 2003 that Govender left Parliament soon after the release of the HIV/AIDS report because of the government's response, or rather lack of response, to its challenges. Losing a high-profile leader like Govender raised significant questions about the continued effectiveness of the committee. As Friedman (2000) found in Venezuela, the success of state feminism is often tied to powerful, strategically placed leaders. The JMC now has two powerful and effective leaders from the ANC at its helm, and all the women in Parliament I interviewed in 2003 indicated that they hope the committee will continue to be a voice for women and maintain its position as a site of cross-party collaboration.

Independent Bodies and Initiatives

The NGM was designed to bridge the gap between civil society and Parliament through two key institutions: the Women's Budget Initiative (WBI) and the Commission on Gender Equality (CGE). The WBI was started by the JMC, IDASA, and the Department of Finance. Based on a related Australian structure, the WBI identifies and tracks the budgetary expenditures of government departments from a gender perspective.[2] One significant difference in the South African WBI is based on a shortcoming of the Australian initiative. The WBI is a joint venture between NGOs and women in Parliament. The link to IDASA, a civil organization, is intended to isolate it from the partisan nature of government (Lowe Morna 2000). Each year the WBI looks at a new level or area of government spending. As members of the initiative recognized, the budget is a critical tool that reflects government priorities, and this organization looks at how much money is being spent on women in all sectors (Budlender 1996). The South African WBI has been heralded by women's movements worldwide and has been duplicated throughout Africa, the Caribbean, and Asia (Lowe Morna 2000). One significant shortcoming of the WBI is that it has no mechanism to assess the impact of such spending.

Several local and provincial governments have started their own projects to monitor spending along gender lines, and IDASA has also launched the Children's Budget Project, which tracks government spending on youth.

The second institution falling between civil society and the government is the Commission on Gender Equality, which was legislated into existence in 1996. The CGE has its national office in Johannesburg and satellite offices in each of the provinces. The CGE has been a consistent voice for women in South Africa, and it has undertaken several highly visible initiatives, such as progress reports on compliance with CEDAW, public education campaigns for women's rights, regular inputs into parliamentary debates, consistent evaluation of government policy, and an ongoing campaign to increase media coverage of and by women.[3]

The CGE has also been at the forefront of debates about the electoral system, strongly favoring a continuation of the proportional-representation system and encouraging all parties to adopt 50 percent quotas for women (Jayiya 1999). One of its most recent programs is a land-restitution project that will target rural women and directly confront patriarchal power systems. Traditional land-restitution programs give land to men or groups headed by men. The CGE hopes to bypass this system while simultaneously fostering development projects selected, designed, and implemented by rural women (Daniels 2001).

Two challenges continually hinder the CGE's full operation. The first is funding. Although Gay Seidman has asserted that the CGE budget is "clearly sufficient to ensure that the commission could make significant interventions in national policy discussions in the future" (1999, 302), the CGE received significantly less funding than other national commissions, such as the Youth Commission and the Truth and Reconciliation Commission (Haffajee 1997). Consistent underfunding has left the CGE facing ongoing difficulty in filling vacant positions and dependent on the whims of international funding and support (Baden, Hassim, and Meintjes 1999). Another ongoing challenge for the CGE is the regular, intense scrutiny of it by the media and at times by the government's Office of the Public Protector. Two former CEOs of the CGE have been placed under investigation, and its commissioners feel that the inquiries and the concomitant press coverage are "part of a 'disinformation campaign' aimed at discrediting the commission" (Magardie 2001b).

Implications of Using the State for Feminist Gains

What can the South African case teach us about the formation of state feminism in African states and other developing nations in a postliberation context? The advancement of gender priorities has been considerable, and at the very least, a solid framework has been created. Yet continued patriarchal norms in politics, parties, and governmental institutions have threatened each step women have taken. While any conclusions about the South African NGM must be highly tentative, several trends are relevant for research on comparative state feminism in general.

Centralization versus Decentralization

The goal of the NGM was to mainstream gender issues throughout government, Parliament, and civil society. The goal of the leading women parliamentarians who envisioned this machinery was to avoid marginalization of women's issues in a single department (Mabandla 1994). Clearly marginalization has been avoided, because discussions and expectations of gender issues now are present in the budget, in policy making, and in government offices. A less anticipated but equally great threat, however, is that the women's movement has been spread too thin. The plethora of structures has concerned external observers as well as parliamentarians themselves. As one MP stated, "All of the parliamentary-type women's structures so far have not worked. . . . There is a proliferation of bodies. Heaven forbid we are getting into the position that they are proliferating because each original one is not functioning properly." Since the resources of the new South African government are limited, having such diffusion among national commissions, government departments, and parliamentary committees has left many women in Parliament wondering how to pay their staffs, finance their projects, and monitor their initiatives. A related and now pressing problem is the increasing workload created by the dispersion of institutions. As I have stressed throughout this book, women in the South African parliament feel that they are excessively burdened by their lives as MPs and that they carry a disproportionate workload. Partly because of this, a great many gender institutions now need leaders, participants, and staff.

Executive versus Legislative

Women have been most successful in making gender issues visible within the legislative process, most centrally through the JMC. The success of this parliamentary committee provides an interesting contrast to claims in the literature on comparative state feminism. Much of the current literature asserts that the most effective branch for promoting policy formation is the executive, under the head of state, not a "subsidiary part of another ministry"

(Friedman 2000, 52). In fact, the South African case is more in line with the Chilean case. Baldez (2001) found that women's organizations there did not meet with greater success when working with the executive branch. Sawer (2000) indicates that a comparable standing committee in Europe has been ideal in helping to "raise awareness of gender issues" there (2000, 370). In Uganda, moreover, legislative committees have constituted one of women's most visible and effective locations for participation in formal politics (Tamale 1999, 131). The effectiveness of the JMC is further evidence supporting the idea that women's use of state feminism may be most effective within legislative bodies rather than executive ones. Interestingly, a Belgian committee analogous to the PWG looks "inwards at the working of the parliament and issues such as family-friendly sitting hours" (370), which is the set of issues initially tackled by South Africa's PWG. One lesson that may be extended from the South African case, then, is that separating these issues—parliamentary culture in the PWG and legislative action through the JMC—may be more effective than pursing them through one body.

Implementation and State Masculinity

South Africa has been highly successful at legislating gender policy and thereby securing rhetorical promises for gender equality and empowerment. But the legislation has not consistently been implemented, and neither the state nor the society has been formally changed, as Goetz argues:

> The relative lack of political leverage of women and feminists both in and outside of the state in Uganda and South Africa has obliged women to seek a bureaucratic form of representation for the gender-equity interest in policymaking. This strategy has had ambivalent results: while it has raised the general level of awareness of gender issues and heightened rhetorical commitments to women's rights, it has not yet resulted in substantive change to the concepts and priorities guiding economic planning, nor has it yet led to a transformation in the structures of bureaucracies and the character of the state. These kinds of changes take time, and it is unrealistic to expect profound change yet. . . . These processes have, however, been slowed by the masculinity of party politics, elite bargaining, and the functioning of state bureaucracies (257).

The advances are visible and notable but have been slowed by the resistant civil service and the lasting impact of state masculinity. Change takes time, and changes from the top take even longer to trickle down if the institutional norms (read: masculinity and hierarchy) and the civil service (read: implementers of apartheid) remain static. The framework and the foundation are now in place, but implementation will be slow to follow.

From Resistance to Governance

In the end, it is difficult for social movements to bring people to office, and running a country is more difficult than drafting a constitution. Women in developing nations face an additional burden of challenging male comrades from national liberation struggles on the gender question. Women in South Africa fought first to gain freedom from apartheid and second to craft a new democracy; they now fight to expand democracy to include women's rights. Women in the 1994 and 1999 South African parliaments have worked hard to create and legitimize structures of state feminism. They have depended on and often worked with a supportive yet autonomous women's movement to pressure the state for funding and power. They have straddled two forms of political participation to accomplish these goals, using methods from their antiapartheid experiences and the new methods of formal political office. They have overcome the initial hurdles to ensure the permanence of the machinery for gender equality and now must work to fulfill the promises of their gender portfolios. They now must face the pressing problems of continued state masculinity, resistant civil servants, and potential leadership vacuum. The revolution for gender equality has started, but it is currently incomplete.

7. The Second Generation:
The Future of Women in Parliament

The women who have remained in or entered Parliament with South Africa's second democratic election, in 1999, are markedly distinct from the women who gained office in 1994. Simply stated, there has been a rapid "professionalization" within this "second generation." Women who are being actively recruited into parties now have political, educational, and occupational profiles different from those of the earlier cohort. Similarly, the women who have stayed in office are among those who were most prepared for the institutional norms and professional expectations of formal parliamentary politics. There are many reasons for this professionalization, including the self-selection of those leaving office, the recruitment of a different type of woman candidate, and an increased emphasis on training women for their lives as MPs.

This professionalization of legislators is not confined to South Africa. First noted in Australia by Sawer (2000), who coined the term, this trend is evident throughout legislatures internationally. It may be less apparent in long-standing industrialized democracies, which have been attracting elite, affluent, formally educated professionals for generations. The trend becomes quite noticeable, however, in states new to democracy. Often these states are formed following a liberation struggle or a revolution, and the first set of leaders is drawn from the ranks of the democratic movement. The demands of office are often a mismatch for these activists, and the call back to grass-roots politics is often too strong to resist. As both Sawer (2000) found in Australia and Camp (1998) noted Mexico, the professionalization of legislatures has specifically gendered consequences. Women who are broadly representative of resistance struggles or women's movements are replaced by women with more affluent occupational backgrounds (Australia) or advanced educational achievements (Mexico).

Geisler (2000) asserts that in the South African case, the very access to professional development and occupational skills necessary to excel in parliamentary life has been gendered. As "the backbone" of the struggle, women activists were focused on supporting the movement's progress rather than their own. Women either found their access to training blocked or chose to focus on different community development skills. In contrast, "the avenues for self-development were . . . more accessible for ANC men" (Geisler 2000, 619). Therefore, men were generally more prepared to meet the demands of fashioning the democratic government and working in it. Tamale (1999, 119–21) discovered a similar trend in Uganda: women, including those in Parliament, had historically been denied access to skills such as public speaking and legislation, whereas men had developed these abilities through their lives in the public sphere. As early as 1996 the women's leadership in the South African parliament began to focus on ending the gender gap within that institution through skills training and development (Geisler 2000). The women who remained in Parliament or won office in 1999 have thus received some job and skills training.

From May to August 2003 I conducted additional research to understand the changes, or lack thereof, that had been implemented since the 1999 elections. My methodology was consistent with that of the interviews conducted in 1996–97, although the sample was somewhat smaller, a total of twenty women. Ironically, I encountered the most difficulty in gaining access to the ANC, but my access to the minority parties was almost unrestricted. I interviewed women across a broad ethnic spectrum, but as the subsequent discussion shows, these women enjoyed higher levels of educational and professional achievement than did those in the first cohort.

Most strikingly these later interviews differed distinctly in tone and scope from the earlier ones. First, most of these interviews happened as scheduled, whereas it had usually taken two or three attempts to secure an interview in 1996–97. Second, these interviews lasted from forty-five to sixty minutes, whereas the earlier ones rarely lasted less than an hour and typically ran to two or three hours. Third, the two sets of interviews differed considerably in terms of the professionalism and party loyalty expressed. The women in the later cohort were warm and open, but their answers were generally brief and concise, indicating their previous experience with interviews. The fact that women so strongly maintained their party lines was striking, and it was especially pronounced within the ANC. On two occasions I was asked to turn off my tape recorder, each time following a question about the ANC's policy on HIV/AIDS. In both instances the MPs silently gathered their thoughts and then asked me to resume taping before answering the question. Such professionalism further indicated experience with interview situations and an understanding of the political impact of their answers, neither of which was universally present in the 1996–97 interviews.

Professionalization of Parliament

The interviews with the 1999 cohort indicated ten major differences between women in the "first generation" and those in "second generation." No one of them indicates a transformative shift, but taken together these ten differences represent a qualitative change in the recruitment strategies of political parties, a refinement of the role of women in office, and the increased viability of women as incumbents.

Prior Officeholders

A majority of the women interviewed indicated they had held prior political office at a local or provincial level. As a result, they had at least some experience with the responsibilities and institutional norms of holding political office. Since they had held lower political offices, all these women had made the transition from their lives as activists, academicians, and unionists several years before they reached national office. Their prior political experience prepared them for their roles as legislators, allowing them to hit the ground running. In part, this change should be expected. Prior to 1994 black South African women were formally excluded from political office, and many white and coloured women were informally discouraged from holding office. With the 1994 election women moved to fill all levels of formal political space, not just the national. They composed the first generation of women politicians, especially from previously disadvantaged groups, who were able to work their way up through traditional political ranks. Again, the majority of women who entered office in 1994 came directly from their various roles in the struggle.

Preparation for Time Commitment

Most of the women I interviewed stated—without prompting—that they were prepared for the demands of their current positions, especially the time commitments. Almost all these women had held jobs with demanding hours, such as owning their own businesses, or had been in office at a lower level. While none of them were pleased with the long hours, none were surprised.

Despite the reforms made by the first-generation MPs, several in the second generation voiced concern that debates were ending at later times. What had been "family-friendly" hours were now becoming less and less accommodating for evenings at home. Perhaps because of the awareness of the time commitment, none of these women spoke of having babies at home, and most commented that the job makes having small children nearly impossible. This attitude contrasts starkly with that of first-generation women, many of whom had infants or small children or were supportive of those who did.

Advanced Education and Occupations

Most of the second-generation women I interviewed had attended university; some held postgraduate degrees. This was remarkable, for 30–40 percent of the women in the first generation had ended their formal education after the standard ten or eleven years. The degrees were in various subject areas, but all the women I interviewed were fluent in English, both written and verbal. Professionally, women most often occupied nontraditionally female jobs before coming to Parliament; they had been, among other things, journalists, academicians, businesswomen, medical professionals, or administrators. Very few worked in the employment sectors to which women were traditionally assigned, such as teaching, nursing, domestic work, farming, or secretarial occupations. Only one woman described herself as a "home executive"; she had stayed at home to raise her children before coming to Parliament. She was also one of the most educated women in the sample.

Institutional Learning

Women from all parties clearly indicated a deep appreciation of the advances made by women in the 1994 parliament. Current members were well versed in the institutional and cultural changes made by these women, including instituting "family-friendly" hours, altering the parliamentary calendar to fit the school calendar, building the day-care facilities, increasing the number of toilets, and ensuring places for women in office and on committees and task forces. Women in the 1999 cohort recognized that things were much harder for their predecessors. All MPs but one indicated that men in their parties are much more accepting of women's participation or at least are silent in their opposition to it. Women from every party were unabashedly thankful for the ANC quota—even more so than they were in 1996–97. Many acknowledged that their own parties would not adopt such quotas, but they all indicated that the ANC's effort had pressured and would continue to pressure the parties' male leaderships. Interestingly, one member of the African

Christian Democratic Party stated while her party did not support quotas, she could see that "God was using an ungodly government" to make a positive difference in women's lives.

Training

All MPs who came into office in 1999 had positive responses to the job training they received when they initially entered Parliament, including the training specifically focused on the challenges they would face as women MPs. I found one major gap in training, however: no programs were available for women who came to national office months or years after the 1999 elections to fill a slot opened by retirement or resignation. One such woman from an opposition party described them as "learning with their eyes closed." Despite this deficit, each of the women I interviewed indicated that she was supported and mentored by the other women and the men in her party or by women in opposing parties.

Cross-Party Collaboration

Women from each of the parties expressed hope that cross-party collaboration would be fruitful. While they supported the concept of collaboration, a few members of the Democratic Alliance were the only women who indicated the potential pitfalls of such cooperation. Women MPs indicated that cross-party collaboration happens both informally and formally. As regards informal cooperation, two women from very small parties told me that they frequently work with women in other small parties to understand legislation and develop their positions. As regards formal cooperation, women mentioned the Joint Monitoring Committee on the Improvement of the Quality of Life and Status of Women and the "multiparty women's caucus." Although the JMC is quite productive, the caucus had done very little in months, and no one could articulate a single issue that the body had taken up.

Favorite Part of Job

Again, this category provided an interesting contrast to the 1994 cohort. Women in the 1999 cohort found all aspects of their job beneficial and productive, but whatever their parties, they were most fond of the debates in chambers and committees because of the humor of debates, the opportunities to speak their minds, and "the give and take" among parties. Debates had been the least favorite part of the job for those in the 1994 cohort; many women were either nervous about the debates or found them to be meaningless in the face of constituency problems.

Issues and Goals

All the women interviewed referred specifically to their legislative and policy goals. They spoke clearly about using legislation to advance the cause of women or to develop society as a whole. The women of 1999 asserted that they took their role and agenda to be policy legislation, not implementation or hands-on development work. From a "Western" or "Northern" perspective, this seems apparent: Parliament is the legislative body, not the implementing body. Yet this sentiment is distinctly different from that expressed by the women in the 1994 generation, who most often spoke of their specific projects or development ideas. Implementation remains the focus for a handful of women, mainly from the Democratic Alliance, African National Congress, and the Inkatha Freedom Party, but even they seek primarily to facilitate funding and legislation to help their projects instead of pursuing implementation itself. Somewhat in contrast to the 1994 cohort, women from all backgrounds and parties in the later group had a broad list of issues they wished to address, including the status of women and the quality of their lives, violence against women, HIV/AIDS, housing, unemployment, health, education, the number of women in political office, child abuse, and the environment; in addition, one member from the African Christian Democratic Party wanted "to fight humanist tendencies in government."

Sexual Harassment or Gender Discrimination

Only one woman, in an opposition party, voiced clear discomfort with the men in her party, stating they were obstructionist and that women had to fight for every position they had. Every other woman I spoke with told me that the climate for women had improved. The most interesting response to this line of inquiry by women in the ANC was "there are no problems in the ANC" or "there are no problems with men in the ANC." This is a remarkable inversion from the 1994 generation, when all but one woman found that their gender presented an additional burden or obstacle to their work. Further, in 1994 most women felt that the men in their parties were hostile to women's participation. As stated earlier, two-thirds of the 1994 sample experienced some form of discrimination or harassment while in office. This means either that the climate for women has improved or that women are less likely to criticize the men in their party publicly.[1]

Professional Needs

Unlike the first generation women, who had an endless laundry list of needs, this generation had only two. The 1994 generation needed a full range of training and assistance: policy training, basic education, staff support, research support, support for the double workday, support from male MPs, computer training, management training, and training in budgeting. The 1999 generation needed only two things: research support or project funding for constituents. They needed research support to actualize their professional goals and to excel in debates and committees. They needed funding to help constituents meet their goals and to prove to the voters they were doing their jobs. Each of these again points to the professionalization of women in Parliament, for both knowledge and funding are political resources used by politicians throughout the world to ensure their political survival and to advance their political agendas and ideas.

2004 Elections

At the time I was writing this book, the 2004 election had just occurred. This third election also marks ten years of freedom in South Africa, and many see it as a benchmark in the democratic consolidation process. There were few surprises in the overall results, given the extensive and reliable polling data in the months before the election. The ANC swept the election with an overwhelming majority, just under 70 percent, for a total of 279 seats. For women in the ANC, this meant continued electoral success as well, because the ANC maintained its commitment to reserve at least one-third of the seats on its list for women; in fact, 35.4 percent were assigned to women. Given the placement of women on the party lists and the high percentage of seats won by the ANC, the party may see women holding as many as 37 percent of its parliamentary seats in 2004 (Gender Links 2004b). The ANC continues to debate the possibility of a 50 percent quota in the future, but for this election, it maintained its one-third rule.

Women's-rights throughout South Africa are praising President Thabo Mbeki, of the ANC, on his selection of women as four of the nine provinces' premiers. Hitherto there had been only one woman premier, and many see this as a significant step forward by President Mbeki in terms of placing women in positions of executive and administrative power (Sebelebele 2004).

Additionally, the 2004 election lists demonstrate that the ANC seems to have responded to the criticism that activist women MPs were ranked low on party lists. As discussed in chapter 2, the ANC faced these criticism after it had placed many women's rights advocates low on its list for the 1999 elections.

According to Gender Links, a South African gender-related advocacy organization, several key women have improved their places on the party lists.

The biggest surprise following the 1994 elections was the retirement of Frene Ginwala as the Speaker of the National Assembly. Although the full reasons remain unexplained as I write, reports indicate that this resulted from a mutual agreement between Ginwala and the ANC. Her former Deputy Speaker, Baleka Mbete, then assumed the top position. Ginwala, who will no longer be an MP, has said she will remain in South Africa, intimating she will not assume an ambassadorship or enter the African Union parliament. All newspaper reports indicate she is not likely to enter a cabinet position, leaving many questions as to what she will do next.

Attention now focuses on the overall percentage of women in Parliament, which will likely increase, perhaps by as much as 10 percent according to the preelection party lists. This increase will be due mainly to the ANC's efforts and continued dominance. Even though most opposition parties increased the number of women on their party lists as well, they often placed them in unwinnable positions. Thus, as a party's percentage of seats drops, so too does the number of women representing that party in Parliament (Gender Links 2004b).

Following the April 15, 2004, elections, the Democratic Alliance became the main opposition party, taking a total of fifty parliamentary seats, an increase of twenty-one seats from the last government. The Inkatha Freedom Party is the third-largest party in the 2004 parliament, winning a total of twenty-eight seats. Although they continue to renounce quotas for their lists, both the DA and the IFP actively recruit women for Parliament. The DA is set to increase the number of women in Parliament, from six MPs (43% of its seats) in 1999 to thirteen (26%) in 2004 (Gender Links 2004b). Based on its lists, the IFP may decrease the number of women representing it in Parliament, reflecting the party's loss of seats overall and its continued placement of women in lower positions on its lists.

The surprise of the election is that Bantu Holomisa's United Democratic Movement has now become the fourth-largest party represented in national office, winning a total of nine seats. The UDM also boasts the rare distinction of having the second-highest percentage—not the highest number—of women in Parliament. The UDM is expected to have women in 44.4 percent of its parliamentary seats—four out of nine—which is higher than its preelection party lists indicated (Gender Links 2004b).

The balance sheet on the remaining opposition parties is mixed. The Independent Democrats, founded and led by former Pan African Congress member Patricia de Lille, won their first seats in this election. The Independent Democrats tied with the now increasingly marginalized New National

Party, the two parties winning seven seats each. The ID will likely bring three women to Parliament, or 43 percent of its MPs, including de Lille. The NNP brings only one woman to Parliament (Momberg and Sapa 2004).

The African Christian Democratic Party won six seats, one of which is filled by a woman, though some controversy in election results could result in a seventh seat. The party had two women MPs in the last parliament. The ACDP went from eight to six seats in this election, so the reduction may simply reflect the loss of seats.

The Freedom Front Plus won four seats, all to be held by men. AZAPO won two seats, both to be held by men. The Pan African Congress won three seats, one of which will be filled by a woman.

The Minority Front won two seats, one of which will be held by a woman, making women 50 percent of its MPs, the highest percentage of any party. In the 1999 parliament the party's only seat was held by a woman, Sunklavathy Rajbally. She will remain in office, and its second parliamentary seat will be occupied by the party's leader, Royith Bholla (Momberg and Sapa 2004).

The 2004 election results reveal interesting trends. Most parties, especially opposition ones, increased the number of women on their preelection party lists. This reflects the contagion effect discussed in chapter 2. Again, Matland and Studlar (1996) argue that women's representation levels increase more rapidly within multimember proportional-representation systems because parties within such systems respond more quickly to the pressure of a rival party's nomination of women. This was true in the 1999 election, and it is even more apparent in the 2004 election lists.

However, most opposition parties continue to place women lower on their lists, so that the first few parliamentary seats they win often go to men. Parties may boast that women appear on their lists, yet they frequently do not appear in office. As the ANC grows and other parties lose seats, those lost positions are the ones that would often be held by women. Even though the 2004 party lists for opposition parties held more women than was the case in previous elections, the opposition parties taken as a whole will see an overall decrease in women in office in 2004.

There are notable exceptions, such as the Democratic Alliance, the Minority Front, the Independent Democrats, and the United Democratic Movement. These parties not only have women on their lists but also will have significant numbers of women in Parliament, either because the parties won enough seats to include women at lower position on their lists or because women were listed sufficiently high to gain one of the few seats won. And the Democratic Alliance is increasing the number of women it will have in office. Yet many parties, such as the IFP, the PAC, AZAPO, the ACDP, the Freedom Front Plus (formerly the Freedom Front), and the New

National Party (formerly the National Party), had more women on their party lists than they will be bringing into office. For these parties, women were hurt because the parties won fewer seats or they placed women low on their lists.

Implications for the Future of Women in Parliament

My conversations with women in the 1999 cohort and the 2004 election results suggest several long-term implications for women's roles in the South African parliament. First, both the "natural selection" and the active recruitment of women from increasingly professional backgrounds indicate that the South African parliament is rapidly becoming similar to parliaments globally, which tend to overrepresent individuals from higher socioeconomic classes and advanced occupational, educational, and political backgrounds. Part of this demographic change is a highly positive outgrowth of the democratization process. Since the demise of apartheid, all women now have the opportunity to advance through traditional paths of local and provincial political office to national parliament. Nonetheless, the recruitment of women into the opposition parties reflects both a recognition of the skills necessary to function as a national legislator and these parties' needs to increase the number of women on their lists so that they can remain competitive with the ANC. Politicians of this type typically fill legislatures and parliaments, however revolutionary the nation's founding happened to be. And there has been an active focus on the training of all women once they arrive in Parliament, through the Women's Empowerment Unit, so that they can not only survive in office but also thrive there. The speed with which this trend toward professionalization has appeared in South African is poignant.

While there is no doubt that the overall focus of the women in the South African parliament is progressive, the women pursuing that focus are increasingly distinct from the general population. One benefit of this change is that these women are more likely to remain in Parliament as incumbents, and this can strengthen them individually as political actors and collectively as a political force. One significant disadvantage is that the wealth of local knowledge, the diversity of experience, and the representative nature of the 1994 cohort have been abridged by those women's choices to leave office and the new patterns of recruitment and electoral advancement.

What, then, can we conclude about the future of women in the South African parliament and about the field of transitionology in general? By focusing on elites, institutions, and processes, orthodox transitionology has rendered women's participation in democratic transitions invisible. But women in the South African parliament have made themselves quite visible, creating new space for women in governance. As I have shown, women can play and have played a pivotal role in democratization by participating in social movements and by using their work in civil society to keep pressure on new democracies. Orthodox democratization studies have dismissed the importance of such movements or have even advocated their suppression, arguing that they may serve to destabilize unproven regimes. By ignoring the vitality of women's participation, however, we misunderstand and misinterpret how transitions originate, germinate, and become viable.

During the apartheid era women in South Africa developed an identity of conservative militancy, which simultaneously preserved and utilized the power they had in the domestic sphere. Drawing strength from their resistance organizations, political training, and international experiences, women were able to influence the language of the constitution, to raise gender equity as a national issue, and to pressure political parties for increased representation for women. This move toward the public sphere challenged the idea that women were merely the "silent strength" and the "backbone" of the movement, for they began to lead the nation as policy makers. As a result, women gained 26 percent of the seats in the national parliament.

Despite the increase in their numerical representation and their new roles in political processes, women continue to face disproportionate challenges that hinder their full participation and foster a high turnover of women in office (Geisler 2000). A continuation of this turnover could reduce the long-term impact of women within Parliament, for those in each new cohort must spend time learning the ropes, which may impede reaching the goal of women's equality. Indeed, the attrition rate could have been much higher had the Women's Empowerment Unit not made a concerted effort in 1996–98 to train and retain women MPs (Geisler 2000).

The women most dissatisfied with Parliament, those most likely to leave the institution, came from previously disadvantaged backgrounds and had neither the training nor the experience to function properly as legislators or comfortably as national political figures. This means that elites have in many ways already come to dominate the institution, for the nonelites chose to leave office. Of course, elites tend to dominate national political institutions around the globe, but the speed of the nonelites' decline in the South African case is significant, even though the ANC has made efforts to retain women from disadvantaged backgrounds. The parties therefore must decided whether to recruit women with the training and experience to function in the institution or to change the institution to accommodate the needs of nonelites and utilize their knowledge. Clearly, the opposition parties have already made that choice.

Regardless of the challenges they face, women in the South African parliament have made remarkable legislative and institutional advances during the short period since the transition in 1994, advances that in many ways far outstrip the progress made by women in more institutionalized industrialized democracies. Women have been responsible for the creation of national governmental institutions and the implementation of key pieces of legislation intended to promote gender equity, such as extending abortion rights to all South African women and legislating clear guidelines regulating pornography. The long-term advancement promised by the National Gender Machinery is perhaps the greatest achievement by women in Parliament, who worked collectively with women in civil society to envision this framework.

Students of women's political participation internationally will further want to know how the conflation of ethnic, class, educational, and professional identities affect the type of women who are in office. This dynamic can obtain despite political parties' rhetorical and substantive commitments to diversity. Focusing on recruitment from a broad spectrum of women does not necessarily translate into the retention of that diversity. As the South African case demonstrates, the rapid homogenization of the type of women in office will have significant ramifications for policy initiation, creation, and implementation. In the long run, this shrinking diversity may widen the gap between women politicians and their constituents in general and may ultimately threaten the legitimacy of both the women's movement and the political parties themselves.

The information presented in the previous pages calls into question the narrow focus of the critical-mass literature, which has captured a great deal of attention in the field of women and politics. This literature often adopts the myopic assumption that greater numbers of women in office will be a panacea for reducing women's inequality and gender discrimination. As the South African case indicates, getting women into office is an important and productive effort; however, merely increasing the number of women does not fundamentally alter the gender system within Parliament and may not have an immediate or lasting impact on legislation or its implementation. Numerous other factors, such as cultural norms, the financial limitations of fledging democracies, and the partisan constraints of political life, play an equally important role.

Although it is still too early to draw any broad conclusions, women in Parliament have become increasingly separate from women in civil society in South Africa (Geisler 2000; Van Donk and Maceba 1999). This situation parallels others across the world, yet South African women seem to be trying to narrow this gap through joint workshops and collaborative initiatives between government and NGOs. The women of South Africa are aware of this trend internationally and are working to prevent it.

The fact that women in South Africa are talking to and learning from women's movements elsewhere leads to another important lesson for students of gender and democratization. The South African case indicates an important new day for the global women's movement. The collective body of comparative research has had an impact on the goals, timing, and strategies of women in democratizations. Women have met and learned from one another. They have studied the comparative literature and have implemented specific mobilization strategies, lobbied for particular electoral systems, and designed innovative institutional arrangements. A broader process of collective learning is occurring within women's groups domestically and the women's movement internationally.

Further, the data previously adduced demonstrate that a nation's first free election does not complete the democratization process. On the contrary, transitions are evolutionary and uneven. Women as a group progress through fits and starts, however unified they may be as a collective force. Indeed, the South African case shows that women's movements are often not unified, and therefore securing additional commitments for gender equality becomes even more difficult. Collective action, while not an impossibility, becomes an even scarcer commodity within the halls of Parliament.

As has been the case internationally and is also apparent in South Africa, women often first come to popular movements through their gender identities—specifically, as wives and mothers. Yet this perpetuation of maternal identity is only one aspect of their involvement, and they are able to use their participation in social movements to pressure the state and the political system for change. As I have shown to be true in South Africa, the methods and strategies they develop within the movement are often utilized long after the transition to democracy has been completed. It is exactly those methods of resistance that women in South Africa are currently using to challenge the foundations and assumptions of their culture's gender system. Women continue vigorously to engage the structures of power within Parliament, the larger government, and civil society. Despite their victories, much work remains. Women are now reclaiming the tools of resistance, tools that are better forged for their current endeavor.

The biggest task women face is ensuring that the content and purpose of the women's movement is not relegated solely to legislative reform. Women have already achieved much of that reform and have institutionalized a great deal of that framework. Women still feel isolated, however, and subject to systemic discrimination. A new revolution, complete with new strategies and ideologies, must be waged on the domestic front so that South African women can actualize the legal rights they have secured formally.

South African women traveled an enormous distance in gaining access to the institutions of state power, which was the culmination of decades of struggle against a racist regime bent on the complete domination of the African majority and the suppression of women of all ethnic groups on religious and cultural grounds. The achievement of electoral success ought to have been an event to be celebrated and a time to reflect on the years of loss, sacrifice, and violence. Yet this was not the moment to pause; instead, the leadership of the women's movement took the opportunity created by the end of apartheid to secure lasting institutions and structures for women's equality. This progress of state feminism will be vital for the eventual empowerment of women in South Africa, but the struggle to actualize these changes and utilize these institutions continues. Ten years of democracy have brought remarkable progress, yet it may take several more decades of consistent leadership to fulfill the promises made by the first generations of women in Parliament.

Methodological Appendix

I modeled my methodological path on the work of Glaser and Strauss (1967), Charmaz (1983), and Emerson, Fretz, and Shaw (1995) and used three qualitative methods: intensive, semistructured interviews; participant observation; and archival research. The two periods of formal fieldwork for this text took place from August 1996 to May 1997 and from May to July of 2003. These trips were preceded by three other trips to South Africa, one I made as a student activist (1990), another as a research assistant (1992), and a research trip I made prior to actual fieldwork (May 1996).

Interviews

INTERVIEW PROCESS

During the 1996–97 research I interviewed 30 percent of the women in each of the parties in Parliament, for a total of thirty-nine women (see table A1). This was a targeted sample determined by ethnic, geographical, and socioeconomic background. The interviewees's backgrounds were similar to those of the population and the parties, making the sample representative (see the final subsection for a complete breakdown by race, age, exile status, and geographic location). The audiotaped interviews were conducted in English. For the women's protection, I did my own transcriptions and used randomly assigned pseudonyms.

Interviewees from the ANC represented every racial category, including white, black, coloured, and Asian, as well as each of the nine provinces. I interviewed equal numbers of white and black women in the IFP, primarily but not exclusively from the KwaZulu-Natal province, where the party has its strongest representation. I interviewed white, black, and coloured women of the NP from three provinces. The racial background of women from the DP and the PAC is limited, for each party had only one representative. The DP representative is white; the PAC representative is coloured.

Table A1. Interviews by Party

National Assembly	Women Seated	Party's Total Representatives	Number Interviewed
African Christian Democratic Party	0	2	0
African National Congress	86	251	25
Democratic Party	1	7	1
Freedom Front	0	9	0
Inkatha Freedom Party	10	43	4
National Party	9	81	3
Pan Africanist Congress	1	5	1
Total			34

National Council of Provinces	Women Seated	Party's Total Representatives	Number Interviewed
African Christian Democratic Party	0	0	0
African National Congress	15	60	4
Democratic Party	0	3	0
Freedom Front	0	5	0
Inkatha Freedom Party	1	5	1 (moved to NA)
National Party	0	17	0
Pan Africanist Congress	0	0	0
Total			5

Because I sought to understand, describe, and analyze only women's experiences during the transition and their strategies of political activity, I had not intended to interview any men. While a study of male versus female experiences and attitudes holds much merit and potential, the nature of my study called for as much focus as possible within my sample group. Gaining a representative sample of women was my primary focus. That said, as my work progressed and I was confident of reaching my targeted sample of women, I decided to interview a small number of male MPs. This did not in any way constitute a control group or a representative sample, and no general theories or models can be drawn from these interviews.

Although they are not included in the study, I interviewed several women in four provinces from the IFP, ANC, NP, FF, ACDP, and the DP (twenty-two in total). Most important for this project were the interviews with women from the FF and the ACDP, for these parties do not have any women at the national level. Again, wherever relevant I have included these women's comments as representative of their parties. Additionally, I tracked eight women's organizations during the research period. Both the provincial interviews and the women's organizational studies as a whole fall outside the scope of my research and lay the foundation for additional scholarship. During the 2003 fieldwork, I also interviewed members of the gender units in six government departments, members of the Office on the Status of Women, several members of the Commission on Gender Equality, a member of the Films and Publications Board, and numerous members of eight organizations working to end violence against women.

The women from each party had socioeconomic, educational, and professional backgrounds that corresponded to their parties' membership profiles. The widest spectrum of socioeconomic and educational backgrounds came from the ANC and the IFP. Women from these parties represented every level of educational achievement, from only a grade-school education to advanced degrees in law and the social sciences (again, see the breakdown of interviewees' backgrounds in the appendix's final subsection). These women differed widely in their careers and training: some had been poor rural farmers or domestic workers; some, middle-class teachers and nurses; and some, upper-class professionals and activists. Women from the NP and DP were college-educated and middle to upper class, indicative of their party's members. Professions were various but correlated to education and class. The wealthiest women had been journalists, lawyers, and businesswomen. Most of the women had moderate education and had been teachers, social workers, or nurses. Several women had received little or no formal education and were domestic servants, industrial laborers, or housewives and farmers. Occasionally within the ANC, and frequently with the NP, white women in higher-class brackets had been active socially but not professionally. In the NP many of these women had been leaders in women's civic clubs or voluntary associations. In the ANC many of these women were involved in women's political organizations or movements.

Within the NP and the DP women had often worked their ways through traditional party structures, and they were viable and experienced political candidates for the May 1994 elections. This was often not true of women in other parties, such as the ANC, PAC, and IFP, who were active in struggle politics and did not follow a path resembling traditional party politics. Because these organizations were outside the legal political sphere during the apartheid regime, they were not necessarily part of well-entrenched parliamentary politics.

OBTAINING INTERVIEWS

The women in Parliament were generally open and accessible, although there were undeniable racial and class differences in scheduling and obtaining interviews. Typically, contacting thirty women resulted in only three interviews: I would manage to speak directly with ten of those thirty women and schedule five of those ten for interviews; of those five, only three would make their scheduled appointments. Part of the difficulty in contacting the women was the lack of support staff. Often six members or delegates shared one secretary. As such, the basic logistics of contacting women, scheduling appointments, and remembering the scheduled meetings were beyond the capabilities of such a skeleton staff. The women who declined interviews almost without reservation stated they were too busy.

This lack of support staff and of experience in scheduling appointments often meant that women from disadvantaged backgrounds were unavailable at interview times. White women or members of the cabinet were almost without exception available at their scheduled times; if they became unavailable, they would call to reschedule. Although I often had to schedule interviews with cabinet members weeks in advance, these leading women had sufficient staff to assist them. Given all this, I soon realized that if I met only with women who kept their scheduled appointments, my sample would be skewed toward white or elite women or experienced politicians accustomed to interviews.

I thus developed another strategy for obtaining interviews: "squatting." For at least two out of any five scheduled appointments, I would go to the women's offices and wait for them to return. Since they had scheduled the interviews for that day, I supposed it likely that they were in the building. Because I had developed a trusting relationship with the security staff, they would either page the MP or allow me to wait at a relevant office, the MP's or her secretary's. Often, after waiting—sometimes up to two hours—the member or delegate would return to her office to find me waiting. She would often have little recollection of making the appointment, but once this face-to-face contact was established, I had a much better chance of conducting the interview then or at least of getting her to show up for a rescheduled interview. I had success with sympathetic secretaries, who became accustomed to my waiting in their offices. Often they went to great lengths to find the MPs or would work to ensure a rescheduled interview was remembered. The staff was tireless and dedicated, just much too small. Clearly, using the squatting method was the only way to gain a truly representative sample, but it also called great attention to the vastly inadequate resources given to members of Parliament. The approach I developed to meet this obstacle to access is most akin to Fonow and Cook's (1991) "using the situation at hand" method of feminist research.

For women who would not return phone calls, I tried to meet them at committee meetings. Once they met me, my age and manner seemed to put them at ease, and they often consented to an interview. Women would recommend other women to me, which proved a successful entryway to other interviews. This combination of networking (Epstein 1992) and "squatting" was especially helpful for filling various racial, class, or geographic categories and was invaluable for obtaining interviews with less experienced members, who may have been hesitant to meet with a researcher from the United States. Most interviews were scheduled within the week of initial contact. I found attempts to send introductory letters fruitless, unless specifically requested by a member or delegate or her secretary.

Only one woman stated she was not interested in being interviewed because my research focused on gender. This woman held a top position in Parliament and was openly antagonistic to being grouped with other women based on gender alone. She has occasionally expressed similar sentiments to the press, suggesting that such gender-based grouping lends credibility to the clearly unfounded critique that women were in Parliament only as tokens or to fill a quota. What was most interesting about this particular refusal was that her secretary was initially quite promising about setting an interview time. After she had explained the nature of my project to the MP, however, she had to call back and awkwardly explain why the interview would not be granted.

No other woman, especially in her party, had a similar hesitancy to participate. To the contrary, most women felt they had a great deal to share, and several explicitly indicated that they felt they had much to teach the United States. Nonetheless, only time will tell whether such enthusiasm will continue or whether a male backlash will eventually inhibit women's participation. As a leader in Parliament and her party, this woman certainly heard criticisms of women's participation frequently—perhaps more frequently than did rank-and-file members—and her lack of participation was understandable. Were they to become the norm, such refusals would raise significant questions about the future of feminist projects, especially those focused on women's knowledge and experience, a problem Kirsch (1999) has discussed.

INTERVIEW LOCATION, LENGTH, AND STRUCTURE

Most initial interviews with parliamentarians occurred in their offices. Three interviews took place during a meal in one of the parliamentary cafeterias. This setting was awkward, for the processes of ordering and eating the meal distracted from the interview. One of these interviews was with a member of the IFP, and the other two were with members of the NP. I initially had difficulty scheduling a meeting with these women, so I was grateful for the opportunity to meet them despite the awkwardness of this setting.

The average interview lasted between one and one-half to two hours. Interviews often ran longer, but only occasionally over three hours. A handful lasted only forty-five minutes or so. These without exception involved women holding top positions in Parliament or their parties. Several women welcomed sequential interviews, supplemental phone calls and faxes, or visits to their constituency offices. The lengthiest of these visits was a weekend trip with an MP to her rural constituency.

I conducted intensive, in-depth, focused interviews. The flexible and open-ended format was directly focused on eliciting the narratives of the women's lives and work. My intention was to have women tell the stories of their lives both during apartheid and as parliamentarians. We discussed several key aspects to their lives as MPs, including the institutionalization of the women's movement, the forces of assimilation experienced by women, the strategies they used to participate as individuals and as a group, and their views and understandings of the National Machinery for Gender issues. An extensive interview outline is offered later.

As did Maria Mies (1991), I found that the women in Parliament were interviewing me, too, during our sessions, with the interviews becoming discussions. Of her interviewees Mies writes: "They wanted to know whether we [members of the research team] were married, had children, what we did during menstruation, whether all the women in my country wore trousers, why we were doing this research, what a woman rural worker earned in my country, whether the people there also ate rice, etc." (71). Dialogue thus became a critical way to reduce, but obviously not erase, the power imbalance in my interviews. The women wanted to know my age, my family background, my relationships, my political affiliations, my experiences of their nation, and my experiences in the townships. I focused on the narratives of their lives, but they, too, wanted to know something of me.

Not only did I intend my interview methods to lessen the divide among women;

in addition, the in-depth and dialogical interviews were intended to create a situation of mutual attachment and closeness. Being asked by an MP to visit in her home constituency and to stay with her family is just one of many examples of this extension of hospitality. It was also a way to see this woman fully shine, for she was much more comfortable and politically effective there than when working under the formal rules of Parliament. Moreover, I was asked to share meals with MPs or attend special meetings. This closeness—or at least this hospitality—may seem problematic to researchers subscribing to more "scientific" approaches or who espouse "objectivity." Within feminist research in general, however, such invitations and exchanges are essential to gaining a complete and comprehensive understanding of such women as political actors, as members of the women's movement, and as politicians, and all this was especially true for my study specifically.

CONFIDENTIALITY

The women were open and honest. At times I felt they revealed more than they should have. Women often told me how their personal beliefs or experiences directly conflicted with their parties' policies or philosophies. Some of these women told me that if their names were ever publicly attached to these positions, they would be reprimanded or disciplined by their parties. Some even feared that public dissent from their parties would result in their removal from office or worse. This fear has some basis in fact, for MPs have been asked to leave parties or Parliament following their critiques of party direction or agenda. The review boards of both Syracuse University and Mississippi State University required me to destroy my interview tapes following the conclusion of my research. Given the women's frankness and the still tense and often violent postapartheid context, this requirement seems justifiable.

Protecting these women is the most important professional commitment I have, and I would never intentionally jeopardize their lives, careers, or political reputations. Erring on the side of caution seems more than justifiable, and I feel my decision is supported by a long line of qualitative and feminist researchers who have gone before me (I. E. Seidman 1991; Finch 1984). As Kirsch argues, "scholars who use interactive, collaborative approaches to research are more likely than traditional scholars to gain participants' trust, establish close relations with them, and learn confidential, emotionally charged information. . . . [Research methods] can have different, unforeseen and at times far-reaching consequences; they can affect participants' emotional welfare, reputation, and safety" (1999, 47, 51). Since my methods focused largely on increasing the connections I had with these women MPs, and since these women will face uncertain political futures for years to come, working within tight and overly cautious boundaries for confidentiality is paramount.

I have continually gone to great lengths to preserve their anonymity. Since some parties (e.g., the DP, the PAC, and to a lesser degree, the NP and the IFP) have so few women representatives, associating party affiliations with specific statements might reveal a women's identity, regardless of any pseudonym. I thus refer only to women "from an opposition party." (I interviewed so many women in the ANC that

their identities are not revealed by party identification.) This anonymity has negative consequences. Many of these women have exceptionally few opportunities for
public recognition, and most of what they said might well aid them publicly and
within their parties. One woman and most of the men specifically asked that I use
their names in connection with their remarks. With only one exception, however, I
have avoided their names to protect them from any unanticipated negative issues.

Ethical considerations, which are fundamental to a feminist methodology, are pivotal in considerations of confidentiality. Indeed, protecting confidentiality may be
more essential in qualitative studies than in quantitative ones, for the intimacy and
hospitality created in the research process mask power imbalances (Stacey 1991). If
feminist methodology is to be focused on a shared understanding of research and
overtly emancipatory in its goals, confidentiality clauses need to be at the foundation of such work.

Archives

The records of women's organizations are either nonexistent or overwhelmingly
comprehensive. The events of the Women's National Coalition, beginning in the
early 1990s, were meticulously recorded, and all those records have been carefully
stored. This material shows how the strong leadership and a commitment to consensus building calmed the contentious multiparty organization. The material also
carefully documents the relationships among race, class, and gender issues in the organization in a scholarly fashion. In contrast, the archival records for the ANC
Women's League and other women's organizations within the resistance are skele-
tal at best. The league's records were made available only at the end of my fieldwork, and the archivist indicated that little material was on file. Such an absence of
written documentation makes intuitive sense, for this was a revolutionary movement
operating under a totalitarian regime. To keep records of any kind often meant certain arrest, if not death. Even in less violent states, women's organizations often leave
few records and subsequently are underresearched or underanalyzed.

The most comprehensive history of the women's movement during apartheid accordingly comes from secondary sources or from oral histories. I obtained several
such histories during my research period, as I interviewed former leaders and members of these organizations. I have attempted throughout to integrate the historical
material from my interviews with secondary sources.

In the new South Africa government documents and parliamentary records are
readily accessible, a sharp contrast to the apartheid era's control of information. In
an effort to make the government as accessible as possible, the price for government
documents is minimal. Because the debates were available only in printed form and
lack a comprehensive indexing system or sophisticated search mechanism, a comprehensive content-analysis of the debates fell outside the scope of my research.
Rather, I focused on several specific tasks. First, I coded the opening speeches of parliament since the May 1994 elections to obtain a longitudinal sense of MPs' and delegates' concerns for women's issues as national priorities. Second, I targeted specific

debates dealing with gender issues—namely, those dealing with abortion, pornography, the national gender commission, and violence against women. I traced the debates from the time an issue was introduced until the final vote. For the abortion debates, I was able to access the records from the 1975 debates. This greatly improved my understanding of the roots of the legislation being revised under the new government. Third, the commemorative speeches on National Women's Day, August 9, 1994–97, further indicated how parties, women, and Parliament as a whole were framing gender issues and legislation. (A discussion of these debates, as well as the commemorative speeches from National Women's Day, appears in chapter 5). Fourth, I chronicled the speeches of the women I interviewed, which provided an addition avenue to understand these women as public speakers and as party members. Much of this material helped me understand women's political roles, as discussed in chapter 4. These speeches, often serving as official party positions, were particularly helpful in understanding parties' positions on elements of the National Gender Machinery, such as the women's budget and the gender commission. Similarly, many speeches from the National Women's Day celebrations focused specifically on the integration of women MPs, the institutionalization of women's issues in national legislation, and the platform for action they were planning to implement.

Observations and Participant Observations

To understand more fully how the women operated in Parliament and in their parties, I watched each of them speak in chambers or read their speeches in Hansard (the equivalent of the U.S. *Congressional Record*). The meetings of the National Assembly and the National Council of Provinces provided a good sense of the processes and procedures of Parliament's daily functions. I was able to better understand how the institution had changed and become much less formal and stoic since the end of apartheid. Attending debates on specific gender legislation was much more valuable than observing debates at random. I found that debates not dealing explicitly with gender issues or women's issues generally omitted any discussion of women's issues whatsoever, although one exception was notable. ANC MP Shope asserted the necessity of black women on the committee in charge of water issues. This was remarkable in that there was no gender analysis within the legislation at hand. As I discovered, however, and as MP Shope asserted that day, access to clean water is perhaps one of the most important women's issues in South Africa (see chapter 2 for a discussion of this speech).

Committee meetings revealed how women in general were operating in the legislative process. Women often had a much stronger voice in committees, and these meetings were the primarily locations for policy debate and creation.

Visiting women in their constituency offices was invaluable. As with committee work, constituency work was a place where many women found their strength. Working with their constituents and with local organizations was central to many women's political identity. During my months in Pretoria, Johannesburg, and Durban, I attended as many meetings and functions of women's organizations, youth organizations, and women's branches of political parties as I could. I also found this to be an excellent way to observe parliamentary women outside Parliament and to understand how women functioned within these various roles. On at least two occasions I scheduled interviews with a leader of a women's group only to find out during the course of the interview that the woman was also a parliamentarian. This reinforced the finding, discussed later, that leadership of women's organizations and the women's movement had been "decapitated" because most of the leadership of women's groups had been "taken wholesale" into Parliament.

Annotated Interview Schedule

I took a topic outline into my interviews, but the format and timing of the questions changed with each interview. My goal was to have the women tell their stories of life before, during, and after the transition to democracy. I attempted to cover each issue with every interviewee, but the nonscheduled nature of my interviews allowed exceptions to this goal. I started with one broad question for each area, and then I asked other questions as needed. What follows is an annotated interview schedule and a list of sample questions.

INTERVIEW AREA 1: PERSONAL POLITICAL NARRATIVE

The following indicate the sort of questions and prompts I initially posed to the interviewees:

—Tell me about your background and when you got involved in politics.
—Were you involved in the struggle? How and why?
—What was your career (education/training) before coming here?
—What were your central goals as an activist (community worker)?
—Who was influential in your work as an activist (community worker)?
—How did gender politics fit into your work with racial politics?
—What did your party do for gender issues?

I found the best way to begin the interview was with a broad prompt relating to their personal history. This was a comfortable place for most women to begin, and I would explore various themes as they presented or failed to present themselves. This portion of the interview typically took between twenty-five and forty-five minutes.

Within this period we discussed the interviewee's socioeconomic, political, and racial background, her point of politicization, career choices or options, and level and form of political activity during the apartheid era. We talked about how, when, and why women became political or became aware of themselves as political entities.

Often this last question elicited stories of familial involvement in resistance politics or in parliamentary politics, stories of politicization during school or in their professions, or stories of childhood poverty and racism, which they later identified as systemic oppression. I was interested in discovering what ideologies and movements—such as Marxism, classical liberalism, Christianity, and black consciousness—had shaped their initial involvement.

I was also particularly interested to learn whether and when a gender analysis entered their activism. For most women, racial oppression or the awareness of racial difference was the first point of political knowledge and activism. Gender issues came second. Women discussed how they had constructed gender issues and deconstructed feminism, and they discussed in some detail how their gender activism was received by their male counterparts in politics.

INTERVIEW AREA 2: TRANSITION TO PARLIAMENT

The following indicate the sort of questions I posed subsequent to the first batch:

—What has the change from your life before Parliament to becoming an MP/Rep been like?
—What committees are you working on? Are you involved with the Parliamentary Women's Group? The Violence against Women taskforce?
—What challenges do you face in Parliament?
—Do men and women face the same challenges?
—What is the most rewarding aspect of your work?
—What skills do you need? What training did you receive?
—What is your main goal for your work as a parliamentarian? What are your top priorities?
—How has your party changed since the transition? The government? The nation?
—What organizations are you involved with outside Parliament?
—Will you tell me about your work in your constituency?
—What are the central women's issues?
—What is your assessment of the debate on abortion? Pornography?

The second broad area was thus a discussion about these women's lives as parliamentarians, focusing on the impact of the transition for them personally, politically, and professionally. We talked about how the transition affected themselves, the government, their party, and the nation. Given the nature of this project, I was particularly interested in the process of political learning for these women. We discussed how they experienced the transition from resistance politics to parliamentary politics, specifically examining the challenges they faced and the skills the developed to become policy makers. The women presented their ideas about parliamentary politics, party politics, and political leadership.

INTERVIEW AREA 3: ASSESSMENT OF THE CURRENT STATE OF GENDER POLITICS AND PREDICTIONS FOR THE FUTURE

The following indicate the sort of questions I posed in the final portion of the interviews:

—Are women mobilized around gender issues?

—How has the transition changed the way you see yourself as a political actor?

—Which is most important to you (your party/the nation)—gender, race, ethnicity, class, sexual orientation?

—How has the transition affected the national status of women?

—How has the push toward racial reconciliation affected women?

—How has the affirmative-action issue affected women?

—Is there (should there be) a national movement for gender issues?

—Is there a national leader on gender issues?

—What is the relationship of organizations in civil society to the government?

—Are women able to work together across generations, races, classes, and parties in Parliament? In society?

Analysis of Sample by Interviewees' Race, Age, Exile Status, and Geographic Origins

The racial composition of my sample for the 1996–97 interviews ran as follows: black, twenty-one; coloured, four; Indian, four; white, nine. White women are overrepresented in this sample, primarily because of racial imbalances in the parties themselves. The representatives of the National Party were overwhelmingly white, and the sole representative of the Democratic Party was white. Interestingly, several members of the Inkatha Freedom Party were white. Within the African National Congress, the racial composition of the membership is most reflective of the population at large. According to *Britannica On-line,* "Black Africans make up three-fourths of the country's total population, and whites account for about one-eighth, with people of mixed race (including Cape Malay) and of Indian descent most of the remainder."

One woman in my sample was between twenty and thirty years old, ten were between thirty and forty, eight were between forty and fifty, eleven were between fifty and sixty, and eight were between sixty and seventy. This distribution of ages is representative of all the women in Parliament. While the age statistics are not publicly available, there are few women in the twenty-to-thirty range, and several women are fifty or older. I did not specifically ask women's ages during the interviews, but several women volunteered the information. Assigning ages based on information given in the interviews (dates of education, participation in specific political events, age of children, physical appearance) was a fairly simple task.

Fourteen women came from rural backgrounds, nineteen came from urban ones, and five were originally from rural areas but were representing an urban constituency or had chosen an urban area as their location or vice versa. Women in this last group were able to speak from both experiences with such fluency that they defied categorization as either rural or urban. Unlike urban women, who often spoke for rural women, women from dual locations spoke with women from each area.

Finally, ten women in the sample had spent time in exile; twenty-eight had not. This was a difficult category to track, however, because exile status is not a publicly recorded statistic. The number of exiles is inflated here because I included all women who left the country for any length of time for political reasons, so that it comprises both self-imposed exile and exile forced by the apartheid government. Also included are women who accompanied their husbands in exile. These women became active in party structures in exile even though their reasons for leaving the country may not have been directly related to their own political affiliations or actions before exile. At least three of these ten were outside the country only briefly for a specific forum or training or for personal safety.

Notes

Chapter 1: Women and the Struggle for Liberation

1. See the appendix for a detailed discussion of my research methods.

2. In an extensive linguistic study, by contrast, Oyewumi argues that "gender was not an organizing principle in Yoruba society" and that the "fundamental category 'woman'—which is foundational in Western gender discourses—simply did not exist in Yorubaland prior to its sustained contact with the West" (1999, 31, ix). While such an analysis applies to western Africa (specifically Nigeria, Togo, Benin, and Sierra Leone) and not to southern Africa, Oyewumi's assertions have important implications for any analysis of all precolonial Africa.

3. This area of southern Africa was originally inhabited by two groups of people: the San, a hunter-gatherer group; and the Khoikhoi, a pastoral group. These groups eventually established themselves in the cape region.

4. Capitalism depends on a mobile, ready, and able labor pool. Slaves are capital; they must be purchased and sustained through food, housing, and so on. Europeans thus found labor cheaper than slaves (Saunders 1992, 127).

5. Following an ancestral prophesy relayed by a young girl named Nongqawuse, the Xhosa people killed all their cattle (most of which had been infected with a lung disease) and destroyed their corn crops, believing this would bring forth from the earth a new herd of healthy cattle and productive corn. The British governor, Sir George Grey, traded food for labor contracts with the starving population and quickly dominated any resisters (Peires 1991, 30–33).

6. This pattern of violence and, more specifically, gender-based assault has continued until the present; South Africa has led the world in reported incidences of sexual violence since 1996.

7. Over 14,000 Afrikaners took part in the Great Trek.

8. These republics became known as the Orange Free State and the Transvaal.

9. These indigenous nations were far more developed than the Khoikhoi and the San; originally known as Bantu-speaking people, each group had progressed from Iron Age peoples

and had sophisticated systems of religion, government, and family relations. The settlers first encountered the amaXhosa, the nation furthermost east and nearest to the cape. These nations are thought to have migrated from northern Africa between A.D. 300 and 700. Originally there were two large language groups, the Nguni and the Sotho, and two smaller language groups, the Venda and the Tsonga. The Xhosa and Zulu people speak a derivative of the Nguni language. The Basotho, Pedi, Lobedu, and Tswana people all speak a form of Sotho (Saunders 1992, 11–12, 62). Today the South African constitution recognizes eleven official languages, nine of which being the major indigenous languages still spoken.

10. The Afrikaners built the Voortrekker Monument to immortalize the trek and the Battle of Blood River. Each year on December 16 a beam of light from the sun strikes a large stone in the bottom of the towering monument. This sunbeam is considered to be God's yearly reaffirmation of the covenant to rule and Christianize South Africa.

11. The roots of the war began on April 12, 1877, when the British declared that they had annexed the Afrikaner's South African Republic and that the republic no longer existed. The war lasted from 1889 to 1902.

12. Neither the British nor the Afrikaners officially enlisted black soldiers, although unofficially both sides used them in "armed and support roles" (Saunders 1992, 245).

13. According to a progressive Afrikaner contact in South Africa, many believe that the British invented apartheid, but the Afrikaners perfected it. This idea is also applied to the concentration camps, which were invented by the British during the Boer War but perfected by the Germans, close relatives to the Afrikaners, during the Holocaust.

14. Although no such system of categorization currently exists, apartheid has left a historical legacy in links between race and socioeconomic status.

15. For the women's protection, I did my own transcriptions and have used randomly assigned Western pseudonyms. See the appendix for an extensive discussion of my methodology.

16. One such mainstream organization was the Black Sash, which I discuss more specifically later in this chapter.

17. Much of the Afrikaner resistance to British rule was linked to the colonists' abolition of slavery in 1834. Slave labor had been a mainstay of Afrikaner farm production. Similarly, the Afrikaners viewed this encroachment onto their political and economic life as they had the encroachment of British settlers onto their land since their arrival in 1820. Some five thousand Boers, or Afrikaner farmers, embarked on the Great Trek, starting in the cape colony and moving northward and inland. They traveled by ox-driven covered wagons and occupied or seized the land from the indigenous population.

18. The members of the FF describe the Afrikaner people as members of an "Afrikaner nation."

19. Similar patterns appear worldwide. Terborg-Penn (1990) determined that even within the 1960s civil rights protests in the southern United States, a similar pattern of women's mobilization, leadership, and involvement in political action was embedded in women's roles as mothers and wives. Although their political action fell outside their scripted gender roles and involved mass action and direct confrontation of state repression, it was not as overtly militant or militaristic as those activities within South Africa. Jad (1995) has shown how women within the Palestinian liberation movement sought to focus their activities on areas traditionally seen as "women's work": crafts, child care, and education. Basu's cross-cultural case studies present consistent evidence that many women's

movements are fed by a non-Western feminism that is a "hidden form of subversion enacted to protect families and communities rather than undermine them" (1995, 7).

20. Temma Kaplan (1982) discussed this term, "female consciousness," in her analysis of the collective action of women in Barcelona, 1910–18. Kaplan stresses that most interpretations of collective action are too simplistic or too myopic to capture the complexity of the events. In her analysis, female consciousness denotes a group of women's ability to mobilize to ensure their rights on the basis not of a shared class or racial bond but of a shared acceptance of the gender roles in their society: "Those with a female consciousness accept the gender system of their society. . . . The collective drive to secure those rights . . . sometimes has revolutionary consequences insofar as it politicizes the networks of everyday life" (545). Rather than simply embrace the material roles they were given, women in Barcelona used such roles to force the state to fulfill its obligations to them.

21. These protests increased dramatically in the 1970s. For a detailed autobiographical account of women in the labor unions, see Mashinini 1991.

22. Women's work and experiences in the labor unions have been of utmost importance in their training and militancy for postapartheid government service. See chapter 5 for a discussion of how women's work in labor unions has prepared them to be parliamentary leaders in postapartheid South Africa.

23. Her narrative underscores how and why apartheid is now being seen as a crime against humanity; see Asmal, Asmal, and Roberts 1997.

24. Debbie Budlender informed me that Ruth First was one of the main instigators of the potato boycotts. A white English-speaking journalist and political activist, First publicized the horrors of the potato practices. First was detained for 119 days and eventually assassinated.

25. Apartheid's practices extended to the exclusion of people of color from white hotels. Black hotels did exist, but they were often too expensive for most South Africans.

26. Similar patterns of maternal militancy appear within the nationalistic struggles in Northern Ireland (see Roulston 1997) and in Palestine (see Gluck 1997; Najjar 1992).

27. For the last four individuals, see, respectively, Joseph 1986, First 1965, Mashinini 1991, and Kuzwayo 1985.

28. For an extended discussion of the intersections of race, class, and gender for South African women, see Cock 1980.

29. For a discussion of the founding and the philosophy of the Black Sash, see Duncan 1991.

30. Women constituted much larger percentages in other armed African liberation conflicts. In the Eritrean People's Liberation Front, for example, women made up 40 percent of the fighters, 30 percent of the combat forces, and similarly high percentages of the support and technical forces (Hale 2001, 354).

31. Although again, opportunities for women in military forces were often much greater elsewhere in Africa, as in the case of the Eritrean People's Liberation Front (Hale 2001).

Chapter 2: Party Politics in the Transition to Democracy

1. Hale (2001) describes the same process of political learning among women combatants in Eritrea. They looked to struggles throughout Africa and learned tremendously from observing South Africa's arguably more successful process.

2. For a complete discussion of the WNC unity, see Britton 2002a.

3. There were periods of conflict and dissension, especially concerning issues that were religiously charged (e.g., abortion) or culturally sensitive; see Ballington 1999b.

4. As of October 30, 2004, the international rankings of women in legislatures included seven countries from Africa in the top thirty: Rwanda is first with 48.8 percent; South Africa is twelfth with 29.8 percent; Mozambique is fifteenth with 30 percent; the Seychelles are sixteenth with 29.4 percent; Namibia is twenty-first with 26.4 percent; Uganda is twenty-sixth with 24.7 percent; and Tunisia is twenty-eight with 21.4 percent (Inter-Parliamentary Union 2004).

5. In its goals and impetus, the WNC bears a striking similarity to the Pro-Femmes/ Twese Hamwe umbrella women's organization in post-1994 genocide in Rwanda. Although the situation in Rwanda was indisputably much more severe, the process of unification was similar. Following the genocide, women in Rwanda joined with returning exile women to rekindle the umbrella group; Hutu and Tutsi alike, they came together to focus on a plan of rebuilding their nation. The Rwandan group did not specifically seek to place women in office, but they did draft a "Campaign for Peace" document to guide their activities and action, making it much like the WNC's Women's Charter. This plan worked not only to bring peace and reconciliation but also to challenge poverty and gender discrimination (Newbury and Baldwin 2001).

6. For an extensive discussion of the IFP and ANC collaboration, see Britton 2002a.

7. Women constituted 18 percent of the delegates to the Ugandan Constituent Assembly; many of these delegates were active in the women's caucus (Tripp 2000b, 77).

8. There is some evidence that party magnitude, not district magnitude, matters most in this instance. For an extended discussion, see Matland 1993.

9. Okin (1979) counters this line of thinking by asserting that women cannot simply be added to the traditional categories and political systems to achieve parity. Merely changing election rules and shifting institutional mechanisms to accommodate women may prove insufficient in rectifying the political exclusion and domination of women.

10. Dene Smuts was not the only person interviewed who wanted me to use her name. While I quote her extensively throughout the book, I have chosen to protect her identity in all other cases. I have used her name here because she is the only woman representative of the Democratic Party at the national level, so that readers could identify her by the content of the quotation. Further, she is known to hold such a view, and her remarks are at times complimentary to her party. She was open to having her name used because she sees herself and her party as playing an important role as an opposition to the ANC majority.

11. With respect to women in government, gendered media coverage includes, for example, an unequal attention to "their family situation, their appearance, and their position on women's issues" (Swers 2001, 171).

Chapter 3: Women's Integration into Parliament

1. Halisi and O'Meara (1995, 408) presented much higher figures for the nation as a whole, claiming that more than 15,000 politically motivated murders occurred.

2. Toyi toying is a marching form used during protests. It involves jumping back and forth from one foot to the other. One simultaneously moves up and down and side to side.

3. See Liebenberg 1995 for examples of the type of work such consultants performed.

4. The second factor Hassim (2003) finds is the ANC's dominance, which limits democracy broadly defined. This will be discussed later in the chapter.

5. See the appendix for a discussion of the educational, economic, professional, ethnic, and geographic backgrounds of the women interviewed.

6. The conference was hosted by the Gender Advocacy Programme, the Association of Women in European Parliaments in Africa, and the South African parliament's Women's Empowerment Unit.

7. Many women interpreted this as a backslide of ANC support. Members are required to vote according to the party line, and the ANC supported the Termination of Pregnancy Act. Several members voiced mainly religious objections to abortion, however, so that the ANC allowed members to abstain from voting. Some women felt that allowing members to abstain from voting showed that the ANC was backsliding on its support of this issue. A similar privilege of abstention was not afforded women who objected to an equally contested vote for the Films and Publications Bill, which initially allowed notably liberal standards for pornography.

8. A woman was in line for the position of chief whip, but she was passed over for a man. One woman I interviewed said she had heard "rumblings" that the men thought women had too many power positions, for they already occupied the seats of Speaker and Deputy Speaker of the National Assembly.

9. Investigations of the U.S. context indicate that congresswomen are professionally and politically disadvantaged by exclusion from often-unstructured informal situations, such as the cloakroom, the gym, softball games, and drinking or hunting parties (Gertzog 1995; Considine and Deutchman 1996). In the recent 2001 U.K. elections, the Labour Party held a candidate-selection meeting in a male-only bar (BBC News 2000).

10. See, for example, Valerie O'Regan's talk entitled "Critical Levels of Female Policy-Makers in the Industrialized Nations," presented at the Midwest Political Science Association's annual meeting, April 1998. Cases have been made in support of the critical-mass theory in studies of nations across the globe, perhaps most recently for Australia (Sawer 2000).

Chapter 4: Class Structure, Role Differentiation, and Gender Identities

1. The attrition rate could have been much higher, however, had there not been a concerted effort to train and retain women in office through the Women's Empowerment Unit in 1996–98. The brainchild of the then Speaker of the National Assembly, Frene Ginwala, this organization was started specifically to assist women from disadvantaged backgrounds obtain the skills and training they needed to survive in office (Geisler 2000).

2. Gertzog delineates three gender-role orientations for congresswomen: the gentlewoman, who is "accustomed to performing subordinate, traditionally female responsibilities"; the neutral woman, who is "inhibited about exhibiting behavior calling attention to her identity as a woman"; and the feminist, who is "unself-consciously proud of her identity as a woman and insistent on equality with men" (1995, 251). He argues that, while all three types of women may be present at all periods of legislative history, gender roles generally have moved from traditional definitions of womanhood in the early 1900s to progressive models of feminist activism in the 1970s.

In her study of women legislators in the United States, Thomas divided these women into three distinct categories depending on how they assessed the way their gender affected their legislative roles: the "avoiders," who denied that gender had an impact; the "accepters," who recognized that gender had an impact on their legislative roles and attempted to transform that impact; and the "resigned and frustrated," who were aware of the impact but too burdened or exhausted to confront the system.

3. Hirschmann (1991) delineated a similar typology for women's political participation in Africa that broadened the political sphere to include nongovernmental activities and informal organizations. Hirschmann disaggregated the traditional definitions of politics and women to give a full view of the latter's political activities. Hirschmann's typology included key women, such as wives of leaders or other highly placed women; women in the bureaucracy; women in Parliament; women in the political parties; women in decentralized agencies; women at the village level; and women interacting with extension officers or fieldworkers. In this way Hirschmann challenges researchers to reexamine both where and how women participate politically.

4. A similar tension was found within the debates of the Commission on Gender Equality.

5. For a comprehensive analysis of the domestic-worker industry in South Africa, see Cock 1980.

6. This MP dismissed the residual effects of apartheid on South Africa, and she resisted acknowledging any structural or systemic obstacles facing women. For example, she stated, "For the ANC to blame everything on apartheid is crap. The ANC doesn't have clean hands in this either. Kids in the rural areas were unaffected by the school burning and got a proper education." She thus suggested that children involved in the school boycotts and burnings in the townships, such as the Soweto uprising of 1976—and not the apartheid government—were responsible for their own lack of education.

7. Little, Dunn, and Deen (2001) stress the importance of background conditions for the legislative agendas of U.S. state legislative leaders. They find that nonwhite legislators are more likely than white legislators to support an agenda addressing women's needs and issues. They also found that southern legislatures were also more interested in issues of particular significance for women, because of "the higher demand for social services in the South in light of the higher levels of poverty, illiteracy, and limited access to quality health care" (43).

8. The issue in Britain arose in part from the change in the Labour Party's women-only short lists, which were scrapped as illegal in 1998 but remain up for review. Fewer women were placed in winnable seats and many others chose not to run again (see BBC News 2001).

Chapter 5: Institutional and Legislative Transformation

1. South African women are not the only ones to push for such changes. Following the 1997 elections and the influx of women MPs due to the now illegal Labour Party women-only short lists, women made similar attempts to change institutional culture (BBC News 2001).

2. Much of the gender-oriented legislation of this first parliament fits within the three categories developed by Gertzog in his analysis of U.S. affirmative-action legislation, which attempts to overcome gender hierarchies and patriarchal social norms; Gertzog as-

serted that such legislation addresses gender discrimination through symbolic, economic, or social measures (1995, 146–59).

3. For a comprehensive history of the road to the 1975 Abortion and Sterilization Act, see Cope 1993. The legislation was achieved through the dedicated work of Cope's Abortion Reform Action Group and was championed in Parliament by Helen Suzman of the PFP.

4. The National Council of Provinces replaced the Senate. The NCOP is intended to increase communication between the national parliament and its provincial counterparts by allowing debate on legislation at both levels and by having designated members move between the two on routine basis.

5. Fedler maintained: "South African women are in a state of mourning because no matter what commitments the government undertakes (and it has undertaken many), women and children continue to be raped, assaulted and murdered. It is almost as if the rate of violence against women and children has been inversely proportional to the democratization of our society and the commitment to gender-sensitive politics. Our legal system is rotten to the core, staffed with inefficient and overworked civil servants, who blame the system when whoops!, another real criminal slips through the loopholes and another little corpse finds its lonely way to the mortuary. Magistrates and judges continue to hand down judgments in femicide, rape and batter cases which are comical in their misogyny. Seemingly these days, the legal system is softer on pedophile murderers than on tax-evaders. Or traffic fine defaulters. . . . It is time that the government recognised that unless it acts to end violence against women, the only 'national machinery' that will work is state-funded AK-47s for women, so that we can protect what the government has promised it will protect" (1997, 1–2).

6. Take, for example, the South African Labour Appeal Court's recent decision that "it is fair for employers to reject work applications for senior positions from women because they are pregnant" (qtd. in Magardie 2000a).

Chapter 6: Implementing Gender

1. Dene Smuts is a leading member of the Democratic Party. She is a progressive liberal, white, well-educated, former journalist, and mother. She has been active in most debates and structures dealing with women's issues and championed the Bill of Rights.

2. Several women MPs mentioned a fact-finding mission to Australia, where they encountered that nation's version of the budget initiative.

3. See the Commission on Gender Equality's homepage, http://www.cge.org.za/.

Chapter 7: The Second Generation

1. I tend to believe the latter, that women are less likely to criticize the men in their party publicly, because a male MP made a harassing, sexual comment to me while riding in a Parliament elevator.

Works Cited

African National Congress. N.d. "A Short History of the ANC Women's League." Available at http://www.anc.org.za/wl/docs/history.html. Accessed September 29, 2003.

Albertyn, Cathi, Shireen Hassim, and Sheila Meintjes. 2002. "Making a Difference? Women's Struggles for Participation and Representation." In *One Woman, One Vote: The Gender Politics of South African Elections,* ed. Glenda Flick, Shelia Meintjes, and Mary Simons, 24–52. Johannesburg: Electoral Institute of South Africa.

Altenroxel, Lynne. 2000. "Thousands Still Resort to Illegal Abortions." *Johannesburg Star,* July 20, pp. 1–2. Available at http://www.iol.co.za/.

Amadiume, Ifi. 1997. *Re-inventing Africa: Matriarchy, Religion, and Culture.* New York: Zed Books.

Asmal, Kader, Louise Asmal, and Ronald Suresh Roberts. 1997. *Reconciliation through Truth: A Reckoning of Apartheid's Criminal Governance.* 2d ed. New York: Saint Martin's.

Baden, Sally, Shireen Hassim, and Sheila Meintjes. 1999. *Country Gender Profile: South Africa.* Prepared for the Swedish International Development Cooperation Agency (Sida), Pretoria, Republic of South Africa. Available at http://womensnet.org.za/links/genderpr.htm. Accessed March 2004.

Baldez, Lisa. 2001. "Coalition Politics and the Limits of State Feminism in Chile." *Women and Politics* 22, no. 4:1–28.

Ballington, Julie. 1999a. "Gender Considerations in Electoral System Reform." *The Election Bulletin.* 6th ed. *Women'sNet* 1 (Aug.). Available at http://womensnet.org.za/election/eb6–esysreform.htm. Accessed March 2004.

———. 1999b. *The Participation of Women in South Africa's First Democratic Elections.* Johannesburg: Electoral Institute of South Africa.

———. 1999c. "Party Representation—The Women's Profile." *The Election Bulletin.* 6th ed. *Women'sNet* 1 (Aug.). Available at http://womensnet.org.za/election/eb6–esystem.htm. Accessed March 2004.

———. 1999d. "Women to Break through 30% Critical Mass Barrier." *The Election Bul-*

letin. 1st ed. *Women'sNet* 1 (May 14). Available at http://womensnet.org.za/election /leadstory.htm. Accessed March 2004.

———. 2002. "Political Parties, Gender Equality, and Elections in South Africa." In *One Woman, One Vote: The Gender Politics of South African Elections*, ed. Glenda Fick, Sheila Meintjes, and Mary Simons, 75–101. Johannesburg: Electoral Institute of South Africa.

Bashevkin, Sylvia. 1985. *Toeing the Line: Women and Party Politics in English Canada.* Toronto: University of Toronto Press.

———. 2000. "From Tough Times to Better Times: Feminism, Public Policy, and New Labour Politics in Britian." *International Political Science Review* 21, no. 4:407–24.

Basu, Amrita, ed. 1995. *The Challenge of Local Feminisms: Women's Movements in Global Perspective.* Boulder, Colo.: Westview.

BBC News. 2000. "Labour 'Lacks Female Candidates.'" July 10. Available at http://news. bbc.co.uk/hi/english/uk/wales/newsid_825000/825976.stm. Accessed March 2004.

———. 2001. "Labour to Change Women Shortlist Law." May 6. Available at http:// news.bbc.co.uk/hi/english/uk_politics/newsid_1315000/1315814.stm. Accessed March 2004.

Beckwith, Karen. 2000. "Beyond Compare? Women's Movements in Comparative Perspective." *European Journal of Political Research* 37:431–68.

Berger, Iris. 1983. "Sources of Class Consciousness: South African Women in Recent Labor Struggles." *International Journal of African Historical Studies* 16, no. 1:49–66.

Bermeo, Nancy. 1990. "Rethinking Regime Change." *Comparative Politics* 22, no. 3:359–77.

Bernstein, Hilda. 1990. "The Real Challenge of Feminism." *The African Communist: Journal of the South African Communist Party* 122, no. 2:96–100.

Bop, Codou. 2001. "Women in Conflict, Their Gains and Their Losses." In *The Aftermath: Women in Post-Conflict Transformation*, ed. Sheila Meintjes, Anu Pillay, and Meredeth Turshen, 19–34. New York: Zed Books.

Bozzoli, Belinda. 1991. *Women of Phokeng: Consciousness, Life Strategy, and Migrancy in South Africa, 1900–1983.* Portsmouth, N.H.: Heinemann.

Britton, Hannah. 2002a. "Coalition Building, Election Rules, and Party Politics: South African Women's Path to Parliament." *Africa Today* 4, no. 49:33–68.

Brown, Alice. 1996. "Women and Politics in Scotland." *Parliamentary Affairs* 49, no. 1:26–40.

Brown, Alice, Tahyna Barnett Donaghy, Fiona Mackay, and Elizabeth Meehan. 2002. "Women and Constitutional Change in Scotland and Northern Ireland." *Parliamentary Affairs* 55, no. 1:71–84.

Budelender, Debbie. 1996. *The Women's Budget Initiative.* Cape Town: Institute for a Democratic Alternative in South Africa.

Byanyima, W. 1994. "Women in the Political Struggle in Uganda." In *Women Transforming Politics: Worldwide Strategies for Empowerment*, ed. Jill Bystydzienski, 129–42. Bloomington: Indiana University Press.

Camp, Roderic. 1998. "Women and Men, Men and Women: Gender Patterns in Mexican Politics." In *Women's Participation in Mexican Political Life*, ed. Victoria E. Rodriguez, 167–78. Boulder, Colo.: Westview.

Castles, Francis. 1981. "Female Legislative Representation and the Electoral System." *Politics* 1:21–27.

Caul, Miki. 2001. "Political Parties and the Adoption of Candidate Gender Quotas: A Cross-National Analysis." *Journal of Politics* 63, no. 4:1214–29.

Charmaz, K. 1983. "The Grounded Theory Method: An Explication and Interpretation." In *Contemporary Field Research*, ed. Robert Emerson, 109–26. Prospect Heights, Ill.: Waveland.

Clayton, Ian. 1999. "Key Challenges Lie ahead for Women." *Johannesburg Mail and Guardian*, April 30, pp. 1–2. Available at http://archive.mg.co.za/. Accessed March 2004.

Cock, Jacklyn. 1980. *Maids and Madams: A Study in the Politics of Exploitation*. Johannesburg: Raven.

———. 1991. *Colonels and Cadres: War and Gender in South Africa*. Cape Town: Oxford University Press.

Coetzee, Alice. 1999. "Gender Activists Too Low on Party Lists." *The Election Bulletin*. 1st ed. *Women'sNet* 1 (May 14). Available at http://womensnet.org.za/election/1storystar.htm.

Connell, Dan. 1995. "Eritrea: Starting from Scratch." *Monthly Review* 47, no. 4:29–40.

———. 1997. *Against All Odds: A Chronicle of the Eritrean Revolution*. Lawrenceville, N.J.: Red Sea.

Considine, M., and I. Deutchman. 1996. "Instituting Gender: State Legislators in Australia and the United States." *Women and Politics* 16, no. 4:1–19.

Cope, June. 1993. *A Matter of Choice: Abortion Law Reform in Apartheid South Africa*. Pietermaritzburg: Hadeda Books.

Croucher, Shelia. 2002. "South Africa's Democratisation and the Politics of Gay Liberation." *Journal of Southern African Studies* 28, no. 2:315–30.

Daniels, Glenda. 2001. "Rural Women to Fight for Their Right to Land." *Johannesburg Mail and Guardian*, June 1, pp. 1–2. Available at http://archive.mg.co.za/.

Darcy, R., and James R. Choike. 1986. "A Formal Analysis of Legislative Turnover: Women Candidates and Legislative Representation." *American Journal of Political Science* 30 (Feb.): 237–55.

Darcy, R., and S. Schramm. 1977. "When Women Run against Men." *Public Opinion Quarterly* 41:1–12.

Darcy, R., Susan Welch, and Janet Clark. 1994. *Women, Elections, and Representation*. 2d ed. Lincoln: University of Nebraska Press.

Davis, Gaye. 1996. "ANC to Act over Abortion Vote." *Johannesburg Mail and Guardian*, November 15, pp. 1–2. Available at http://archive.mg.co.za/.

Deegan, Heather. 2001. *The Politics of the New South Africa: Apartheid and After*. New York: Longman.

Duncan, Sheena. 1991. "Forced Removals Mean Genocide." In *Lives of Courage: Women for a New South Africa*, ed. Diana E. H. Russell, 312–28. Oakland: Basic Books.

Duverger, Maurice. 1955. *The Political Role of Women*. Paris: United Nations Economic and Social Council.

Eades, Lindsay Michie. 1999. *The End of Apartheid in South Africa*. Westport, Conn.: Greenwood.

Emerson, Robert, Rachel Fretz, and Linda Shaw. 1995. *Writing Ethnographic Fieldnotes*. Chicago: University of Chicago Press.

Epstein, A. 1992. *Scenes from African Urban Life: Collected Copperbelt Papers*. Edinburgh: Edinburgh University Press.

Fedler, Joanne. 1997. "Women's Day: It's Time to End State Neglect of Women." *Johannesburg Mail and Guardian,* August 8, pp. 1–2. Available at http://archive.mg.co.za/. Accessed March 2004.

Feris, Melanie-Ann. 1999. "South Africa Tops in Africa for Women in Power. *Johannesburg Star,* August 8, p. 1. Available at http://www.iol.co.za/. Accessed March 2004.

Fester, Gertrude. 1991. "The United Women's Congress." In *Lives of Courage: Women for a New South Africa,* ed. Diana E. H. Russell, 241–53. Oakland, Calif.: Basic Books.

Finnemore, Martheanne. 1994. "Negotiating Power." In *Agenda* 20:16–21.

First, Ruth. 1965. *117 Days.* New York: Stein and Day.

Fonow, Mary Margaret, and Judith A. Cook. 1991. *Beyond Methodology: Feminist Scholarship as Lived Research.* Bloomington: Indiana University Press.

Fox, Diana, and Naima Hasci. 1999. *The Challenges of Women's Activism and Human Rights in Africa.* Lewiston: Edwin Mellon.

Friedman, Elisabeth. 2000. "State-based Advocacy for Gender Equality in the Developing World: Assessing the Venezuelan National Women's Agency." *Women and Politics* 21, no. 2:47–80.

Gaitskell, Deborah. 1990. "Devout Domesticity? A Century of African Women's Christianity in South Africa." In *Women and Gender in Southern Africa to 1945,* ed. Cherryl Walker, 33–47. Cape Town: David Phillips.

Geisler, Gisela. 1995. "Troubled Sisterhood: Women and Politics in Southern Africa: Case Studies from Zambia, Zimbabwe, and Botswana." *African Affairs* 94, no. 377:545–78.

———. 2000. "'Parliament Is Another Terrain of Struggle': Women, Men and Politics in South Africa." *Journal of Modern African Studies* 38, no. 4:605–30.

Gender Links. 2004a. "More Women on Lists, but Major Gains Unlikely," Press release, April 7. Available at http://www.genderlinks.org.za/gelections/pressrelease.asp?nid=3. Accessed March 2004.

———. 2004b. "Number of Women in New Parliament up by Ten Percent." Press release, April 19. Available at http://www.genderlinks.org.za/gelections/pressrelease.asp?nid=5. Accessed March 2004.

Gertzog, Irwin. 1995. *Congressional Women: Their Recruitment, Integration, and Behavior.* 2d ed. Westport, Conn.: Praeger.

Ginwala, Frene. 1991. "Women and the Elephant: The Need to Redress Gender Oppression." In *Putting Women on the Agenda,* ed. Susan Bazilli, 248–55. Johnnesburg: Raven.

———. 1992. "Non-racial Democracy—Soon; Non-sexism—How?" Speech given at the Women's National Coalition National Workshop, April 25–26.

Glaser, B., and A. Strauss. 1967. *The Discovery of Grounded Theory: Strategies for Qualitative Research.* Hawthorne, N.Y.: Aldine de Gruyter.

Goetz, Anne Marie. 1998. "Women in Politics and Gender Equity in Policy: South Africa and Uganda." *Review of African Political Economy* 76:241–62.

———. 2003. "Women's Political Effectiveness: A Conceptual Framework." In *No Shortcuts to Power: African Women in Politics and Policy Making,* ed. Anne Marie Goetz and Shireen Hassim, 29–80. New York: Zed Books.

Goetz, Anne Marie, and Shireen Hassim, ed. 2003. *No Shortcuts to Power: African Women in Politics and Policy Making.* New York: Zed Books.

Goldblatt, Beth, and Sheila Meintjes. 1998. "South African Women Demand the Truth."

In *What Women Do in Wartime: Gender and Conflict in Africa,* ed. Meredeth Turshen and Clotide Twagiramariya, 27–61. New York: Zed Books.

Gordon, April. 1996. *Transforming Capitalism and Patriarchy: Gender and Development in Africa.* Boulder, Colo.: Lynne Rienner.

Govender, Pregs. 2001. "Gender Budgeting Was Removed Not Committee's Funding." *Johannesburg Mail and Guardian,* August 17, pp. 1–2. Available at http://archive.mg.co.za/. Accessed December 9, 2004.

Guy, J. 1990. "Gender Oppression in Southern Africa's Precapitalist Societies." In *Women and Gender in Southern Africa to 1945,* ed. Cherryl Walker, 33–47. Cape Town: David Phillip.

Haffajee, Ferial. 1997. "Women's Day: Big Hopes, Little Funding." *Johannesburg Mail and Guardian,* August 8, pp. 1–2. Available at http://archive.mg.co.za/.

———. 1999. "Who'll Cook for the Women MPs?" *Johannesburg Mail and Guardian,* February 19, pp. 1–3. Available at http://archive.mg.co.za/.

Hale, Sondra. 2001. "The Soldier and the State: Post-Liberation Women: The Case of Eritrea." In *Frontline Feminisms: Women, War, and Resistance,* ed. Marguerite R. Waller and Jennifer Rycenga, 349–70. New York: Garland.

Haroz, Audrey. 1997. "South Africa's 1996 Choice on the Termination of Pregnancy Act: Expanding Choice and International Human Rights to Black South African Women." *Vanderbilt Journal of Transnational Law* 30, no. 863:865–901.

Hassim, Shireen. 1999a. "Consolidating Representation: Post-Election Challenges." *The Election Bulletin.* 6th ed. *Women'sNet* 1 (Aug.). Available at http://womensnet.org.za /election/eb6–postelect.htm. Accessed July 2000.

———. 1999b. "From Presence to Power: Women's Citizenship in a New Democracy." *Agenda* 4:6–17.

———. 2002. "The Dual Politics of Representation: Women and Electoral Politics in South Africa." In *One Woman, One Vote: The Gender Politics of South African Elections,* ed. Glenda Fick, Sheila Meintjes, and Mary Simons, 102–15. Johannesburg: Electoral Institute of South Africa.

———. 2003. "Representation, Participation, and Democratic Effectiveness: Feminist Challenges to Representative Democracy in South Africa." In *No Shortcuts to Power: African Women in Politics and Policy Making,* ed. Anne Marie Goetz and Shireen Hassim, 81–109. New York: Zed Books.

Hendricks, Cheryl, and Desiree Lewis. 1994. "Voices from the Margins." *Agenda,* 20:61–75.

Henn, J. 1984. "Women in the Rural Economy: Past, Present, and Future." In *African Women South of the Sahara,* ed. M. Hay and S. Sticher. New York: Longman, 1984.

Hirschmann, D. 1991. "Women and Political Participation in Africa: Broadening the Scope of Research." *World Development* 19, no. 12:1679–94.

Inter-parliamentary Union. 2004. "Women in National Parliaments." Available at www .ipu.org/wmn-e/classification. Accessed December 10, 2004.

Issel, Shahieda. 1991. "Balancing Motherhood and Politics." In *Lives of Courage: Women for a New South Africa,* ed. Diana E. H. Russell, 307–11. Oakland: Basic Books.

Jayiya, Eddie. 1999. "Commission Calls for More Women in Government." *Johannesburg Star,* October 21, pp. 1–2. Available at http://www.iol.co.za.

Joint Monitoring Committee on the Improvement of the Quality of Life and Status of

Women, Parliament of South Africa. 1999a. Introduction. *Second Annual Report January 1998–March 1999.* Available at http://womensnet.org.za/parliament/intro.html. Accessed July 2000.

———. 1999b. Welfare. *Second Annual Report January 1998–March 1999.* Available at http://womensnet.org.za/parliament/welfare.html. Accessed July 2000.

Jones, Mark P. 1996. "Increasing Women's Representation via Gender Quotas: The Argentine Ley de Cupos." *Women and Politics* 16, no. 4:75–98.

———. 1998. "Gender Quotas, Electoral Laws and the Election of Women: Lessons from the Argentine Provinces." *Comparative Political Studies* 31, no. 1:3–21.

Joseph, Helen. 1986. *Side by Side: The Autobiography of Helen Joseph.* Johannesburg: A. D. Donker.

———. 1991. "The National Federation of Women." In *Lives of Courage: Women for a New South Africa,* ed. Diana E. H. Russell, 200–212. Oakland, Calif.: Basic Books.

Kadalie, Rhoda. 1995. "Women in the New South Africa: From Transition to Governance." In *The Constitution of South Africa from a Gender Perspective,* ed. Sandra Liebenberg, 64–78. Cape Town: David Philip.

Kanter, R. M. 1977. "Some Effects of Proportions on Group Life: Skewed Sex Ratios and Responses to Token Women." *American Journal of Sociology* 82:965–90.

Kaplan, Temma. 1982. "Female Consciousness and Collective Action: The Case of Barcelona, 1910–1918." *Signs* 7, no. 3:545–66.

Kemp, Amanda, Nozizwe Madlala, Asha Moodley, and Elaine Salo. 1995. "The Dawn of a New Day: Redefining South African Feminism." In *The Challenge of Local Feminisms: Women's Movements in a Global Perspective,* ed. Amrita Basu, 131–62. Boulder, Colo.: Westview.

Kenworthy, Lane, and Melissa Malami. 1999. "Gender Inequality in Political Representation: A Worldwide Comparative Analysis." *Social Forces* 78, no. 1:235–69.

Kirsch, Gesa E. 1999. *Ethical Dilemmas in Feminist Research: The Politics of Location, Interpretation, and Publication.* Albany, N.Y.: SUNY Press.

Klugman, Barbara. 1994. "South Africa: Women in Politics under Apartheid: A Challenge to the New South Africa." In *Women and Politics Worldwide,* ed. Barbara J. Nelson and Najma Chowdhury, 639–59. New Haven, Conn.: Yale University Press.

Kumar, Krishna, ed. 2001. *Women and Civil War: Impact, Organization, and Action.* Boulder, Colo.: Lynne Rienner.

Kuzwayo, Ellen. 1985. *Call Me Woman.* Johannesburg: Raven.

Lakeman, Enid. 1970. *How Democracies Vote: A Study of Majority and Proportional Electoral Systems.* London: Faber.

Lane, Megan. 2001. "Sisters Are Doing It." *BBC News Online,* June 9. Available at http://news.bbc.co.uk/vote2001/hi/english/features/newsid_1379000/1379658.stm.

Lawless, Jennifer, and Richard Fox. 1999. "Women Candidates in Kenya: Political Socialization and Representation." *Women in Politics* 20, no. 4:49–76.

Little, Thomas H., Dana Dunn, and Rebecca Deen. 2001. "A View from the Top: Gender Differences in Legislative Priorities among State Legislative Leaders." *Women and Politics* 22, no. 4:29–50.

Lodge, Tom. 1983. *Black Politics in South Africa since 1945.* New York: Longman.

Lovenduski, Joni, and Pippa Norris. 1993. *Gender and Party Politics.* London: Sage.

Lowe Morna, Colleen. 2000. "Gender Budget on the Rocks?" *Johannesburg Mail and Guardian,* August 4, pp. 1–2. Available at http://archive.mg.co.za/. Accessed March 2004.

Luciak, Ilja. 2001. *After the Revolution: Gender and Democracy in El Salvador, Nicaragua, and Guatemala.* Baltimore, Md.: Johns Hopkins University Press.

Mabandla, Brigitte. 1994. "Choices for South African Women." *Agenda* 20:22–29.

Magardie, Khanija. 2000a. "Bosses Mustn't Have Babies." *Johannesburg Mail and Guardian,* April 7, pp. 1–2. Available at http://archive.mg.co.za/. Accessed March 2004.

———. 2000b. "Government Fails to Do Its Bit for Rape." *Johannesburg Mail and Guardian,* April 28, pp. 1–2. Available at http://archive.mg.co.za/. Accessed March 2004.

———. 2001a. "Safe Abortions Still out of Reach." *Johannesburg Mail and Guardian,* January 12, pp. 1–2. Available at http://archive.mg.co.za/. Accessed March 2004.

———. 2001b. "Baqwa Probes Gender Commission CEO." *Johannesburg Mail and Guardian,* August 10, pp. 1–2. Available at http://archive.mg.co.za/. Accessed March 2004.

Mallaby, Sebastian. 1993. *After Apartheid: The Future of South Africa.* New York: Random House.

Manby, Bronwen. 1995. "South Africa: Threats to a New Democracy: Continuing Violence in KwaZulu-Natal." *Human Rights Watch* 7, no. 3 (May): 1–62. Available at http://www.hrw.org/reports/1995/Safrica.htm.

Mangaliso, Z. 1997. "Gender and Nation-Building in South Africa." In *Feminist Nationalism,* ed. Lois West, 130–46. New York: Routledge.

Marks, Shula, and Stanely Trapido, eds. 1987. *The Politics of Race, Class, and Nationalism in Twentieth-Century South Africa.* New York: Longman.

Mashinini, Emma. 1991. *Strikes Have Followed Me All My Life: A South African Autobiography.* New York: Routledge.

Matland, Richard. 1993. "Institutional Variables Affecting Female Representations in National Legislatures: The Case of Norway." *Journal of Politics* 55, no. 3:737–56.

Matland, Richard, and Donley T. Studlar. 1996. "The Contagion of Women Candidates in Single-Member District and Proportional Representation Systems: Canada and Norway." *Journal of Politics* 58, no. 3:707–33.

Mayne, Anne. 1991. "Feminism and the Anti-Rape Movement." In *Lives of Courage: Women for a New South Africa,* ed. Diana E. H. Russell, 227–40. Oakland: Basic Books.

Mbire-Barungi, Barbara. 1999. "Ugandan Feminism: Political Rhetoric or Reality?" *Women's Studies International Forum* 22, no. 4:435–40.

McAllister, I., and D. Studlar. 1992. "Gender Representation among Legislative Candidates in Australia." *Comparative Political Studies* 25:388–411.

McLachlan, Fiona. 1987. "The Apartheid Laws in Brief." In *The Anti-Apartheid Reader: South Africa and the Struggle against White Racist Rule.* New York: Grove Weidenfeld.

Meintjes, Sheila. 2001. "War and Post-War Shifts in Gender Relations." In *The Aftermath: Women in Post-Conflict Transformation,* ed. Sheila Meintjes, Anu Pillay, and Meredeth Turshen, 63–77. New York: Zed Books.

———. 2003. "The Politics of Engagement: Women Transforming the Policy Process—Domestic Violence Legislation in South Africa." In *No Shortcuts to Power: African Women in Politics and Policy Making,* ed. Anne Marie Goetz and Shireen Hassim, 140–59. New York: Zed Books.

Michelman, Cherry. 1975. *The Black Sash of South Africa: A Case Study in Liberalism.* London: Oxford University Press.

Mies, Maria. 1991. "Women's Research or Feminist Research? The Debate Surrounding Feminist Science and Methodology." In *Beyond Methodology: Feminist Scholarship as Lived Research,* ed. Mary Margaret Fonow and Judith A. Cook, 60–84. Bloomington: Indiana University Press.

Mikell, Gwendolyn, ed. 1997. *African Feminism: The Politics of Survival in Sub-Saharan Africa.* Philadelphia: University of Pennsylvania Press.

Mohanty, Chandra, Ann Russo, and Lourdes Torres. 1991. *Third World Women and the Politics of Feminism.* Bloomington: Indiana University Press.

Molyneux, Maxine. 1985. "Mobilization without Emancipation? Women's Interests, State, and Revolution in Nicaragua." *Feminist Studies* 11, no. 2 (Summer): 227–54.

Momberg, Eleanor, and Sapa. 2004. "Parties Finalise Parliament Lists." *Durban Mercury,* April 21. Available at http://www.iol.co.za/index.php?sf=2902&click_id=13&art_id= vn20040421042423355C841427&set_id=1.

Mompati, Ruth. 1991. "The Most Powerful Woman in the African National Congress." In *Lives of Courage: Women for a New South Africa,* ed. Diana E. H. Russell, 106–20. Oakland: Basic Books.

Murray, Colin. 1981. *Families Divided: The Impact of Migrant Labour in Lesotho.* New York: Cambridge University Press.

Najjar, Orayb. 1992. "Between Nationalism and Feminism: The Palestinian Answer." In *Women Transforming Politics: Worldwide Strategies for Empowerment,* ed. Jill Bystydzienski, 143–61. Bloomington: Indiana University Press.

National Assemby of South Africa. 1995. *Debates of the National Assembly (Hansard).* First Parliament, 2d session (8 Aug.). Vol. 6. Cape Town: The Government Printer.

———. 1996a. *Debates of the National Assembly (Hansard).* First Parliament, 3d session (26 Mar.). Vol. 4. Cape Town: The Government Printer.

———. 1996b. *Debates of the National Assembly (Hansard).* First Parliament, 3d session (28 May). Vol. 7. Cape Town: The Government Printer.

———. 1996c. *Debates of the National Assembly (Hansard).* First Parliament, 3d session (29 Aug.). Vol. 12. Cape Town: The Government Printer.

Nelson, Barbara, and Najma Chowdhury, eds. 1994. *Women and Politics Worldwide.* New Haven, Conn.: Yale University Press.

Niven, David. 1998. *The Missing Majority: The Recruitment of Women as State Legislative Candidates.* Westport, Conn.: Praeger.

"No Free Vote for Abortion." 1996. *Johannesburg Mail and Guardian,* July 12, p. 1. Available at http://archive.mg.co.za/. Accessed September 1996.

Norris, Pippa. 1985. "The Gender Gap in Britain and America." *Parliamentary Affairs* 38:192–201.

———. 1987. *Politics and Sexual Equality.* Boulder, Colo.: Lynne Rienner.

O'Regan, V. 1998. "Gender Matters: Female Policy Makers' Influence in Industrialized Nations." Paper presented at the annual meeting of the Midwest Political Science Association, Chicago, Ill., April 23–25.

Oyewumi, Oyeronke. 1997. *The Invention of Women: Making an African Sense of Western Gender Discourses.* Minneapolis: University of Minnesota Press.

Parpart, Jane L., and Kathleen Staudt. 1989. *Women and the State in Africa*. Boulder, Colo.: Lynne Rienner.

Peires, J. B. 1991. "Suicide or Genocide? Xhosa Perceptions of the Nongqawuse Catastrophe." In *History from South Africa: Alternative Visions and Practices*, ed. Belinda Bozzoli, Joshua Brown, Peter Delius, Patrick Manning, Karin Shapiro, and Jon Wiener, 29–38. Philadelphia: Temple University Press.

Phillips, Anne. 1991. *Engendering Democracy*. University Park: Pennsylvania State University Press.

Pitkin, H. F. 1967. *The Concept of Representation*. Berkeley: University of California Press.

Ramgobin, Ela. 1991. "An Indian Woman Confronts Apartheid." In *Lives of Courage: Women for a New South Africa*, ed. Diana E. H. Russell, 133–42. Oakland: Basic Books.

Ranchod-Nilsson, Sita. 1994. "'This Too Is a Way of Fighting': Rural Women's Participation in Zimbabwe's Liberation War." In *Women and Revolution in Africa, Asia, and the New World*, ed. Mary Ann Tetreault, 62–88. Columbia: University of South Carolina Press.

Reinharz, Shulamit. 1992. *Feminist Methods in Social Research*. New York: Oxford University Press.

Republic of South Africa. 1996a. Commission on Gender Equality Act. *Government Gazette*. Vol. 373, no. 17341 (24 July). Cape Town: The Government Printer.

———. 1996b. Films and Publications Act. *Government Gazette*. Vol. 377, no. 17560 (8 Nov.). Cape Town: The Government Printer.

———. 1996c. Choice on the Termination of Pregnancy Act. *Government Gazette*. Vol. 377, no. 17602 (22 Nov.). Cape Town: The Government Printer.

Reynolds, Andrew. 1995. "Constitutional Engineering in Southern Africa." *Journal of Democracy* 6, no. 2:86–99.

———. 1999. "Women in the Legislatures and Executives of the World: Knocking at the Highest Glass Ceiling." *World Politics* 51, no. 4:547–72.

Rosenthal, Cindy Simon. 2000. "Gender Styles in State Legislative Committees: Raising Their Voices in Resolving Conflict." *Women in Politics* 21, no. 2:21–45.

Rule, Wilma. 1981. "Why Women Don't Run: The Critical and Contextual Factors in Women's Legislative Recruitment." *Western Political Quarterly* 34:60–77.

———. 1987. "Electoral Systems, Contextual Factors and Women's Opportunity for Election to Parliament in Twenty-three Democracies." *Western Political Quarterly* 40:477–98.

Rule, Wilma, and Joseph F. Zimmerman, eds. 1994. *Electoral Systems in Comparative Perspective: Their Impact on Women and Minorities*. Westport, Conn.: Greenwood.

Russell, Diane, ed.. 1989. *Lives of Courage: Women for a New South Africa*. Oakland: Basic Books.

Salie, A. 1997. "No Rush for Abortions under New Law." *Cape Times*, February 4, p. 5.

Sapa. 2002. "45,000 Babies Aborted in SA Hospitals in 2001." *Cape (Town) Argus*, February 27, p. 1. Available at http://www.iol.co.za./. Accessed August 2002.

Saunders, Christopher, ed. 1992. *Illustrated History of South Africa: The Real Story*. 3d ed. Cape Town: Reader's Digest Association.

Sawer, Marian. 2000. "Parliamentary Representation of Women: From Discourses of Justice to Strategies of Accountability." *International Political Science Review* 21, no. 4:361–80.

Schwartz, H. 1994. "Women in the South African Process of Change." Speech to Democratic Women's Club, Washington, D.C.

Scott, Catherine. 1994. "'Men in Our Country Behave Like Chiefs': Women and the An-golan Revolution." In *Women and Revolution in Africa, Asia, and the New World,* ed. Mary Ann Tetreault, 89–108. Columbia: University of South Carolina Press.

Sebelebele, Matome. 2004. "Gender Activists Praise Appointment of New Female Pre-mier Elects." *Pretoria BuaNews,* April 22. Available at http://allafrica.com/stories /200404220407.html. Accessed May 2004.

Seidman, Gay W. 1993. "'No Freedom without the Women': Mobilization and Gender in South Africa, 1970–1991." *Signs* 18:291–320.

———. 1999. "Gendered Citizenship: South Africa's Democratic Transition and the Con-struction of a Gendered State." *Gender and Society* 13, no. 3:287–307.

Seidman, I. E. 1991. *Interviewing as Qualitative Research.* New York: Teachers College Press.

Senate of South Africa. 1996. *Debates of the Senate (Hansard).* 3d session. No. 14 (10 Oct.). Cape Town: The Government Printer.

Sharoni, Simona. 2001. "Rethinking Women's Struggles in Israel-Palestine and in the North of Ireland." In *Victims, Perpetrators, or Actors? Gender, Armed Conflict and Political Vi-olence,* ed. Caroline O. N. Moser and Fiona C. Clark, 85–98. New York: Zed Books.

Sheldon, Kathleen. 1994. "Women and Revolution in Mozambique: A Luta Continua." In *Women and Revolution in Africa, Asia, and the New World,* ed. Mary Ann Tetreault, 33–61. Columbia: University of South Carolina Press.

Sibisi, Harriet. 1977. "How African Women Cope with Migrant Labor in South Africa." *Signs: Journal of Women in Culture and Society* 3, no. 1:167–77.

Sideris, Tina. 2001. "Problems of Identity, Solidarity, and Reconciliation." In *The After-math: Women in Post-Conflict Transformation,* ed. Sheila Meintjes, Anu Pillay, and Meredeth Turshen, 46–62. New York: Zed Books.

Smith, Charlene. 1999. "The Issues That Few Have Yet Addressed." *Johannesburg Mail and Guardian,* May 21, pp. 1–3. Available at http:// archive.mg.co.za/. Accessed August 2002.

Soggot, Mungo. 1997. "Censorship: Too Little or Too Much?" *Johannesburg Mail and Guardian,* July 4, pp. 1–2. Available at http://archive.mg.co.za/. Accessed August 2002.

Staudt, Kathleen A. 1998. "Women in Politics: Mexico in Global Perspective." In *Women's Participation in Mexican Political Life,* ed. Victoria E. Rodriguez, 23–40. Boulder: West-view Press.

Steininger, Barbara. 2000. "Representation of Women in the Austrian Political System 1945–1998: From a Token Female Politician Towards an Equal Ratio? *Women and Pol-itics* 21, no. 2:81–106.

Stetson, Dorothy McBride, and Amy G. Mazur, eds. 1995. *Comparative State Feminisms.* Thousand Oaks, Calif.: Sage.

Steyn, Melissa. 1998. "A New Agenda: Restructuring Feminism in South Africa." *Women's Studies International Forum* 21, no. 1:41–52.

Swers, Michele. 2001. "Research on Women in Legislatures: What Have We Learned, Where Are We Going?" *Women in Politics* 23, no. 1:167–85.

Tamale, Sylvia. 1999. *When Hens Begin to Crow: Gender and Parliamentary Politics in Uganda.* Boulder, Colo.: Westview.

———. 2000. "'Point of Order, Mr. Speaker': African Women Claiming Their Space in Parliament." *Gender and Development* 8, no. 3:8–15.

Terborg-Penn, Rosalyn. 1990. "Black Women Freedom Fighters in South Africa and in the United States: A Comparative Analysis." *Dialectical Anthropology* 15:151–57.

Themba, Priscilla. 2001. "Don't Deny the Role the Women's Committee Has Played. *Johannesburg Mail and Guardian,* April 6. Available at http://archive.mg.co.za/.

Thomas, Sue. 1989. "The Impact of Women on State Legislative Policy." Paper presented at the annual meeting of the American Political Science Association, Atlanta, Ga., August 31–September 3.

———. 1991. "The Impact of Women on State Legislative Policies." *Journal of Politics* 53, no. 4:958–76.

———. 1994. *How Women Legislate.* New York: Oxford University Press.

———. 1997. "Why Gender Matters: The Perceptions of Women Officeholders." *Women and Politics* 17, no. 1:27–53.

Tickner, Anne. 1992. *Gender in International Relations: Feminist Perspectives on Achieving Global Security.* New York: Columbia University Press.

Tremblay, Manon, and Rejean Pelletier. 2000. "More Feminists or More Women? Descriptive and Substantive Representations of Women in the 1997 Canadian Federal Elections." *International Political Science Review* 21, no. 4:381–405.

Tripp, Aili Mari. 2000a. "Rethinking Difference: Comparative Perspectives from Africa." *Signs* 25, no. 3:649–75.

———. 2000b. *Women and Politics in Uganda.* Madison: University of Wisconsin Press.

Turshen, Meredeth. 2001. "Engendering Relations of State to Society in the Aftermath." In *The Aftermath: Women in Post-Conflict Transformation,* ed. Sheila Meintjes, Anu Pillay, and Meredeth Turshen, 77–94. New York: Zed Books.

"Two Top Women Quit Parliament." 2002. *Johannesburg Mail and Guardian,* May 31, 1. Available at http://archive.mg.co.za/. Accessed August 2002.

Van Donk, Mirjam, and Maletsatsi Maceba. 1999. "Women at the Crossroads: Women in Governance." *Agenda* 40:18–22.

Viall, Jenny. 1997. "The Law That Lets SA Women Choose: Abortion Act Welcomed as Clinics and Hospitals Stand at the Ready." *Cape Argus,* February 3, p. 8.

Walker, Cherryl. 1982. *Women and Resistance in South Africa.* Cape Town: David Philip.

Waylen, Georgina. 1994. "Women and Democratization: Conceptualizing Gender Relations in Transition Politics." *World Politics* 46:327–54.

Wells, Julia. 1993. *We Now Demand: The History of Women's Resistance to Pass Laws in South Africa.* Johannesburg: Witwatersrand University Press.

Whicker, Marcia Lynn, and Lois Duke Whitaker. 1999. "Women in Congress." In *Women in Politics: Outsiders or Insiders?* 3d ed., ed. Lois Duke Whitaker, 171–89. Upper Saddle River, N.J.: Prentice Hall.

Whip, R. 1991. "Representing Women: Australian Female Parliamentarians on the Horns of a Dilemma." *Women and Politics* 11, no.3:1–22.

Wolf, Diane L., ed. 1996. *Feminist Dilemmas in Fieldwork.* Boulder, Colo.: Westview.

Women'sNet. "Party Manifestos: How Parties Rate in Key Gender Equality Areas." Available at http://womensnet.org.za/election/manifest.htm. Accessed December 6, 2003.

Zulu, Lindiwe. 1998. "Role of Women in the Reconstruction and Development of the New Democratic South Africa." *Feminist Studies* 24, no. 1:147–60.

Index

HANNAH E. BRITTON is an assistant professor of political science and women's studies at the University of Kansas. Prof. Britton's research focuses on African politics, transnational women's movements, and democratization and development.

The University of Illinois Press
is a founding member of the
Association of American University Presses.

———————————————————

Composed in 10.5/13 Adobe Minion
with Minion display
by Type One, LLC
for the University of Illinois Press
Manufactured by The Maple-Vail Book
Manufacturing Group

University of Illinois Press
1325 South Oak Street
Champaign, IL 61820-6903
www.press.uillinois.edu